# KAFIR SOCIALISM

# KAFIR SOCIALISM
## AND THE DAWN OF INDIVIDUALISM

AN INTRODUCTION TO THE STUDY OF THE NATIVE PROBLEM

BY

DUDLEY KIDD

AUTHOR OF "THE ESSENTIAL KAFIR," "SAVAGE CHILDHOOD," &C.

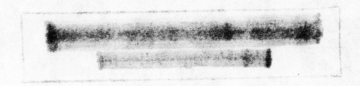

[redacted]

NEGRO UNIVERSITIES PRESS
NEW YORK

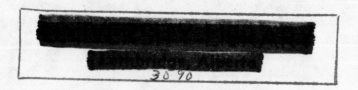

Originally published in 1908
by Adam and Charles Black

Reprinted 1969 by
Negro Universities Press
A Division of Greenwood Publishing Corp.
New York

Library of Congress Catalogue Card Number 69-18985

PRINTED IN UNITED STATES OF AMERICA

# PREFACE

RACIAL questions, democratic ideals, and the problems of Socialism are in the air. The world is filling up fast, and aggregates, whether of nations, races or classes, are now being sifted drastically by the process of natural selection. Aristocracies, majorities, and minorities, whether of races or classes, seem to have entered on the acute stage of their probation. No matter where we turn, whether to South Africa with its Boer and Native problems, to America with its Negro and Japanese difficulties, to Russia with its nightmare, to India and Egypt with their agitations for self-government, to the Balkans with its tangle, to the Congo with its struggles and tragedies amid primæval forests, to Australia with its fear of Kanakas and Japanese, to Mohammedans with their aspirations for Pan-Islamism, to Asia in its awakening, or to Europe with its rising tide of Democracy and Socialism, we are face to face with the struggle for existence that is taking place between groups of men that are fighting for very life. In the case of races and classes, just as in the case of individuals, those that are the most efficient in their adaptation to environment, and not those that simply give expression to the loftiest sentiment, will survive and dominate all rivals; while the weak and inefficient will go to the wall.

We shall be occupied in these pages with but a single

race ; though the future of the Kafir, and our duty to him, will take us into several fields of thought. The present volume deals with but one aspect of the Native Problem, namely, the conflict of Western conceptions of Individualism with the ingrained Socialism of the Kafir. This aspect of the problem is isolated for several reasons.

In the first place, no treatment of all the aspects of the Native Problem can hope to be altogether satisfactory unless it takes the form of a symposium in which experts in native thought, economics, politics, education, and missions combine to present the various aspects of this many-sided problem. There seems to be no person who possesses all the qualities necessary for such a work.

In the second place, so far as I know—and I think I have read every book that has been written on the subject—the very existence of the above-mentioned aspect of the problem has not even been recognised by any previous writer.

In the third place, the conflict of European Individualism with Kafir Socialism constitutes the very heart of the problem. No one has written more wisely about the Native Problem than Mr. Colquhoun ; and yet he not only failed to recognise the existence of this conflict of Socialism and Individualism, but has actually stated that the socialistic ideal is a conception that cannot possibly take hold of the Kafir. I shall quote presently the actual words used by Mr. Colquhoun ; and hope to prove that, so far from being alien to native thought, Socialistic ideals affect almost every conception of the Kafirs, giving colour and form even to their ideas about such widely different things as justice and witchcraft.

There is a further and final reason for not attempting a

complete discussion of the Native Problem. It is a most unsuitable time to make such an attempt, because the present Liberal Government, by reserving the affairs of the Kafirs in the Transvaal and Orange River Colony for its own special care, and by interfering in the native affairs of Natal, is virtually stifling discussion; for what colonist cares to waste his time in presenting a reasoned statement of his views concerning a thousand details of administration when he has every reason for feeling certain that the Party that meditates interference in the domestic affairs of South Africa will be guided, not by facts and sound sense, but by the uninformed sentiment of "moral experts"?

For the above reasons—and assured that Home interference is the transient whim of a political clique rather than the settled will of the people—I have decided to make this volume simply an introduction to, and not a detailed study of, the Native Problem. The native point of view, which I have sought to explain, is of great importance, though it is not the only point of view. Unless we clearly understand native conceptions and ideals, we shall but reckon without our host.

In South Africa we are all aware that we are building up our commercial, industrial, political and social structure at the foot of a volcano; but like all Pompeians, we have become so accustomed to the manifold dangers of the situation that we do not worry very much about our Vesuvius. Every now and then we feel some very disquieting and ominous rumblings beneath our feet, and occasionally see a flash of fire and a puff of smoke, and feel a few ashes falling on our heads; but the anxiety soon wears off; officials assure us that the natives are quiet again; and every one goes about his work as though there were no danger brewing. The problem is so many-sided and complicated that most of us are content to postpone all serious consideration of the subject. We talk about the natives in vague terms, for most of us know but little about the inscrutable Kafirs. There are comparatively few people who have any first-hand and intimate knowledge of the *kraal-life* of the natives ; and so most of us are content to accept the many floating, commonplace statements that abound in our towns and villages. Opinion takes the place of knowledge, and we are apt to adopt a sort of nonchalant optimism based on our national reputation of muddling through most of our difficulties. The law-abiding nature of the Kafir tends to confirm us in the delusion that the natives are reconciled to a rule which we know to be just and fair.

As the result of this attitude towards the subject, the ground is simply littered with half-truths, and with antiquated though inveterate prejudices. The Kafir that the average white man knows is the semi-civilised barbarian who has suffered from the degenerative influences of civilisation in our centres of industry, on our farms, or in domestic service. The visitor to South Africa picks up some specious and delusive myths about such Kafirs, and if he should write a book, he can scarcely resist the temptation to give the most picturesque of these half-truths a fresh lease of life, a wider currency, and an additional distortion due to his imperfect understanding of a strange and alien race. From the nature of the case, it is impossible even for the globe-trotting Member of Parliament to get to the heart of a racial problem in a visit, the brevity of which makes it impossible for the out-of-the-way Kafir kraals to be visited. Yet the writer feels bound to spatchcock into his book a chapter dealing with the subject. It is no cause for wonder that Home criticism should so often be wide of the mark, and that the most ludicrous suggestions should from time to time appear in the Press, or should be proposed in the House of Commons.

In addition to these sources of information, we have some valuable Blue Books—studies in the anatomy of the subject—that only few people seem to read until the contents are boiled down into magazine articles. There are also among the annual crop of South African books some volumes in which the writers manage to find space for a short chapter on the Native Problem. Though writers who are experts in economics or sport, or some kindred subject, naturally view the Native Problem through their own special key-hole, the result is interesting and not without value; for it is of great importance to know the bearing of such a side-issue as the Rand Labour-Supply on the Native Problem, even though the writer may assure us that this side-issue is not only the heart but the whole of the problem. The Kafirs say that no elephant ever felt its own trunk to be a burden, and we may therefore safely take some discount off the opinion of the man with but one idea.

But it is not only the mine-owner who is in danger of ignoring the native in his insistence of the importance of some side-issue of the problem: the philanthropist, the person who asks hysterical questions in the House of Commons, and the members of the Aborigines Protection Society are just as much in danger of forgetting the actual Kafir owing to their concentration on their own hobby.

It is fatally easy to set up in the mind some unreal image of an oppressed and voiceless black man, who is too gentle and peaceable, and withal too guileless, to provoke hostilities except under the most provoking oppression of some wicked white men. This mental image affords a splendid occasion for giving expression to those most pleasurable and luxurious of all emotions, indignation and pity. A meeting is held, and there is set up an emotional storm in many a tea-cup; the actual savage is lost sight of, and the "brutality" of the colonist and the humanity of the people at home are apt to become the twin-centres of what the Kafirs call a crab's dance. The question then ceases to be the *native*, and becomes the *white*, problem. Under the influence of prejudice or passion, the native, who is the subject of the contention, is lost sight of; and the real war is waged round such problems as the moral character of the colonist, the nature of the British Constitution, or the abstract idea of Justice, for every one thinks he knows all about these things. The Kafir becomes the ostensible subject of debate in which people exploit their special and peculiar obsessions. The argument becomes practically independent of the actual Kafir of the kraal, and would not be modified much if the aborigines of South Africa were Siamese, Red Indians or even Martians. Every conceivable side-interest, prejudice, and false analogy is discussed by these people, whom Carlyle would call Professors of Things in General, and who entirely ignore the real wishes of the Kafir.

*The Native Problem is the problem of the native.* This is so obvious when once stated that one would be ashamed to say it unless it were so constantly forgotten. Before we can understand the bearings of the Native Problem we must study native customs and thought. We shall never get any nearer a solution of the problem by concentrating our attention on the relative values of Home and Colonial sentiment and ethical sense, or on political panaceas for imaginary and non-existent needs, for it is the Kafir, and not our emotion, that is the determining factor in the problem.

I have not dealt with the subject of the religious aspect of Missions, though missionaries have done so much to exploit individualism amongst the Kafirs. There is not space available for the treatment of the subject. I fear to say too little or too much, and feel that any inadequate statement would but raise many undesirable misunderstandings. That aspect of the subject must therefore be reserved for a future volume.

I am not without hope that the picture of the "savage" that I present may do something to undermine the distorted mental image that is ordinarily awakened by that word. Many a race has opprobriously called another race, that it did not understand, barbarian or savage; even though that despised race was in some directions the more advanced of the two. The Kafir, contrary to ordinary belief, has the most extraordinarily well-developed spirit of altruism and *camaraderie*, which is very rarely equalled amongst Western nations. Ethnologists are slowly forcing us to admit that the savage is not so savage as has been supposed.

# CONTENTS

## PART I

## KAFIR SOCIALISM



## PART II

## THE DAWN OF INDIVIDUALISM

# PART I

# KAFIR SOCIALISM

## CHAPTER I

### PRIMITIVE SOCIALISM

In discussions as to whether Socialism would or would not stop progress and remove incentives to the strenuous life, appeal is not uncommonly made to the imagination, and opinion is pitted against opinion. When prophets, armed with private revelations, vie with one another, it is hopeless to judge as to the truth or falseness of the opposed predictions by weighing the relative confidence and assurance shown by the contending parties. If we could but leave imagination and prophecy on one side, and examine facts, our position would be much simplified. Ethnology is able, most fortunately, to supply us with such facts.

To all civilised people face to face with the problem of Socialism, a study of the Clan-System of the Kafirs should be of much interest, for it is an attempt on the part of a primitive people to solve on a lower plane problems we are seeking to solve on a higher. The system has been working for ages, and so the socialistic * experiment has had time to bear its characteristic fruit.

In examining Kafir Socialism it may be well to keep before us Rousseau's famous definition of the Social Pact: "To find a form of association which may defend and

* The word socialism is used in these pages to connote an organisation of society in which the means of life—whether production, distribution, or protection—are held in collective ownership.

protect, with the whole force of the community, the person and property of every associate, and by means of which each, coalescing with all, may nevertheless only obey himself, and remain as free as before. . . . Such is the fundamental problem of which the social contract furnishes the solution." * The Kafirs certainly fulfil the conditions of the pact, and the following pages will show how far they have been able to " remain as free as before."

The Kafirs may not have such a complete and highly developed organisation as the Indian village communities, yet they are, nevertheless, thorough-going collectivists. Their very babes are Socialists. The roots of their social policy are to be found in their Clan-System, which must now be described.

## I. The Clan-System

According to this system, the native races of South Africa are divided up into a number of tribes, each of which is composed of a number of clans, each of which, again, consists of a group of families. The children are responsible to the father; he is responsible to the head-man, who, in turn, is responsible to the petty chief; while the petty chiefs are responsible to the Paramount Chief or king. A Paramount Chief, therefore, has to watch the interests of the entire tribe; the petty chiefs have to watch the interests of the various clans; the head-men have to watch the interests of their respective groups of families, and the father has to watch the interests of his family, even when the sons are grown up. Group-association and

" Social Contract." English translation by Tozer, p. 109.

responsibility are therefore the essence of the system. There is considerable latitude as to the details of the plan, and as to the extent of powers committed to these various people in different tribes. In one tribe the chief may be more or less assisted by, and responsible to, a number of old councillors; while in another tribe the chief may be an absolute tyrant. Such a chief can do no wrong. His will is the will of the people, who do not complain about the abuses of his power, because it is the will of the people that the will of the chief should be supreme. It is as though they said to their chief: "We govern ourselves by choosing to do what you tell us." Thus we have the strange phenomenon of self-government taking the form of an Autocracy or Tyranny. In those tribes in which the chief is less autocratic, the people only exert their power very indirectly and occasionally; and even in such tribes it is not true to say, as it has been stated recently in the Home Press, that the Kafirs are a "pure democracy."

Even so careful a writer as Mr. Colquhoun has said strangely that Afrikanders "must see for themselves that to introduce Socialism and Democracy to the Kafir is to destroy their strongest hold on him. The conception is not one which can get any real hold of a people just emerging from the tribal state."* In that sentence two different things are confused—Socialism and Democracy. The Kafirs reject the Democracy with all their nature, while they welcome the Socialism with every fibre of their being. They differ from Western Socialists in the fact that they are the firmest believers in both Autocracy (or should we say

* "The Afrikander Land," p. 118.

Aristocracy ?) and Socialism ; and there is no reason why the socialistic state should not " run " itself through its own chosen autocratic chiefs or councillors.

The various departments of life that have been socialised, or tribalised, by the Kafirs must now be passed under review. It will be seen that so far from the conception of Socialism not being able to get hold of a people emerging from the tribal state, it is the very breath of their life.

(*a*) *The Individual and all his Rights.*—Amongst the Kafirs, the person of the individual belongs in theory to the chief : he is not his own, for he is the chief's man. It is extremely difficult for us, with our advanced conception of the inviolability of the rights of the individual, to appreciate the bearing of this fact. Philanthropists sometimes draw the most unwarrantable conclusions from their imperfect understanding of the native's idea : they catch a glimpse of one aspect of this matter, and their sentiment becomes so deeply affected and engaged that they have not patience to study the subject from the Kafir point of view, but at once cry out for the abolition of this intolerable power of the chief.

The relation of the individual to the chief can be understood from the following statement made by a Zulu, who was describing to a white man the custom of the Festival of First Fruits. He said : " The Zulus, if the mealies are ripe, are not permitted by themselves to eat them. The king must always give them permission before they do so. If somebody is eating new mealies, before the king has given his permission, he will be killed entirely. The white men are wondering about it, and say : 'Is a man not allowed to go into his own garden for harvesting food, which he planted himself, and to eat it?' But the Zulus are not wondering about that, saying: 'We are all the king's men: our bodies, our power, our food, and all that we have, is the king's property. It is quite right that we do not commence to eat new mealies unless the king has permitted it.'" *

"Zulus are not wondering about that": what pregnant words are these! This custom of the Feast of First Fruits has been designed, probably, partly as a taboo to prevent the squandering of the tribal food-supply, and partly as a means of insuring that the *amatongo*, or ancestral spirits, shall get their due, and so be kept well disposed towards the tribe. The native also readily understands that his own impulse of greediness must not be allowed to override his social obligations, for the interest of the clan is really his highest interest: apart from the prosperity of the clan, the individual has no security whatever; consequently the Kafir sees that it would never do for every man to do what is right in his own eyes; if they did that, the tribe would be at the mercy of surrounding enemies who knew how to curb the anti-social or asocial actions of its members.

"Zulus are not wondering about that!" Evidently that which puzzles, and sometimes obsesses, the mind of the white man, and which seems to him so absurdly unjust, is no cause of wonder to the Kafir. To him the matter seems essentially just and reasonable. Let the European but once accept the data which are implicitly accepted by the Zulus, and the conclusion follows, for the logic is not at

* *South African Folk-Lore Journal.* The expression "killed entirely" is used in a somewhat Irish sense, for the disobedient Zulu will probably only suffer considerable gastric disturbance, largely induced by his imaginative fears of breaking a taboo.

fault. Our own progress should teach us that national advance is due rather to the changing of our data as to "rights" than to an improvement in our logic.

When we come to speak of the sense of justice, this saying of the Zulu will be found of value in showing how a Kafir differs from a European in his conception of justice and of "rights." But in this place it is merely given to show how entirely the rights of the clan supersede those of the individual. So fully does the individual belong to the head of the tribe, that a chief, named Shiluvane, issued the decree: "I do not allow of anybody dying in my country except on account of old age." This command was given with a view to the checking of the use of sorcery and witchcraft to murder people; for the chief imagined that old age was the natural cause of death, and that none of his warriors could die in the prime of life unless they were bewitched by some private enemy. But the very expression, "I allow no one to die," shows how completely the people were regarded as the property of their chief. The very existence of the tribe depends upon the existence and maintenance of a great number of mature and able-bodied human beings: and in this sense the people themselves may be regarded as a means of production, for it is they who create and protect the tribe. For this reason, the individuals with all their personal rights must be socialised and brought into subjection to the recognised head of the tribe.

In theory, the entire property of all the members of the tribe belongs to the chief. When bargaining with the Kafirs for such things as assegais, and even snuff-boxes, the native, when reluctant to sell, has said that he had no right to part with the property of his chief. It is true that this line of argument is advanced more frequently when the article the European wants to buy is a weapon of war than when it is such a thing as a snuff-box, which is practically of no tribal value. But Kafirs have advanced this reason to me even when refusing to sell a wooden spoon. However, the Kafir never pushes a thing to what a European would regard as a logical conclusion. He has a sweet reasonableness; and when he covets the object offered in barter, he conveniently forgets all about the theoretical rights of his chief, and readily parts even with an assegai. It should be pointed out, in passing, that in every direction we meet with this disinclination to push principles to their logical conclusions, and a failure to recognise this fact not improbably accounts for some of the conflicting theories with regard to the natives and their customs that have been advanced hastily by some observers.

Since the bodies of all the members of the tribe belong to the chief, any damage done to the person of the individual is regarded as a criminal offence, and restitution has to be made, not to the person injured, but to the chief. Thus if A breaks B's leg, or knocks out his eye, he has to pay damages, not to B, but to the chief. When a white magistrate reverses this procedure, the natives think he is doing the tribe an injury, for he is putting a premium on anti-social selfishness. The action of the white man is therefore regarded as an immoral one. Thus the tables are turned, and instead of Glaucon's objection, "'Tis a city of pigs, Socrates," applying to the socialistic state, it would be used by a Kafir as a remark applicable to our individualistic *régime*.

We come now to the question of personal property, and find that, in this matter also, the Kafirs show their excellent moderation. The people regard their cattle as their own property, for the chief has his oxen, and the people have theirs. We may perhaps say that the cattle form the money of the people; and yet even the cattle are held at the discretion of the chief, who is entirely justified in appropriating them should a man fail in performing his tribal duty. Thus, when a man is convicted of using witchcraft,* and is therefore considered guilty of a grossly anti-social action, he is "eaten up" by the chief, who may either keep the man's cattle for himself or divide them up amongst his councillors. In the eyes of the Kafirs this is not spoliation, for the chief has but taken back what all along was his own. Thus it will be seen that Kafir practice agrees with ancient Roman custom. Maine says: "*Peculium*—a few head of oxen kept apart—was the name which the Romans gave to the permissive separate property allowed to the son or a slave. No principle was more persistent in Roman law than the subjection of the *peculium* to the authority of the paterfamilas or the master, should he choose to exercise it. . . . When the house community is in its primitive and natural state there is no *peculium:* there is none in Montenegro; the dominant notion there is that as the community is liable for the delinquences of its members, it is entitled to receive all the produce of their labour."† It will thus be seen that the Kafirs are in very good company on this subject, and that their system is undeserving

* Not infrequently the accusation of using sorcery is trumped up against any one guilty of anti-social practices, so as to provide an occasion for giving vent to indignation.

† "Dissertations on Early Law and Custom," pp. 251, 252.

of the plentiful abuse that is showered on it by some philanthropists.

Dr. Schäffle, in his " Quintessence of Socialism," explodes a common misunderstanding when he says : " In opposition to all contrary views, which have been very widely spread, it must be emphatically stated that Socialism does not universally exclude either property in general or private property in particular. The principle of collective labour does, indeed, demand plainly, and pretty exclusively, collective capital, but it does not without ceremony deny the admissibility of private property." * The Kafirs, however, only allow people to hold private property and cattle when this does not conflict with the good of the community ; they make short work of the man who grows too rich and who neglects the interest of the clan. Such a man is sure to be accused of amassing wealth by using sorcery, and is consequently " eaten up " by the chief.

Without going further, it should be evident that the Clan-System is based on obligations to be performed by the individual and not on the man's rights. It is the Kafir's primary obligation to sacrifice, if needs be, everything for the good of the clan, and his individual rights are wholly subservient, contingent, and secondary to the performance of his obligations. This sound basis of the social state is undoubtedly one of the main causes of the stability of Kafir society. To do anything that is anti-social is the one heinous offence : nay, it is more, for it is the one hopeless case of " bad form." It is a striking thing that it should be in primitive peoples and amongst English school-boys, the very classes in which there exists the

* *Op. cit.*, English translation, p. 101.

intensest egoism, that the strongest spirit of communism should be found. School-boys have organised their social forces against their common enemy—their masters: it is therefore the height of treachery, for it is utterly anti-social, for a boy to "sneak," and so put his clan at the mercy of the enemy. Similarly a school-boy who fails to do his duty to his school, soon finds himself deprived of many coveted privileges. The analogy need not be laboured, for we all know how strong is the communistic spirit amongst English school-boys, and how much more "sporting" it is than the unchecked individualism of later life. But, in the case of the Kafirs, it may be well to point out an apparent exception that helps to prove the rule. Every Kafir is supposed to be a sort of policeman, and it is his duty to report to his father, or head-man, or petty chief, any violation of clan-interests that he has observed. He is his brother's keeper in fact and not merely in theory. All this might appear to an English boy as an example of "sneaking." But it is not so; for a Kafir only gives information against another man when that person has violated clan-interests: he would never think of doing it in the case of private quarrels.

The tribal solidarity is further strengthened by the regulations concerning marriage. No man is allowed to marry a woman of his own clan, even though she should be but a fifth or sixth cousin; but he must marry within his tribe.* There are few things that scandalise the Kafir more than to hear a missionary approve of the marriage of cousins. The Kafirs are intensely particular in not allowing marriages where any blood-relationship can be traced:

* A tribe may contain more than a hundred clans.

they are also, in their natural condition, very averse from marriages between members of different tribes. All this, naturally, consolidates the clan.

There is a great danger in interfering with racial problems. Largely owing to the natural difficulty that arises from the entire difference in point of view adopted by the Anglo-Saxon and the Kafir, it comes about that our sentiment is offended at the utter ignoring of the "rights" of the individual. We are apt to regard the Kafir as but the chattel of the chief. But this is a great mistake, and easily leads to trouble. Maine has pointed out that: "Wherever servitude is sanctioned by institutions which have been deeply affected by Roman jurisprudence, the servile condition is never intolerably wretched. There is a great deal of evidence that in those American States which have taken the highly Romanised code of Louisiana as the basis of their jurisprudence, the lot and prospects of the negro population were better in many material respects, until the letter of the fundamental law was overlaid by recent statutory enactments passed under the influence of panic, than under institutions founded on the English Common Law, which, as recently interpreted, has no true place for the slave, and can only, therefore, regard him as a chattel."* This is a typical example of the unfortunate effects of Anglo-Saxon action based on a misunderstanding of unfamiliar conceptions. Professor Westermarck points out: "From a moral point of view negro slavery is interesting chiefly because it existed in the midst of a highly developed Christian civilisation, and nevertheless, at least in the British Colonies and the United States, was the most brutal form of slavery

* "Ancient Law," p. 170.

ever known. . . . Through the direct action of Congress it became law that persons known to be free should be sold as slaves in order to cover the costs of imprisonment which they had suffered on account of a false suspicion that they were runaway slaves. This law was repeatedly put into effect. 'How many crowned despots,' says Professor Von Holst—he might have said, how many autocratic Kafir chiefs—'can be mentioned in the history of the old world who have done things which compare in accursedness with this law to which the democratic republic gave birth?'"

Similarly, any ignorant "democratic" interference on our part with regard to Kafir customs based on the conception of the obligations of the people to sacrifice their "rights" for the good of the clan is certain to produce trouble of the most deplorable kind. Later on we shall examine some of the unexpected results arising from this cause.

(*b*) *Military Forces.*—The safety of the tribe—indeed its very existence—depends on the efficient organisation of its military forces. Every individual is therefore compelled to sink his own private wishes and perform his share of military service. Every able-bodied man—that is to say, every man, for amongst the Kafirs in their "raw" state all weaklings are killed off in infancy—is a soldier, and has to go undergo military training. Tshaka, the great Zulu despot, gathered the manhood of his tribe into regiments which lived in military kraals, and which were maintained at public expense. These men were not allowed to marry until the chief gave them permission, for it was essential that their fibre should not be softened unduly by domestic life. The very boys were herded together into military kraals, and had to serve as baggage-carriers for the army. The man who refused to perform his military duties would have been hounded out of his tribe, being regarded as a worthless and anti-social wretch. The Kafirs would stand aghast at the insipid and tepid Socialism of the English Labour Party, for they would regard their anti-military emotionalism as utterly effeminate.

(*c*) ***Hunting***.—Co-operation in hunting has such obvious advantages that it obtains in all primitive societies. The Kafir system of tribal hunting is very interesting. Having elsewhere described at length a tribal hunt,* a brief summary must here suffice. A couple of days in advance of the hunt, the chief sends messengers—usually boys of about sixteen years of age—to tell the people at what hour to arrive at the Great Place, as his kraal is called. These boys are duly accredited as messengers, those I have seen being distinguished by two circular patches of red paint at the top of the arm. On the day appointed, the people arrive at the Great Place, clan by clan, and greet the chief, who pretends not to know who the different people are until one of the councillors pronounces the *isibongo*, or surname, of each clan. On hearing the name, the chief pretends to show great delight and praises the men excessively. The tribal diviners, or doctors, then come upon the scene, working magical practices and investigating the omens. When they pronounce that everything is favourable, the whole crowd scatters, and clan by clan the people take their place as they surround a large district that has been pointed out previously to

* "The Essential Kafir," p. 316.

them. The boys act as beaters; and it is the duty of all the men to drive the game to a common centre where the chief has taken up his position. As the circle gets narrower and narrower, the terrified game grow very wild, and finally turn completely silly, running straight on to the assegais that everywhere surround them. Any one who kills a buck immediately puts it on his shoulder, and, running up to the chief, lays it on the ground at his feet. Possibly half a dozen claimants come up, each maintaining that he has had a hand in the killing of the animal. The chief decides all such claims on the spot, and everybody is satisfied. The man who is judged to have killed the animal carries it away and is allowed to reserve it, not for himself, but for his family or group; but if the chief should happen to have decided that another man's dog helped to hold the animal while it was being killed, then a leg of the animal—it would sometimes need ten legs to satisfy all the claimants—has to be given to the man as his share of the spoil: but even this man does not regard the leg of the buck as his private property, for he shares it with his group of friends. There are times when the natives hunt privately, but the tribal hunts are the great events, for sometimes enormous quantities of game are then secured.

Wild animals originally formed a large part of the food-supply of the tribe: it was therefore thought that the game belonged to the community, and that no private individual had the right to warn people off any private preserve. Thus the hunting of game was socialised, while there was a certain amount of reasonable liberty granted to the individual to hunt privately.

(*d*) *Land.*—All the land owned by the tribe is vested in the chief, who allows every man to use as much ground as his wives can till. No land can be sold, entailed, or devised, and yet a man knows that his gardens will never be taken from him so long as he cultivates them. All unallotted land that is not required for gardens, together with all wood and water, is regarded as common property for the grazing of cattle or for the needs of all the members of the clan. The nationalisation of land is therefore absolute.

It is important to note that it was the sense of the solidarity of the clan that led to the tribalisation of the land. It is easy to imagine the institution of a carefully thought-out plan of land-tenure devised so as to prevent scandalous selfishness and neglect of the good of the people, and also so as to produce and foster a spirit of *camaraderie* and social union: but this is not what happened amongst the Kafirs; for in their case the system of land-tenure is the effect and not the cause of their communism. In their case individual self-consciousness is not fully developed, though the clan-consciousness is amazingly strong. The individual amongst the Kafirs to a large extent confuses (we might say *fuses*) himself with his clan, and therefore has not that strong sense of personal property and "rights" that obtains amongst people who have become acutely conscious of their own individuality.

Again, this nationalisation of land did not arise out of a sense of territorial sovereignty, for the chiefs were not the chiefs of Zululand, Basutoland, nor of any other "land"; they were the chiefs of the Zulus, the Basutos, and so forth. "Territorial sovereignty—the view which connects sovereignty with the possession of a limited portion of the earth's surface—was distinctly an off-shoot, though a tardy one, of feudalism. This might have been expected *a priori*, for it was feudalism which, for the first time, linked personal duties, and by consequence personal rights, to the ownership of land." *

It would be difficult to devise a more complete socialising of land than that adopted by the Kafirs; and no wonder the natives are scandalised when they see a missionary putting up a fence around a certain plot of land and declaring that it is his private property. "But, eh!" says the Kafir, "how the white man eats up our land!"

(*e*) *Administration of Justice.*—In any case of dispute, a man would appeal, naturally, first of all to the head-man of the group: if he were not satisfied with the opinion of the head-man, he would bring the matter before the petty chief, and only in important cases would he make the final appeal to the Paramount Chief. So thoroughly is justice regarded as a thing within the tribe that a man is only responsible for injuries he does to members of his own tribe. In fact there is no court that is competent to sit on an inter-tribal affair. A man who injures a person belonging to a hostile or rival tribe does a meritorious action in the eyes of his own clan. "International law," says Holland, "can subsist only between States which, on the one hand, sufficiently resemble one another, and are close enough knit together by common interests to be susceptible of the uniform pressure of public opinion, while, on the other hand, they are not so politically combined as to be controlled by the force of a central authority." †

* Maine: "Ancient Law," 10th edit. p. 108.
† "Jurisprudence," p. 370.

There can therefore be no inter-tribal law in the case of the Kafirs.

Every now and then a chief may send a daughter to another chief with the view of forming an alliance, or of compelling him to admit his dependence on the sender of the girl. The chief must either accept the girl as wife, and so accept the alliance, or the position of subordination, as the case may be, or he must drive back the girl and prepare for war. This demand for alliance or submission is perhaps the nearest approach the Kafirs can show to international law.

If a person feared that he was going to be "eaten up" by his chief, he might escape and take refuge with the chief of another tribe—"Live under his shadow," as the Kafirs graphically say. In that case he would have to pay a number of cattle to the new chief as a guarantee for good behaviour. When the new chief accepts the cattle he becomes, *ipso facto*, responsible for the protection of the fugitive, who, having failed in his old tribal obligations of course loses his old tribal privileges. The only peaceable way in which the original chief can get back his escaped subject is by paying a greater number of cattle to the chief with whom the man has taken refuge. Should this prove ineffective, the only other appeal is to war. A recent writer, wishing to make out a case against her own nation, has recently revived an unsavory episode that took place in Natal more than thirty years ago. But her case could not be made out without inventing the existence of a "fundamental" inter-tribal law, forbidding a chief from following a fugitive. It was therefore evolved from the imagination, the writer forgetting that the very existence of the Clan-System indicates a social condition anterior to the recognition of "frontiers," or of local contiguity as a political bond. Had she but understood Kafir thought, she would have seen that no Kafir would be scandalised at our action, which was in keeping with native custom. Mr. Brownlee, writing in 1858, says: "About forty years since, it was lawful to put a man to death for the act of adultery; but Gaika abolished this law and ever since, bloodshed, in a case of this nature, is punished as murder. . . . A man is punished for taking the law into his own hands; and in no case is he justified in doing so, even in a case of retaliation. There is this to be observed, that the above remarks refer to people of one tribe; but if the case were between people of different tribes, and the injured person obtained no redress, he would retaliate on any one of the other tribe who came within his power, and in this would be supported by his chief until redress was obtained; but there does not appear to be any law to sanction the custom."* Thus tribal law may restrain a man from injuring a member of his own tribe, but there is no constraint in connection with violence or injury done to a person outside the closed circle of the tribe. It is strange that Brownlee did not see that there could be no "law" in such a case; for in the first place, a custom needs no law for its support, as in primitive races custom supports the law which it creates; and in the second place, a law only holds good within the tribe, as there is no vestige of machinery for international or inter-tribal law. In such matters might is the only right. We thus see that the administration of justice is, in the fullest sense of the word, tribalised.

McLean's "Compendium of Kafir Law."

(*f*) *Magic.*—There are three errors that are so deeply ingrained in European minds that one almost despairs of eradicating them: they are, first, that magic in the eyes of savages is regarded as a use of *supernatural* forces; secondly, that magic is the same thing as witchcraft; thirdly, that witch-doctors are sorcerers, witches, or wizards.

With regard to the first of these errors, it cannot be too clearly stated that the savage regards magic as no more supernatural than such a thing as the rising of the sun, or the growing of the crops, or the falling of a stone to the earth. Magic is no more supernatural than is the electrical dynamo, though it may pass the wit of a plough-boy to conceive how the cunning machine works. The machine may be beyond the comprehension of the lad, who does not, however, imagine that it therefore works by supernatural forces, for he is aware that it was made by men who know more about the laws of this strange universe than he does. In the eyes of the Kafir, the diviner is simply a cunning man who understands, better than ordinary people, the inner working of nature. It follows, as a matter of course, that the diviner can use forces for the service of man in ways that pass the understanding of ordinary folk.

With regard to the second error, magic is the legitimate social use of these forces of nature, while witchcraft is the private and illicit anti-social use of such forces. The State regulates the use of the secret knowledge of nature's ways, and sees that it is used for the common good of the tribe. The tribal *diviner*, or *magician*, therefore, not only confounds the politics but also frustrates the knavish tricks of the common enemy. He is the bulwark of society. The person who uses witchcraft, however, is supposed to have found out some of these secrets of nature which he (or she) uses so as to avenge injuries, or to secure illicit and immoderate gain, purely for personal and anti-social ends.

With regard to the third error, the *sorcerer* (the witch or wizard) is the person who either uses these secret forces of nature for his own ends, or who secretly sells his knowledge, or puts it at the disposal either of the enemies of the tribe or of people who wish to pay out their own personal grudges regardless of public interests. He is the enemy of the tribe, for he has no regard to its interests. The diviner—the so-called witch-doctor—is the man appointed by the State to use all these tremendous forces of nature for the common good of the tribe. He knows how to ward off evil from the tribe, how to doctor the army, how to form a veritable ring of defence around a kraal or a country into which charmed circle no wizard who is the enemy of the clan, and no disease, can enter. This clever man knows how to make charms to induce the crops to grow; he knows how to kill the locusts; and he knows how to prevent the spread of disease, and, in short, to secure the well-being of all the members of the tribe. He is the sworn enemy of the sorcerers; and it is one of his main functions to detect and "smell out" these anti-social charlatans. All these excellent functions are rarely united in the person of one human being, for there is, as a rule, the duly appointed crops-doctor, the locust-doctor, the witch-detecting doctor, the rain-doctor, the medicinal- or herb-doctor, the war-doctor, the lightning-doctor, and so forth.

There is a class of magical practices that comes between these two divisions of tribal magic and personal witchcraft.

The Kafirs are for ever using such innocent things as love-charms, which are neither regarded as detrimental to the clan nor as of much use to it. There is thus a sort of neutral zone which is regarded as quite harmless; native girls or young men will even go to white traders to buy such things as magnets or the prismatic glasses of chandeliers with which to attract and hold the affections of some other person.

It should now be clear what it is that the Kafir condemns in connection with witchcraft. He does not think it wrong to use the hidden forces of nature, but he thinks it extremely base for a person to use these forces for anti-social purposes. Magic is socialised, and the private individual must recognise this fact. Let us imagine for a moment that some Englishman were to discover such a thing as the Heat Ray of Mr. Wells's Martians,* wherewith he could frizzle up whole crowds of men and entire regiments of soldiers. Would not there be a popular outcry that the State, instead of allowing an irresponsible person to make havoc of our population, should interfere and control this force? In the eyes of the Kafir the witch or wizard has somewhat similar powers at beck and call, and the natives naturally desire such a force to be socialised or controlled by the tribe.

The Rev. H. A. Junod, in a most interesting and valuable paper on "The Theory of Witchcraft amongst South African Natives," has thrown much light on the subject. Yet towards the end of his paper he says: "It may seem

* Reference might also be made to the fears of people half a century ago concerning mesmerism and its possible use for criminal purposes.

inexplicable that millions of human beings who possess a fair amount of reason and of common sense . . . can entertain such absurd, dreadful ideas. But let us remember that three centuries ago European tribunals were condemning wholesale hundreds of poor people accused of witchcraft. There, however, was a capital difference. The white witches, our ancestors, who were burnt by thousands all over Europe, were supposed to have made a pact with Lucifer, the Prince of Darkness. That sin was considered as essentially diabolical in its origin. The Bantu have no idea of Satan, and that aspect of witchcraft is entirely absent from their mind."

I do not believe this distinction can bear examination. If anything, the theory and practice were more reprehensible in the case of the Europeans than in the case of the Kafirs. M. Junod seems to me to fail to see that the indignation shown against witchcraft all the world over is due to a hatred of anti-social tendencies. The essence of our European satanic theory of witchcraft would seem to be quite in keeping with Kafir conceptions. The witch or wizard was supposed to make use of mysterious and uncanny forces. Europeans, no less than Kafirs, had to interpret the thing in terms of their own thought. In Europe the explanation of such a thing was naturally tinged and coloured by the overpowering religious conceptions of the times. Yet the priests in mediæval days worked magic in a dozen different ways, and were held in great respect and reverence on that very account. They were able—so the common people thought—to bless the arms of the military forces of the nation; they were able to effect cures by means of relics; they forgave sins and granted indulgences; they controlled miracles; blessed the crops; stayed plagues; and in a dozen different ways performed the most amazing feats that Kafir diviners also are thought to perform. But their actions were all regulated by authority, and were supposed to be used for the good of the State; but the witches, who used very similar powers, were supposed to work for private, immoral, or anti-social ends, without submitting to the regulations of the authorities. They were therefore regarded as the enemies of mankind; and, since any stick is good enough to beat a dog with, they were accused of working through evil agencies. Moral indignation takes on a different colour in different races. The satanic theory of witchcraft not only arose as a natural explanation, but was also obviously suited to justify the treatment meted out to these poor wretches. But even in Europe there was a class between these two great types, for there were numbers of Thaumaturgic mystics whose practices were so neutral from a social or moral point of view that it was almost a toss-up whether they came to be regarded as social, neutral or anti-social in their tendency. One of these mystics might be made into a saint, another left unnoticed, and a third condemned by the authorities to be burnt to death.

In the case of the Kafirs, the man who uses the forces of nature in a cunning way to the advantage of the tribe is regarded as a public benefactor, while the man who uses precisely similar forces for private and anti-social ends is regarded as an enemy to the tribe, and consequently unfit to live. Between these two there is a class that uses similar practices for harmless and innocent purposes, and such people are left alone to go their own way unmolested but unpraised. We shall never understand Kafir conceptions as to the odiousness and crime of using *witchcraft* or *sorcery*, and the beneficence of the users of *magic*, until we clearly grasp the essential fact that the use of magic, no less than the use of land, has been socialised. Legitimate and public-spirited use of magic makes a man a *diviner;* the illegitimate and selfish private use of magic makes a man a *sorcerer*.

(*g*) *Religion.*—It is but natural that religion in a primitive race should crystallise round the axis of the tribe. To change the metaphor, the conception of the tribe is the spine of the whole body of native thought. In the eyes of the Kafir there are few things more important than the maintenance of the religious customs of the tribe.

There is no need to labour the fact that religion has sometimes been, if not a retrograde force, at least a cause of stagnation at certain epochs in the history of the world. The old enmity between science and religion may be given as an example. Yet ethnology, whatever light it may throw ultimately on the exclusive claims of certain religions, has undoubtedly helped us to appreciate the great benefits the world has received through religion. Even magic, which we had generally regarded as inimical to the good of society, has been shown by Dr. Westermarck (in the second volume of "Sociological Papers") to have contributed in no small way to the amenities of life: by attaching great importance to a curse, it has strengthened filial obedience to parents; it has encouraged charity to the poor; it has upheld and intensified the claims of hospitality; it has broken down the selfishness of the savage about his food; it has upheld the right of sanctuary for the oppressed.

Thus, by appealing to reverence, awe and fear, it has restrained the grossest evils of savage life. And if magic has tended in the direction of civilisation, how much more must religion have done so? Religion has restrained the turbulent impulses of the savage, and has given him ideals to live for. Mr. Jevons has pointed out, in his "Introduction to the History of Religion," that it is quite possible we owe such things as the culture of wheat and other grains, as well as the domestication of the ox and the sheep, to totemism. His idea seems to be that when men felt a bond of sympathy with such things, they regarded them as totems, and sought to secure the growth of the grain by preserving the seed, and began to protect the sheep and oxen from undue struggle for existence. It is therefore quite possible that the man who rails at religion may owe the very bread he eats to the totemism of his ancestors. Were it not for primitive religion there would probably be no civilisation to-day. The religion of primitive races may not be lofty in a spiritual sense, but it is at least more effective in the direction of restraining the impulses of primitive peoples than is Christianity in curbing the vices of European races. It is hardly too much to say that a savage never knowingly disobeys his religious belief or conviction. Within the narrow area of its operations, the religion of a savage is intensely effective, and is something like a law of nature.

The religion of the Kafirs is a blend of a decadent form of totemism, an elementary type of ancestor worship, and an all-pervading fetishism. No idols of any sort are worshipped; while the belief in a Supreme Being, to say the least, is vague and uncertain. It is important to remember that religion, in the case of a primitive people like the Kafirs, is mainly an affair—and a public affair—of the men, for the women play a very subordinate part in it.

It is but natural for the people to think that when the chiefs and head-men die they still retain the interests in the tribe or clan that they ever showed during life. They therefore think that the *amatongo*, or spirits, of such people preside over the destinies of the clan and are in a large measure responsible for its fortunes. It is of the utmost importance that the tribe or clan should maintain an intimate relationship with such ancestral spirits. Religion is therefore socialised.

The founder of the tribe is the one common ancestor who binds the members of the different clans in religious unity: while the deceased head-men of the different clans cement the family tie and strengthen the bond of consanguinity. Thus ancestral worship is a means of strengthening the tribal and family ties.

To the European, the Kafirs seem singularly devoid of reverence in their worship of the ancestral spirits, for the meat-feast, which forms one of the chief ceremonies of their worship—"We pray by eating beef," said a Kafir to me once, "just as white men pray by using words"—is not the type of thing that we are accustomed to. Kafir religion, like the religion of the Israelites in early times, does not seem to us to be an inward or subjective religion of the heart, for it is occupied rather with outward action than with inward motive and ideal. There is, however, a good deal more in the religion of the Kafir than meets the eye of the average European observer. A Kafir when on a journey, or when hunting game, or when entering on any important enterprise, prays inwardly to his *itongo*, or special ancestral spirit, and repeatedly expresses his religious emotions in ejaculatory prayer. Boys pray to the cord used in making bird-traps ; anoint it with medicine and beg it to catch birds nicely; and having done this, they pray to the *amatongo*, whom they have heard their fathers address. When a man is offered beer, he will spill a few drops from the full pot on to the earth, saying, "Chiefs"—addressing his ancestral spirits as he offers the libation. He will also, when offered snuff, take a little pinch and drop it on the ground as an offering to the ancestral spirits. When he has received an unexpected boon, he will laugh, and will repeatedly thank his *itongo*. A dozen similar occasions occur on which a man shows that, though he may not be demonstrative in his emotions, his religion is yet very far from being devoid of heart. The man's religion is, it is true, largely confined to questions of clan-taboo, coupled with the desire to hold communion with his tribal ancestors. In their way, the people are all religious until civilisation undermines their customs, and they are influenced by their religious beliefs more than they are aware, and very much more than most missionaries imagine. Amongst the natives, Church and State are one and indivisible, and everybody is religious in one and the same way—new theologies, nonconformists, and blatant sceptics being unknown. All such things would be regarded as anti-social; and proselytising Christian Kafirs are regarded as unpatriotic men who are willing to sacrifice the good of their tribe for personal whims and fancies. Kafirs think that missionaries inoculate the people by means of medicines and potent charms, turn them silly, and persuade them to be sacrilegious to their tribal ancestors. It is sometimes thought to be a device of the white man to undermine the tribe. It is difficult to see how this can be helped since the Kafirs have socialised their religion. A native who breaks with the religion of his clan appears basely to fail in his fundamental duty to his fellows.

(*h*) Finally, we must say that all such things as food, beer, private earnings, blacksmithing,* matrimony, &c., are more or less tribalised. When the people are eating food or drinking beer, any member of a clan or tribe who happens to be passing invites himself to the feast; there is no need for him to wait until he is asked to join the party. But this only holds good for members of the tribe. Scattered about the country at the side of the pathways, there are frequently to be found small heaps of stones called *isivivane*, about which there has been very much speculation, into which we cannot enter in this place. When natives pass one of these heaps, they pick up a stone, or a twig, and throw it onto the *isivivane*. They do this, amongst other reasons, to ensure the finding of plenty of food along their journey. But it is noticeable that they only throw stones on to such heaps as are in their own territory. If a member of some rival tribe, travelling through the country, were to throw a stone on to the heap, he would almost certainly be noticed by many sharp eyes that are for ever watching; and at the first kraal he stopped at, he would be told in unmistakable language that there was no food for him in that district.

* This art is rapidly disappearing under the influence of our trade.

In ancient days when white men wanted labour, they would sometimes go to a chief, who would order a number of his men to go and work for the white man; and the chief would take as much of the earnings of these men as he wished, for all that his men earned was so much tribal property, and therefore at the disposal of the chief.

Coupled with all this, the people have a clear sense of the responsibility of the corporate body for the deeds done by the individuals of the tribe. We shall return to this subject later on. In surrendering their "rights," they may seem to us to pay heavily for this privilege, but in their own eyes they think they drive a very good bargain, as they are thus freed from half the responsibilities and fears of life.

It will be clear now that the tribe is a highly socialised community, being what the Greeks would call *πολίς αὐτάρχης*, that is to say, a self-sufficed State without any imports. It is complete in itself, and the essence of its government is group-association. The tribe, and in some measure the clan, may be regarded as an organism; for it is a sort of enlarged individual, and has a solidarity that is almost absolute. It is a closed society into which the young men are introduced by a special rite when they come of age; and when any man in any way fails to perform his obligations, he finds that his privileges vanish. Thus when a man becomes a Christian, he practically cuts himself adrift from his clan, and has to shift for himself as best he may, If he is a good-natured fellow, his lot is not made unpleasant, for the natives value and respect good-nature very highly.

The Clan-System of the Kafirs is of great value because it is the seed-plot in which the altruistic sentiment develops

It is most striking to notice how there is much less selfishness and much more *camaraderie* amongst the "heathen" Kafirs than amongst the ruck of the "Christian" converts. The Clan-System simply could not exist without a strong sense of the brotherhood of the members of the tribe; and it might be well for European Socialists to bear this fact in mind. No system of collectivism that is imposed from without upon a selfish, licence-loving people can hope to succeed. To be successful it must be the spontaneous outcome of strong altruistic feeling. Until Europeans can base the structure of their society on a sense of obligations to be performed, rather than on rights to be received, they must remain unfitted for Socialism, and could, at the best, but make the "have nots" change places with the "haves." It is not a little surprising that those who are fighting the Socialists in Europe do not pursue the policy of explaining to the masses that the socialistic state they are asked to help to set up, so far from being a question of extra skittles and beer, will demand the utmost self-sacrifice of fierce individual interests, and will entail almost undreamt-of obligations and restraints on every man. No doubt all self-respecting and intelligent Socialists * recognise this fact; but it has not at all penetrated the intelligence of the average working man, who fondly dreams of a sort of *bourgeois* suburban New Jerusalem, where those who are

* The popular outcry against Socialists, based on trumped-up accusations of irreligion and immorality, is most deplorable. Though in no sense a Socialist, I feel bound to protest against the shameful tactics of those who quote sentences from socialistic writers, while concealing the bearing of the context. At the worst, Socialists are visionary and unpractical people who think too well of human nature, and who imagine that all men are as altruistic and public-spirited as they are themselves. No great crime this!

at present poor are going to be enriched at the expense of those who are now wealthy. Militant Socialism depends for much of its popularity in the gallery on the ignorant assumption of the man who preaches at the street corner that Socialism will mean all privileges and no obligations. No wonder those who have nothing to lose, and who think they may have much to gain without working for it, are tempted to join the cry; for in the general scramble that they think will follow a social upheaval, they hope to get something for nothing. Were it made clear to the working man that he will have to ignore most of his individual "rights" that he is now clamouring for, and will have to accept, whole-heartedly, his obligations to society, he would either accept the fact and set to work to discipline his nature, or else he would have nothing more to do with Socialism. And if Socialism should win the day, the tactics suggested above would be found to have been of great value, for the people would thus have developed their altruistic spirit and minimised the evils that are inseparably connected with every human scheme. Whether or not we can hope the average Briton to rise to the undoubtedly high level of the despised African savage in this respect is open to doubt.

Passing on from the organisation of the clan we must consider the advantages of the Clan-System.

## II. Advantages of the Clan-System

(1) The system has certainly satisfied the bulk of the people, and that is no small achievement. Amongst the raw Kafirs one practically never finds people who are for

ever discontented with, and looking out for causes of complaint against, their rulers. There is no such absurd thing as a Party system, and consequently nobody plays fast and loose with the interests of the tribe. No one ever dreams of asking for the franchise, or for popular control, until white men put the ideas into the heads of the few ill-educated Kafirs, who are naturally hostile to the entire Clan-System and to the chiefs. The system has made the people surprisingly unselfish in the way they sacrifice their own private gain and private ideas for the good of the State. Passive Resisters would be regarded as the most selfish and callous of individualists, and no one dreams of breaking a law so as to attract attention to a grievance. It is only the educated Kafirs who become aggressively selfish, who find their obligations irksome, who press their own ideas, and who foment discontent. If any device that we may have wit enough to introduce will make the bulk of the people even half so contented with the state of affairs, we shall indeed be fortunate.

(2) The system has led to a general and uniform state of medium prosperity, for on the tribal system of land-tenure poverty is virtually impossible. A system that absolutely prevents the formation of a class of paupers has indeed points in its favour. We cannot hope to introduce any plan of individualism which will not inevitably produce a vast amount of poverty, and squalor, and suffering amongst the natives.

(3) The effect of the system has been that the people rise, if they rise at all, *en masse;* therefore the clash of various types, all at different stages of culture, is impossible. There is no war between capital and labour, nor yet any

class of people that regards another as composed of blood-suckers. This universal social harmony is of no small advantage to the people.

(4) There has been no trouble whatever as to taxation. Since, until they are brought into contact with civilisation, the people have no money, they can only be taxed in kind: the chief is supported by the fines inflicted for criminal offences; he can also requisition labour according to his needs; and he receives large "dowries" from the men who seek to marry his daughters. Thus the people readily and willingly pay their way; they support their chiefs, and even glory in the self-sacrifice this entails. I have seen the young Swazi warriors, who would scorn the idea of doing anything so feminine as to hoe in the gardens or fetch wood, do both these things for their king. All the young bloods turned out in regiments and showed the highest delight in doing this work, which was changed from a shame into a glory just because the gardens belonged to the king and not to themselves.

(5) The natives are very frequently satisfied with the decision of the head-man or petty chief; and if they are dissatisfied with that, they are certain to be content to welcome, and abide by, the decision of their chief, whose judgment is the end of all strife. It is scarcely an exaggeration to say that in olden days the man who lost his case was as contented with the chief's verdict as was the man who won it: the chief had spoken, and that was the end of all controversy. It need scarcely be said that our administration of justice can never appear to the Kafir as satisfactory, but must serve as an endless cause of discontent.

(6) The system produced a most valuable method of inculcating the spirit of unselfishness and *camaraderie*. It is almost impossible to over-estimate how valuable such a thing is amongst primitive peoples where a fierce egoism walks naked and unashamed. This spirit of good-fellowship is very evident to one when travelling with a large number of native carriers. I have often been struck at the extraordinary kindness these simple children of the veld showed to one another even under the most trying conditions. After a long day's march in the tropics, men who have carried a 60 lb. load on their head for thirty miles will run the last mile or two of the day's tramp, put down their loads at the camping-ground, and race back to carry the load of some native who happened to be tired. Numbers of similar instances of a spirit of unselfishness could be mentioned.

(7) The system has served the most invaluable of all functions, namely, that of constraining, controlling, and curbing the appetites and passions of the natives. The system has provided what must be regarded as an immensely strong clan-conscience, and it is this function that, above all others, shows us that the system is no mean mode of civilisation. Clan-custom and clan-taboo perform in primitive peoples what religion does, or tries to do, in more advanced nations. Kafir religion may have ethical force in many directions, yet not infrequently the natives make their religious conceptions the excuse for a gross sensualism of which they feel at times not a little ashamed. When wishing to argue with the white man about the undue gratification of some appetite, a man will say: "If *Umkulunkulu* (The Great One) gave me this appetite, it is

not my affair but his if I indulge it excessively." While the native might argue thus about some semi-bestial private action, he would not, even though he knew he could not possibly be observed, entertain even for a moment the thought of doing some comparatively innocent thing that was condemned by tribal custom as being anti-social. A clan-taboo acts as an immensely strong categorical imperative, except where contact with civilisation has weakened the Clan-System.

Instead of every man playing for his own hand, the members of the clan have clubbed together to seek the interest and to advance the prosperity of the social group. The most fundamental of all the appetites, and the one most frequently put into operation, is the desire for food. Now we have seen that instead of each man keeping all the food he can for his own consumption, it is one of the first duties in the clan to let all others share in the food that is being eaten. Few things are thought more base than to refuse to share food with others. To eat in secret is a most base and vile action in the eyes of the Kafir.

Another important department of life the Clan-System took in hand was the regulation of the intercourse of the sexes; and until Europeans broke up the Clan-System this restraint was wonderfully effective within certain limits. Unblushing abuses we tolerate in Piccadilly or Regent Street could never exist under Kafir rule. All who understand the intensely strong sexual instincts of the raw Kafir—and in this matter the Kafir would make Boccaccio, and possibly Apuleius, blush—will see of what infinite value the Clan-System was in curbing this most violent and turbulent of all Kafir impulses. And amongst the worst vices fostered by contact with the white man, the two most pernicious and unlovely are the indulgence in gluttony and greediness in connection with food, and the loss of restraint, and the lack of regulation, of the sexual instincts and impulses. Civilisation pays heavily for the latter, for practically all the outrages on white women are committed by Kafirs who have been for some time in contact with civilisation and out of the reach of clan-control. I have known single white women to live for years all unprotected amongst hordes of raw Kafirs—one American lady lived actually in the kraals—and yet I have never heard of an authentic case of any attempted outrage committed in such cases by the natives. The fear of such lonely white women is that they may suffer at the hands, not of the Kafirs, but of low-typed white men who may be tramping through the country.

(8) The tribal system has been the one thing that has prevented a universal rising of the natives; for, coupled with friendship within the tribe, there exists the intensest jealousy of one tribe towards another. However much we may condemn this narrow-minded hostility, we must admit that it has worked most admirably in our favour. Had the tribes combined in early days, the white man would have had insuperable difficulty in gaining a foothold in the country; and it is only in so far as we have undermined the Clan-System that it is possible for natives to combine against us.

* * * * *

When we weigh up these excellent features of the Clan-System, and then think of the way our philanthropists have pressed upon these people the strange and tangled civilisation of the Western world, with all its sordid accompaniments, we can but pause and say to ourselves:

> I often wonder what the Vintners buy
> One half so precious as the goods they sell.

Before forming a definite opinion on this point, let us pass on to consider the other side of the story, noting the disadvantages of the Clan-System.

## III. The Defects of the Clan-System

There are, it would appear, but two serious accusations that can be brought against the Clan-System. The first is that under it the people are too much at the mercy of their chief. To Europeans, who most conveniently ignore the ruthless tyranny of majorities in a democratic country, this possibility of abuse of power seems a very terrible thing. The Zulu chief Tshaka is a notable instance of such a tyrant. Yet it must be clearly understood that the people very rarely complain of the way their chiefs use their power. There are so many subtle ways of bringing a chief to book that as a rule the man is careful not to offend his people. After looking all round the question, I feel fairly certain that this theoretical abuse of power is not so common as is imagined. There is certainly no doubt that the natives would rather be under their chiefs than be ruled by, let us say, the Committee of the Aborigines Protection Society or an English Radical Government. Yet for all that, in weighing up the advantages and disadvantages of the Clan-System, we must remember the fact that some chiefs abuse their power.

The second accusation seems to be a very much more

serious one. It is often said, with not a little truth, that in a Kafir kraal there is not only no incentive but no room for individual initiative. The consequence of this is that the entire tribe reaches—for it aims at—a low, dull level of mediocrity, in which no one is behind or in front of the mass. The result of this unprogressive state of affairs is seen in the facts that the Kafirs to-day cling to the customs of their ancestors, build the same type of rude hut, use the same primitive implements and methods of agriculture and warfare, and have borrowed little or nothing from the civilisation of the white man. It is therefore thought that the Clan-System is inherently opposed to the whole spirit of progress, and that the chiefs are, as a rule, the bitterest of all opponents to the missionary and school teacher. The Clan-System seems to enshrine a conservatism that is nearly absolute: all innovations are regarded with suspicion, simply because they are innovations; the status of woman will apparently remain low so long as the system continues; polygamy will vanish slowly, if at all; the belief in witchcraft will never die out, and many poor wretches will continue to suffer from this cause; the *lobola* custom, in virtue of which a man receives a number of cattle when he gives his daughters in marriage, will probably remain the woman's one defence and safeguard—and it is not a noble one, though it is surprisingly effective.

Such is the second accusation that is brought against the Clan-System. Before we try to weigh up the advantages and disadvantages of the system we must glance at the means by which it has been broken up.

## IV. The Disintegration of the Clan-System

It is not infrequently stated in the Home Press, and also in books on South Africa, that we are not destroying the Clan-System, but are conserving everything that is good in it. For example, in a recent book on the native problem we find these words at the close of a two-page description of the Clan-System:

"Such then, briefly, was the tribal system, which has been modified and moulded into the forms thereof in existence at the present time in British South Africa. . . . So we see that all that was excellent in the original forms of native government was to remain, embodied in British rule and necessarily under British protection." It might as well be maintained that after having cut out several square yards from different parts of a balloon we had not destroyed its efficacy. The Clan-System depends for its success upon its completeness, and the removal of essential elements destroys the value of the organisation. We have undermined the Clan-System right and left, and have riddled its defences through and through with the explosive shells of civilisation; we have removed nearly all the old restraints which curbed the people, and have disintegrated their religion, and so rendered it, comparatively speaking, useless. It is not to be wondered at that the various tribes are in chaotic and confused condition, ready to listen to any nonsense the Ethiopians choose to put before them. The savage under real self-government is in no sense the same thing as the savage with his customs and government broken up by the presence of white men in the country.

With the Clan-System have gone, or are going, some of the best traits in Kafir character.

We have set up an absurd legal fiction in virtue of which some white official is pompously called the Paramount Chief of some native tribe, and we insist that the natives shall salute this person with the forms and ceremonies used to the real Paramount Chief. The natives are so very courteous by nature that they readily show all the signs of outward respect we demand from them, but when our backs are turned they laugh and ask what these inconsequent white men will want next.* The white man, however, looks at this ridiculous silk tassel that he has fastened on to the ruined balloon, and asks us to believe that the emasculated system of patchwork we have left behind is the Clan-System.

It may be well to point out how we broke up the Clan-System, looking at this matter of course from a native point of view. We started by undermining the power of the chief, and in striking a blow at him we struck a death-blow at the very heart of the system, for it is in him that all the main girders of the structure are centred. First of all we took away the chief's power of making war against rival clans, and thus dishonoured or insulted him in the eyes of his people. Having done that we set up white magistrates, who took the law out of the chief's hands and refused to allow him to exercise the power of life and death. We then gave him a subsidy, payable only on condition of good behaviour, and thus made it less necessary for the

* It is interesting to note that this fact has been recorded by Mr. Bryant in his excellent Zulu dictionary, which work is evidently unknown at the Colonial Office, for the new Constitution of the Transvaal keeps up the fiction in all seriousness.

people to support their chief; and since people lose interest in what they cease to pay for, the people lost some interest in their chief. Then we deposed one chief and put up another, and departed from native conceptions of hereditary right; as a consequence it sometimes happened that there were two Popes within the clan, each hurling the Kafir equivalents of Bulls and anathemas at one another. Then we finally pretended that a white man was the Paramount Chief. Thus we discredited the chieftainship. It must be remembered that we are not yet discussing the question as to whether we were wise or not in doing these things, but are merely showing that as a matter of fact we have undermined the system.

Having effectively broken the power of the chief, we set to work to break up, in many districts, the tribal system of land-tenure. We did this largely in the interest of ourselves and of the few natives who welcomed our civilising influences. Sometimes also we did this with the definite intention of inserting the thin end of the wedge so as to break up the Clan-System. In some districts, as, for example, in Swaziland, large tracts of land were sold by chiefs for a mere nothing as concessions to Europeans; and it is quite possible that the chiefs did not realise what they were doing until it was too late, for the Kafirs generally say that the chief has no right to alienate land from the tribe. As soon as Europeans began to press in upon lands hitherto held by the natives, every conceivable kind of modification had to be made as to land-tenure. White men needed labour, and so natives came to live on farms, in towns, and on Mission Stations. Native reserves were formed in which land was held by communal tenure. In some parts of the country, as in most parts of Bechuanaland, Zululand and Basutoland, the land was retained almost wholly for the natives.

In other parts, as, for example, in the Transkeian territories, a larger proportion of white men held land, and villages or small towns were laid out in some districts. In Natal much land became vested in the Native Trust; while in other parts Kafirs owned land individually, having either bought it from white men or (in Cape Colony) having been granted plots in return for services rendered to the State. Natives began to squat on farms, on Mission Stations, or on unoccupied Crown lands, and in certain districts they were allowed to settle on private farms on condition of putting in a certain amount of work in lieu of paying rent. Native syndicates, as in Natal, sprung up, and began to buy up land which had hitherto been the property of the white man. Mr. Rhodes conceived the Glen Grey Act, which is too well known to need description, and which was, confessedly, introduced so as to break down the power of the chief and the corporate spirit of the clan, which were thought to be inimical to progress.

At our mines we have had to deal with the natives as best we could, with the result that these men, after being under our control, return to the kraals and feel disinclined to submit to the restraints of the clan, which they begin to feel irksome.

Missionaries, of course, directly aimed their blows at the system; and every convert, by the very action of professing Christianity, is cut adrift from the clan-life, and yet remains in the country with, at best, divided allegiance to his former chief.

We next interfered by stopping some of the grosser tribal customs. It was almost necessary for us to do this, but it is to be doubted whether we quite understood the inner meaning and outer effect of some of the customs we put a stop to: the effect of our interference, however, is not subject to doubt.

Finally, we brought about the dawn of economic individualism. We gave the Kafirs an example—that most potent kind of lesson—of a new kind of liberty, which some of them, naturally, thought excellent. The natives began to be reluctant to part with individual gains. We taught them the value of thrift and of personal property; we created new wants and urged the natives to labour for us in return for wages—which, of course, was an entirely new thing to them, for in olden days they only worked so as to provide for their actual needs. Traders persuaded the natives to bring them skins, or grain, or wool, or other produce; and so we introduced a new economic era. Previously there had been but little division of labour, and no production of commodities. The people did not distinguish between use-values and exchange-values, but under our tuition they began to see the value of growing things, not for purposes of consumption, but for utility of exchange. We taught them the use of money. We thus brought in the era of economic individualism, and, since a Kafir loses self-control when plunged into an entirely new environment, we sapped the very foundation of the spirit that had hitherto constituted the motive-power in clan-life. If by these means we have not utterly undermined the entire structure of the Clan-System, it is difficult to see what we have done.

## V. The Results of our Policy

The advantages and disadvantages of breaking up the Clan-System are so interwoven that it is difficult to differentiate and assess them accurately, and he is a clever accountant who can draw out a balance-sheet. I heard the other day of two clerks who, on the way to town in the train, were discussing the question of Free Trade and Colonial Preference. Said one superficial gentleman: "Oh, it did not take me two minutes to make up my mind: I decided at once for Free Trade." There are hundreds of people in South Africa who decide the great question as to the relative benefits of the Clan-System and the native franchise with a similar amount of thought.

It is frequently said that we gained considerably by breaking up the Clan-System, for, by undermining the power of the chief just sufficiently to make it difficult for him to fight, and yet not sufficiently to break down tribal jealousies, we avoided a number of little petty wars. It is very doubtful whether our action did not have exactly the opposite effect; but be that as it may, we quite forgot that our policy, by breaking down tribal jealousies, might possibly lead to an ultimate and united native rising worse than fifty small local wars. It certainly looks as if we had now squandered all our initial advantages, and were beginning to feel the more awkward consequences of our hasty action. The scales seem to be turning against us now, and we are reaping the fruit of our half-considered action. Our past action may be likened to a policy that was adopted in the early days in Australia. It is said that during a bad drought in Queensland the farmers cut down a certain bush which they thought absorbed too much water. When they had destroyed an immense amount of the shrub, they found that it was a preserver of water, and that sheep could live on it in times of drought. In their panic, they had destroyed their best asset. The story may be apocryphal, but it is, none the less, an excellent illustration. The Cape, in granting a native franchise, may have destroyed much of its water-preserving bush; but we need not, in our desire for symmetry, set to work to cut down by panic legislation all the rest of the bush throughout South Africa.

But the question before us is not whether *we* gained by our action, for there were obviously certain initial advantages in our policy; what we need to find out is whether or not our action was for the good of *the natives*.

The Kafirs certainly reaped some advantages from our action. The main advantage has been that by limiting the power of the chiefs and by stopping inter-tribal wars, we have made life and property more secure, and have abolished, at least theoretically, death by torture in the case of people found guilty of using witchcraft. In talking with old Kafirs, I have invariably found that it is this that has struck them as the one beneficial result of our rule—though they have always been quick to add that they would rather go back to the old *régime*, with all its disadvantages, than continue as at present. The second advantage is that we have rendered progress possible, while under the Clan-System stagnation was the rule. It must be admitted that there is a great amount of truth in this contention, though it is extremely difficult to avoid all the fallacies that lie in wait for us when arguing thus.

On the other hand, there is but little doubt that progress has been one-sided, superficial, and far too rapid. The civilised Kafirs carry too much sail for their very scanty ballast. We have entirely failed to get the bulk of native opinion on our side, and have made no serious attempt to utilise the immense force of custom. If we had but given them time, the Kafirs would have invented their own restraints suitable to their changed condition. It has been pointed out above that we have broken down the religious and clan-restraints of the people; it must now be added that we have provided no adequate substitutes. To ask a Kafir to accept the restraint of a precept in the Sermon on the Mount is as unpractical as to ask a Member of Parliament, or the German Emperor, to do the same thing in Party, or International, politics. It may be said that we have sought to restrain the people through their fears. That shows how we fail to understand how little a Kafir fears our punishments compared with the consequences of breaking a clan-taboo. We may flog a Kafir, but such an action demeans the white man who gives it more than it disgraces the Kafir who receives it. I speak of course from the native point of view. The one point on which we can touch them is their cattle, and a substantial fine in that direction has more effect than half a dozen floggings, for the men soon forget their pains, but never cease to regret the loss of their beloved oxen.*

* For outrages on white women it may be, and I think is, necessary to flog the natives: in such cases it is generally a half-civilised Kafir who is guilty, and he needs somewhat different treatment from that suited to the raw native.

No doubt we thought that we should be able to provide restraints as effective as those we removed. We forgot the Kafir proverb which says that the well ahead is not to be depended on. We fully intended to substitute strong restraints; but having forsaken the well behind us, we found but dry country ahead. A chain is no stronger than its weakest link, and our weakening of certain links of the Clan-System has spoilt the efficacy of the whole chain. The worst elements of our civilisation are being absorbed by the youth of the Kafir tribes. The young men, on returning to their kraals from the goldfields, or Mission Stations, or towns, refuse to submit to the old clan-restraints, and decline to obey the orders of their betters, for they have lost their sense of reverence—a thing almost unheard of in olden times. The young men become lax and lawless, and are a serious peril to all order and decency in the kraal. This spurious liberty and impudent swagger are very contagious, and even the children become infected. In olden days, for example, only men of mature age were allowed to drink beer and to smoke Indian hemp. Quite small boys do both these things nowadays, and the old people are powerless to prevent them. Sexual irregularities, which were only allowed between young men and their betrothed lovers in ancient days, are now practised freely even by children. Excesses of this nature were rendered very rare in olden days, because all the girls of the kraal were examined by a court of old women before and after great dances. The girls now refuse to submit to these examinations, and threaten to go and complain to the white magistrate if they are examined against their wish. The old men know quite well that the magistrates know but little of native custom, and that they will look at this matter with European and hostile eyes; so they are powerless to compel obedience from the children. It is hopeless—so the Kafir thinks—to obtain anything but opposition from the white magistrate, who is filled full with his ideas of the rights of the individual. Even the missionary cannot provide suitable restraints. Here and there a few Kafirs grasp the essential spirit of Christianity, and in such cases the new restraints are effective. But the average Church member is but little influenced, with regard to his fierce sexual impulses, by Christian ideals. It is no wonder that the old men sigh for the good old days with all their drawbacks.

As bearing out the above remarks, it may be pointed out that the Rev. F. Roach, giving evidence before the Native Commission upon the native view of British methods of government, said: "The heathen Zulu, I think, compares it unfavourably with his own form of government, before the war. I have had impressions on that point from native head-men themselves, who are heathen, old heathen *Izunduna* or head-men, and they say: 'No, we prefer the old system.' They say that in these days *Indab itengiwe* (bribery) is practised; that evil-doers occasionally get off scot-free; and that children and young fellows get entirely out of hand, because the magistrate's courts uphold them very often in cases of disputes between themselves and their parents. In these three ways they say the government of the present time is inferior to their old system of government. I do not put that as my own opinion; that is the expression I have got from the natives." I entirely agree with this evidence, and have heard the same thing from natives in many other districts.

The Kafirs certainly are an unprogressive race. Of that there is no doubt. They have developed no art, the rude attempts of the children to model in clay not being indulged in, as a rule, after puberty; they have developed no architecture, for Zimbabye, if indeed it be of Kafir origin, cannot be regarded as anything but primitive; they have developed no poetry, their attempts in this direction being chiefly limited to absurd and fulsome praise of their chiefs or of themselves; they have developed no writing—not even knowing the use of pictographs or ideograms —taking over this art but very slowly from the white man; they have developed no form of money or of currency; they have developed no music, not aspiring to anything better than to play the most monotonous jingles on rude instruments; they have developed no national unity, being split up into rival clans and tribes; they have developed no lofty religion, being satisfied with a crude and but slightly ethical ancestor worship, combined with a modified form of totemism and a belief in magic and fetishism; they have developed no philosophy, accepting the crudest hedonism, and giving up the problem of existence as not worth seriously troubling about; they have developed no lofty ideals of any sort, being frankly content with abundance of cattle, beer, and women.

With regard to the alleged necessarily unprogressive nature of the Clan-System, I would point out that there

It is stated that the Malayan races have developed no less than nine alphabets—a striking contrast to the Kafirs, and one that shows how impossible it is to use the Malay States as an analogy.

are probably several factors that have led to the unprogressive condition of the Kafirs. We observe some symptom that arises from half a dozen causes, and are so occupied with one cause that we ignore the rest. All Kafirs have brown-black eyes, but he will be mistaken who puts that fact forward as the cause of the stagnation in Kafir society. Building the huts in circles and using wattle and mud as materials are not parts of the Clan-System; they result from the fact that such materials are ready to hand, and that building in circles leads to simplicity of construction, for angles are difficult things for builders to negotiate. It is extremely difficult to persuade the ordinary Kafir to plant and take care of fruit-trees, or to make any agricultural improvements. That does not seem to be due to the Clan-System, but to the fact that the people have only to scratch the ground to get all the food they require. The use of the plough is becoming more general, and thousands of raw Kafirs—in spite of the Clan-System—are adopting the implement even when living far away from white men. We might take all the points enumerated above, and could show that it is at least doubtful whether they resulted from the Clan-System, though they were concomitant with it. The way chiefs become envious of men who grow rich, and the devices they adopt to get them "smelt out" and "eaten up," are not essential parts of the Clan-System, for such things occur under individualistic forms of government. Those who propose the entire destruction of the tribal-system make much capital out of the fact that when trouble between whites and blacks comes to a head, the chief is found to be at the head of the movement. Of course he is. We might as well propose to abolish Crown and Parliament because they are found, when European wars break out, to be involved in the declaration of war. It seems to be held by opponents to the Clan-System that the chiefs are going to remain for ever selfish, oppressive, and opposed to progress. It is forgotten what an immense change has come about in this respect during the last thirty years. Chief after chief is coming to realise that there are advantages in education; and the old hostility to progres is beginning to vanish—I think a little too quickly.

There seem to be several causes, other than the Clan-System, to account for the lack of progress. There is, for example, the intrinsic nature of the race. Even when freed from the Clan-System, the educated natives show almost no initiative; they start no manufactures, but borrow everything from the white man; they seem incapable of steady progress without constant supervision; the moment this supervision is removed, the men relapse into squalor and indolence. If all this happens when the man is freed from his clan, it is difficult to see how the evil complained of can be due to the clan—unless it is the after-effect of a vicious system. Again, there is the belief in witchcraft, which throws its shadow over the entire life of the people. What is the good of adopting new methods of agriculture, and so growing rich, if it is but to lead to a charge of using sorcery? The relation of witchcraft to the Clan-System is not by any means simple. It may be the belief in magic, and not the socialistic ideas of the people, that is the trouble in this matter. But, yet again, possibly it is the fact that rich men become anti-social that drives the people to hunt round for some accusation to justify them in curbing such a tendency;

thus, it may be, after all, the Socialism of the people, and not their belief in magic, that is really at the bottom of this open sore. The subject can be looked at from two different points of view, and I rather doubt whether any white man can hope fully to understand the matter.

Again, there is the improvidence of the people which obviously leads to stagnation; and there is also sheer ignorance as to how to improve land, to say nothing of the natural dislike of innovations of all kinds, a trait that is found everywhere even amongst Englishmen. None of these points that have just been mentioned seem to be *organic portions* of the Clan-System, which, purged of its defects, might yet become progressive.

One thing seems quite clear, and it is that there is room for great advance under the Clan-System. If we take the Indian village communities, we see how progressive primitive Socialism can be. "The constitution of these communities varies in different parts of India. In those of the simplest form, the land is tilled in common, and the produce divided amongst the members. At the same time, spinning and weaving are carried on in each family as subsidiary industries. Side by side with the masses thus occupied with one and the same work, we find the 'chief inhabitant,' who is judge, police, and tax-gatherer in one; the book-keeper who keeps the accounts of the tillage and registers everything relating thereto; another official, who prosecutes criminals, protects strangers travelling through, and escorts them to the next village; the boundary-man, who guards the boundaries against neighbouring communities; the water overseer, who distributes the water from the common tanks for irrigation; the Bramin, who conducts the religious services; the schoolmaster, who on the sand teaches the children reading and writing." *

It is after examining such a system that Maine has said: "Nobody is at liberty to attack several property, and to say at the same time that he values civilisation." † If he had said "Western," or "Rapid" civilisation, the sentence would hold good. The Kafirs have a very long way to go before they become as civilised as the people living in these Indian village communities; and as far as one can see, if we had retained the Clan-System in its fulness, we might have led the Kafirs on along the path of civilisation as far as they are ever likely to reach with safety. No civilised Kafirs have advanced to the level of such Indian village communities: in fact they are yet far behind the stage of culture reached in India.

The question of the relative values of different systems of land-tenure has been left purposely for the close of our chapter on Primitive Socialism; and to it we must now turn.

The question of land-tenure, as the recent Native Commission states, "dominates and pervades every other question," and is "the bed-rock of the natives' present economic position." It certainly has the most intimate connection with the tribal system. The natives cannot be said to make good use of their land, which, coupled with the genial climate, easily affords the people all they require. It is interesting to note that in the manifesto of the Fabian Society we find it stated that: "The practice of entrusting the land of the nation to private persons in the hope that

* Karl Marx, "Capital," p. 351.
† "Village Communities," p. 230.

they will make the best of it has been discredited by the consistency with which they have made the worst of it." * Whatever may be the truth or exaggeration of such an accusation with regard to England, the statement could not be made with regard to South Africa with even the vaguest semblance of truthfulness.

It is very difficult to say for certain whether the *agricultural* progress observable wherever individual tenure holds in South Africa is due to the system of tenure adopted or to some collateral factor. It is quite common for people to point to the Glen Grey experiment as a proof of the value of individual tenure; yet it is permissible for one who regards the experiment as, on the whole, a great success to point out that there are some peculiar conditions which make it difficult to be sure we are tracing the right cause when we place the success to the credit of individualism. Up to the present it has been possible to select suitable natives for the experiment. Only natives keen to own land and develop it have been selected. When the system becomes universal, this great advantage of selecting suitable Kafirs will vanish. At present no native who believes that crops can only be increased by magical charms applies for land. Thus the commonest cause for indolence is not operative. There is no reason why such a belief should be wedded to any special system of land-tenure. We can no more argue from the success of the Glen Grey Act to the advisability of destroying the system of tribal land-tenure, than we can argue from the success of some land scheme in which selected white men are sent, let us say, to the Orange River Colony, to the wisdom of shipping all our home indolent out-of-

* Tract No. 2

works wholesale into the Transvaal. Selection is the secret of success in both schemes. The unfit are weeded out before the experiment is begun; but it is the unfit that will cause trouble when the scheme becomes adopted universally.

Not a little of the success of the Glen Grey Act has also arisen from the caution, the slowness, the restrictions, and the excellent wisdom with which the scheme has been worked. We could scarcely hope to do so well with a gigantic plan. It is not only the wisdom of a scheme, but it is also the way it is applied and administered, that determines its success or failure amongst the Kafirs. A bad scheme applied with tact will often work amongst primitive people better than a perfect scheme stupidly administered. Our danger is in being premature and in doing excellent things in the wrong way.

In thinking of the benefits of the Glen Grey Act, we are apt to forget that when individual tenure is the rule rather than the exception, there will be considerable progress in suitable cases and appalling failure in bad cases. Poverty will probably increase *pari passu* with the increasing adoption of the plan, and there will also be a great increase of selfishness which will undermine one of the best features in the character of the raw Kafir. Aristotle has censured the community of property as tending to repress industry, and as doing away with the spirit of benevolence; but amongst the Kafirs, whatever may be the result with regard to industry, it is individualism and not collectivism that saps the spirit of benevolence. The raw socialistic Kafir appears to be a philanthropist when compared to the individualistic educated native.

It is very difficult to say what will happen when all the natives enjoy individual tenure; some people think that this change will lead to the Kafirs forgetting their other grievances, for they will be so engrossed—so it is argued—with their interests in the land that they will not have time to listen to agitators. And certainly any one who has become intimate with the Kafirs knows that it is as useless to expect to get a Kafir to think about his other duties, when he has to see to his sowing, or ploughing, or reaping, as it is to get a decent day's work out of an Italian youth when he falls in love. The man becomes obsessed with his one interest. But for all, that there would seem to be another possibility, and a rather grave one. It is just as likely that having once tasted the sweets of owning land, the natives will get greedy for more land; and their land-hunger may make them cast eyes more envious than ever on the districts occupied by white men.

It is fairly certain that in introducing individual land-tenure we shall make as many difficulties as we shall remove; for the change will act like the shaking of a dice-box, and there are sure to be unlooked-for results. It is quite possible that we might gain all the advantages derived from the Glen Grey Act by a different system, which would at the same time conserve what is good in native character. I have seen natives living under the Clan-System and communal land-tenure roused to considerable energy by a sensible missionary who introduced to them new kinds of vegetables, and then took the trouble—a thing very few seem to care to do—to see the experiment tided over the initial difficulties.

Whatever may be done finally, it is to be hoped that

arrangements will at least be made so that those natives who prefer to live on land held by communal tenure may be free to do so. Any enactment should be permissive and not obligatory.

It has been urged that owing to the nature of the land in the native reserves it is not practicable to institute individual holdings. It is possible that some Crown lands may be available; but there is another possibility which seems to be less reactionary, less risky, and more suited to the people. The land might be broken up so that the natives held it by family or group tenure. If that were done, and if the family owned land in perpetuity, all improvements would be kept as family assets. Such a system might appeal to natives who do not wish for individual tenure; for the plan is in keeping with the genius of the people. The natives in Natal show considerable desire to own land by syndicate—that is, by group-association.

Differences as to the value people attach to Socialism may after all resolve themselves in the last analysis into temperamental differences of outlook upon life. Does a man's life consist in the abundance of the things which he possesses, or in his sharing all things with others, and in possessing his soul in contentedness and peace? Of course in one sense it consists in neither of these alternatives, for "We live by Admiration, Hope and Love." But when we have these, what next? Shall we find life in the feverish quest of possessions and contrivances, in the enjoyment of luxury and rapid motion, or, on the other hand, shall we find it in the "Simple produce of the common day," and in "Joy in widest commonalty spread"? The reply to that question will depend upon the temperament of the man who answers. In the West, progress, action, luxury—though they can only be reached through strife, competition and a divine discontent—are the ideals most men cherish: in the East, men prefer placid contemplation, quiet enjoyment and the simple social life. William Morris may sigh for a paradise in which energy and the quest of beauty are combined with self-sacrifice and a spirit of human fellowship. He would take what appeals to him as highest and best in the West and root the flower in what is highest and best in the East. And well has he called his vision "News from Nowhere," for after all,

> East is East and West is West
> And never the twain shall meet.

In England we have long since passed through the socialistic stage, and to go back to it would probably mean regression to semi-barbarism. In spite of the proverbial kindness of the poor to one another, we have too little altruism to ensure the success of collectivism. In our present state of culture we shall get much of the good and none of the evil Socialism would give us, through group-association and a system of co-operative enterprise designed so as to give ample room for individual energy, ambition, and initiative. Amongst the Kafirs the institution of individualism might no doubt lead to certain types of progress; but the people are in a stage of development in which, I think, they will gain more from a Socialism they are accustomed to than from an individualism suited to a highly developed people. They have so much altruism that it seems almost a crime to break down their own system, and with it to destroy the finest qualities of the savage. Communism has been the breath of their life for ages, and they regard the simple life as the best. Shall we, because our nerves are tingling with the desire to hustle everybody on, take these backward people and put them through a process that may possibly lead to some progress, but which must lead also to much suffering and peril? If the Kafirs prefer to lie down in the shade, cannot we leave them alone and go our own hot, bustling way?

I think that we should do better rather to return to the Clan-System and to Kafir modes of thought than to plunge the native races of South Africa into the vortex of our democratic and industrial life. However, if, as seems probable, we decide to push individualism, we should be more than ever anxious to develop all the various sides of the native's character so that he may be prepared for his new life under the changed conditions. White men, whether engaged in industrial or missionary work, must not merely develop one or two sides of the Kafir's nature, but must draw out all his capacities so that he may survive the flood we let loose in the land. When missionaries pay less attention to the apex, and more attention to the base, of the native's character, they will find more stability and intelligence in their converts. And the same thing is true of those who are anxious to gather the Kafirs into our industrial system.

My own view of the matter is that politicians act for Party ends without due forethought, and that there is but little hope that they will mend their ways in this special matter. It looks therefore as if Kafir Socialism were, unfortunately, doomed: but I feel it to be of the very utmost importance that we should retard rather than hasten the process. It is late, but not too late, to conserve many of the finest traits in Kafir character: therefore we should not break up the Clan-System in any district more than we are absolutely bound to do, but should conserve it wherever we can. When the people have outgrown the system, it will drop off of itself. We pass on to trace the effect of socialistic ideals on the Conception of Justice.

# CHAPTER II

## KAFIR CONCEPTIONS OF JUSTICE

THERE is an unmapped region that is bounded in one direction by legal duty, in a second by moral obligation, in a third by social usage, and in a fourth by instinct or habit. It is a sort of no-man's-land, for it is beyond the frontier lines of jurisprudence, sociology, ethics and biology. Since racial custom is so intimately interwoven with conceptions of what is right and fitting, ethnologists have recently annexed this hinterland of the four sciences enumerated; and it is already evident that a study of this region will prove of great interest and importance to all who would rule or civilise the backward races of mankind. If we would help such people to rise out of their backward condition, we must cease to take it for granted that a course of action that is approved of by our highly specialised sense of justice must necessarily appear obviously right and fitting to primitive races.

The most superficial observer is forced to notice certain individual physical differences as well as certain broad resemblances in the different races of mankind: but it often escapes his observation that there are also mental and moral differences that in some directions outweigh the resemblances. This failure to recognise deep-seated differences is largely due to our insularity of nature, which is apt to shut us off from intimate association with the races we govern.

It is strangely difficult to explain convincingly to people who have never come into close contact with backward or primitive races, how widely Europeans and Kafirs differ in their conceptions of justice. It not only calls for much sympathy, but it also takes time for the mind to accustom itself to the atmosphere of primitive thought. It is extremely difficult for a white man to "think black." The man in the street little realises how slowly his own ideas on morals and legal rights have become crystallised into their existing shapes and forms, and how profoundly his conceptions of justice have been affected by custom and social usages. It is not every one who has the opportunity to study the misty region—that "vanishing-point of jurisprudence."—where, as Holland says, "law and morality are not conceived as distinct."

The average Briton is apt to grow impatient at the mere mention of the fact that human beings differ in their conceptions as to what is just and unjust. "Don't tell me," he is apt to say impatiently, "that there is a single sane human being who does not in his heart of hearts know what is just or unjust: we want none of your theoretical subtleties: just give the Kafir straightforward British justice and see if he will not recognise it at first sight." "The Hebrew prophet," writes Jowett, "believed that faith in God was enough to enable him to govern the world; the Greek philosopher imagined that contemplation of the good would make a legislator. There is as much to be filled up in the one case as in the other." The Briton imagines that the administration of his own ideas of justice will usher in the millennium. It seems to be the peculiar right of an Englishman to constitute his own conception of fair play as a sort of Platonic archetype of Eternal Justice. He seems to be constitutionally incapable of believing that his conception of justice is not necessarily universal. He regards his sense of justice as a sort of *noumenon*, or thing-in-itself, that is independent of time and space: he thinks he comes to his conclusions as to what is just or unjust by means of fixed and infallible "intuitions" that must be shared by all other rational beings. He solves the native problem at a stroke, so he thinks, when he urges us to give the Kafirs simple justice and have done with it. The British are proud of many things: they are proud of their Empire, of their Navy, of their commercial activities, of their free institutions; but there is nothing they are so proud of as their impartial administration of justice to all the races they govern. There may be individual Britons who rail at the Empire, who would reduce the Navy, who condemn our industrial and commercial life, who find fault with our Party system; but there is scarcely a Briton who does not profoundly believe that it is pretty well the whole duty of man to administer British justice to all the subjects of the King. The love of justice is the god of our idolatry; and it is the one thing in which we take refuge when we feel ourselves libelled by some other envious nation as to our territory-grabbing propensities.

Our imagination is so dull that we feel something of a shock when so sane and level-headed a man as Jowett says (in his "Plato's Republic"): "There may come a time when the saying, 'Have I not a right to do what I will with my own?' may appear to be a barbarous (*sic*) relic of individualism. Such reflections appear wild and visionary to the eye of the practical statesman, but they are fairly within the range of possibility to the philosopher."

Our historic memory is so short-lived that we forget that the "infallible intuitions" of our great grandfathers are poles asunder from our own intuitions on such a subject as the justice of burning human beings for using witchcraft; yet it was, comparatively speaking, but yesterday that many European nations considered the justice of that action as beyond question, and appealed triumphantly, as the Kafirs do to-day, to their "intuitions" as being decisive. Nay, we need not go so far back: many things that seemed to us essentially just when we were children appear to us in a very different light forty years later, and we pause and pick our steps carefully where once we would have stepped out boldly. The pain with which we part from the old judgments of childhood might give us pause, if not sympathy, with a backward race that often stands aghast at our twentieth-century conceptions of what is just.

"The business of the jurist," says Holland, "is, in the first place, to accept as an undoubted fact the existence of moral principles in the world, differing in many particulars in different nations and in different epochs: and, in the second place, to observe the sort of sanction by which these principles are made effective." There are, of course, certain broad resemblances, especially in abstract questions, between Kafir and European ideas of what is just, and no one wishes to deny the fact. The Kafir, for example, will admit that it is unjust to punish a man who is admittedly guiltless. But once we leave abstract questions and come to practical details, we are faced with endless difficulties in the most unexpected quarters. For example,

Is it just to punish a man for theft? Is it just to punish a man for breaking a contract? Is a child responsible for the debt of his deceased father? Just as an Irishman and an Englishman may differ as to the justice of cattle-driving, just as a Conservative and a Socialist may differ as to the justice of punishing a starving man for stealing bread, so may Kafir and European differ on the questions just asked. The Kafir sees nothing wrong in stealing from a rival tribe, or in leaving, without giving any notice, his European employer who has entered into a contract with him. In some of the above cases, therefore, the European has the loftier ethical conception, but in others, as, for example, the duty of a son to pay his deceased father's debts, the Kafir surpasses him. The soft and welcome excuses that the European might honestly advance with regard to such obligations would be indignantly scouted by the savage. We may imagine, then, how surprised the Kafirs are to find us looking to them for gratitude when, in a bungling fashion, we feel it our duty to correct what we imagine to be their wrong-headed conceptions. It is pathetic to see how chagrined a European magistrate sometimes is when he has gone out of his way to give the Kafir what he considers the inestimable boon of substantial British justice, only to see the Kafir leaving the court in a grumbling and discontented spirit.

The mistake of the Briton consists in his imagining that human nature is all of a piece, and that even as in all races men are agreed as to the intellectual judgment that twice two make four, so they must be agreed as to moral and emotional judgments.

If justice be defined in Justinian's words as the " constant and perpetual will to render to each one his right," then differences in thought as to a man's "right," will lead to concrete differences in human judgments as to what is just. Professor Westermarck, in his "Origin and Development of the Moral Ideas," * has pointed out that the emotional constitution (perhaps he should have said emotional *judgment*) of man does not present the same uniformity as does the human intellect. It would be interesting to pause at this point and to see whether this dissimilarity in emotional judgment be due to constitutional differences, or merely to variations in the data on which the emotional nature works. Leaving on one side this somewhat academic problem, let us pass under review a few of the more important points in which Kafirs differ from Europeans as to conceptions of justice, and as to emotional judgments.

(1) It is custom and precedent, rather than considerations of abstract fairness, that are considered by the Kafirs in their system of jurisprudence. This arises partly out of their veneration for old men and worship of Ancestral Spirits; partly from a tendency in human nature in virtue of which that which is forbidden by authority comes, in process of time, to be felt intrinsically wrong; and partly because "in the vague and floating order of primitive societies the mere definition of a right immensely increases its strength." †

Professor Drummond's description of the way in which the natives in Central Africa form a pathway across country is an excellent illustration of the way in which laws are

* Vol. i. p. 11.

† Maine, "Village Communities," p. 150.

formed in primitive societies.* He tells us how the natives, clad in a little palm oil and a few mosquitoes, avoid stones, ant-heaps, or small bushes, and thereby form their tortuous pathway. One man goes a little bit out of the way because of some obstacle, and the dozen men following him walk in his erratic footsteps, so that the path maintains in the main the desired direction while incessantly wriggling to left and to right. Even so in the case of savages, the people are conscious of a vague direction in which it is best to go. Some individual meets with a difficulty, and the chief is called in to solve the doubt. The path gets twisted a little to one side. This détour becomes established when, lo, another obstacle is met. Resort is again had to the chief, with the result that the path is again deflected. Little by little customs and precedents get established. In opposition to this idea it is sometimes said by theorists that the idea of a custom must precede that of a judicial sentence: but it seems certain that in primitive races it is the judgment of the chief that generally inaugurates a new custom. Maine has expressed this by saying that "the only authoritative statement of right and wrong, in the infancy of mankind, is a judicial sentence after the facts, not one presupposing a law that has been violated." † The Kafir chief who gives a verdict, within certain limits, makes an action right or wrong in the eyes of the natives; and, consequently, precedents are all-important in their system of law. To controvert, or even to doubt, the justice of the decisions of a dead chief is tantamount to contemptuous behaviour towards the *itongo* or spirit of that

* *See also* Holland, "Jurisprudence," p. 54.

† Maine, "Ancient Law," pp. 4, 5, 7.

ancestor: it is the last thing that the Kafir would dream of doing; and should he reverse the chief's decision by inadvertence, and subsequently discover the fact, he would be prepared to expect untold calamity to the tribe as a most natural consequence of angering the Ancestral Spirits.

In many instances the Kafirs are honestly confused as to the rightness or wrongness of certain actions: they go to their chief with their ideas nebulous, or at least held in solution. As the case proceeds their difficulties get cleared up and their judgments crystallise out into a definite shape, so that new habits of thought are formed. Each party is glad to get his ideas clarified, and though we could not exactly say with Maine that the "person aggrieved complains, not of an individual wrong, but of the disturbance of the order of the entire little society," * yet this socialistic aspect of the case is certainly present in the sub-conscious mind of the Kafir. The important point is that the chief has spoken and resolved the doubt. Every one now thinks he knows what is right. With each act of obedience the new course of conduct becomes easier and confirmed. Just as a bodily habit, by the mere repetition of certain nerve impulses, forms a pathway in the cells of the brain, thus making the action easier and more natural, so does a custom, which is but a public habit, make a pathway in the brain of the body politic. Men tacitly assume that what they have always done is the thing they ought to do. The custom has no sooner become a habit than it comes to be regarded as an obvious rule of conduct: "Custom," as Bacon has said, "is the principal magistrate of man's life."

* Maine, "Village Communities," p. 68.

We are apt to take it for granted that all other nations must desire the progress we are bent upon ourselves. "In spite of overwhelming evidence, it is most difficult for a citizen of Western Europe to bring thoroughly home to himself the truth that the civilisation which surrounds him is a rare exception in the history of the world. The tone of thought common among us, all our hopes, fears and speculations, would be materially affected if we had vividly before us the relation of the progressive races to the totality of human life. It is indisputable that much the greatest part of mankind has never shown a particle of desire that its civil institutions should be improved since the moment when external completeness was first given to them by their embodiment in some permanent record. . . . Instead of civilisation expanding the law, the law has limited the civilisation. . . . The stationary condition of the human race is the rule, the progressive the exception." * Though the Kafir has no permanent record, yet his memory is a very good substitute. I have seen a Kafir chief discussing with a number of aged councillors a precedent made eighty years previously by one of his ancestors. After two or three minutes' discussion the whole case was revived to the satisfaction of all the councillors—so excellent is the memory of the Kafir, and so reliable is tradition in such cases.

When these facts are borne in mind it causes us no surprise to find that the Kafir is a confirmed Conservative: the fact that his grandfathers did a certain thing, or held a certain opinion, is sufficient to recommend it to him and to cause him to reject new ideas. He neither wants to have

* Maine, "Ancient Law," pp. 27, 28.

the equal and placid flow of his life interrupted by the intrusion of new conceptions, nor does he wish to have his system of law improved, for it quite satisfies him. When some European magistrate rules according to Western ideas, giving the people *British* justice, and consequently upsetting all Kafir precedents, there must of necessity be a feeling of discontent in the hearts of the natives. They are bewildered at the pace we insist on, and leave the white magistrate's court with glum faces, for they are incapable of seeing rhyme or reason in the white man's view of the case. It frequently happens that the more the white magistrate thinks that he is just, and the more (where a native and a white man are opposed) he strains the law in favour of the Kafir, the more unjust does the Kafir think him. European reformers and philanthropists may talk to the raw Kafir till doomsday, but they will not change his opinion on this point: the native will either be silent and refuse to waste his breath, or else he will say: "We are going along different roads; your path goes in that direction and mine in this. Let us each go our own way."

Speaking of Kafir jurisprudence, Mr. Dugmore, who had excellent opportunities of studying the subject before the Kafirs had been much brought into contact with white men, wrote: "It would be scarcely correct to speak of a *system* of Kafir law. The laws of the Kafir tribes are but a collection of *precedents*, consisting of the decisions of the chiefs and councillors of bygone days, and embodied in the recollections, personal or traditional, of the people of the existing generation. That these decisions, in the first instance, were founded upon some general notion of right is not unlikely. It is not, however, to the abstract merits of a case that the appeal is now ordinarily made, in legal discussions, but to what has been customary in past times. The decisions of deceased chiefs of note are the guide for the living in similar circumstances. The justice of those decisions is usually assumed as a matter of course, no one presuming to suppose that an Amaxosa *chief*, any more than an English *king*, can do 'wrong.'" *

(2) We are prepared now to see that the Kafir does not regard justice as an abstract thing in the way we do in Europe: to him it is essentially a personal thing, and he cannot abide our Western idea of cold, impersonal, and abstract justice. He likes it to be hot, personal, and concrete. It is the chief alone who can give it to him, for justice is a thing that scarcely exists apart from the chief who creates it. As English children believe—or used to believe, in the good old days—in the necessary justness of all that their fathers do, and consider such decisions to be necessarily final, even so the Kafir, before he is educated, has a passionate faith in the essential rightness of the decision of his chief. It never occurs to him to question the word of his chief, for the verdict instantly inhibits all other action of his judgment. The man does not want abstract justice, but the personal opinion of his chief: and the last thing a Kafir would like to do would be to call in a white man to examine, and possibly to reverse, the decision of his chief, even when such decision had been given against him. The Kafir distrusts our entire machinery of administering justice, and he cannot for the life of him conceive that the white man is in any way justified in

* "A Compendium of Kafir Laws and Customs," MacLean, pp. 33, 34.

forcing natives to bring their cases to white magistrates. He cannot admit that it is just that a white man should come in uninvited and set up his new-fangled authority. He admits that the white man is the very person to decide what constitutes justice for the European, but will never admit that he is capable of deciding what is right for black men. The home sentimentalist is ever saying: "All will come well if you will but give the Kafir what you know to be just." The Kafir says, however, that this is the one thing in the world he does not want, and will not have if he can help it. Can the decision of a usurper make things right or wrong? Is not the very action of the white man in presuming to administer justice an act of injustice? And how can any decision of such an unjust tribunal be anything but discredited in advance? That is the Kafir's natural thought when first the white man sets up his court. Under the influence of time and education, the natives are here and there becoming somewhat reconciled to our rule; but there is still an immense amount of underlying discontent with our administration of justice, which, I hasten to add, is clean and irreproachable from the European standpoint.

The thought of the Kafir should be familiar to us, for are we not accustomed to the argument of the extreme Socialist who defends the starving man when he steals bread, and condemns the judge who punishes the theft? To the rabid Socialist, our entire economic system is a cruel tyranny and a gigantic injustice; and the law is nothing but a device of the men who steal the labour of the poor to render secure their unlawfully gotten gains. These men, so the argument runs, rob the poor of their means of getting bread; and the starving man—or it may be the poacher—

simply takes back what really is his own, but which has been previously stolen from him by the rich. The landlord is supposed to have wrested the land from the poor in a most iniquitous and unrighteous fashion: he then makes and administers the law of the land, which is all in his own interests. Therefore the decision of a magistrate, who is *ex hypothesi* the official of this iniquitous conspiracy, is discredited in advance, whenever a question relating to property comes before him. If we accept this point of view and these data, we cannot for a moment be surprised at the judgment of the Socialist. The starving man has but appealed from legalised tyranny to essential justice, and has but taken that to which he has a perfect right. We may deplore this way of looking at the matter, and may be certain that it is wrong, but that need not prevent us from understanding the position taken up by such an extreme Socialist. In a somewhat similar way the Kafir looks upon the white magistrate as the administrator of a wholly indefensible system. In the eyes of the Kafir the selection of the man who is to administer justice is all-important.

(3) Perhaps the very central conception of Kafir law—a conception in intimate correlation with the whole idea at the base of the Clan-System—is that of collective, or corporate, responsibility. It is a conception most admirably suited to a race that is in a backward condition, for it is a great deterrent from crime in all immature societies. It is also a conception that could be used by us to reduce our difficulties to a minimum.

A striking example of a successful use of the imagination in making laws for subject races is seen in what is known as the Spoor Law. It is true that it was not an original

Kafir conception, but it is in keeping with Kafir ideas. The law came into force early in the nineteenth century, when the natives in the eastern territories were incessantly stealing the cattle of the white settlers. It was found to be useless to try to convict the thieves, or to regain the cattle, for no native would ever tell against another native in such a case. In 1817 Lord Charles Somerset suggested to Gaika that when the spoor of stolen cattle could be traced to within a few hundred yards of a kraal, the white men should give over the pursuit, and should tell the people of that kraal to pay up the stolen cattle or else point out the spoor leading away to another kraal.* Any kraal that obliterated the spoor so as to hide the thief became, *ipso facto*, responsible for the theft. The natives raised no objection to the plan, for it was a brilliant piece of imaginative legislation, as it appealed to the conception of collective responsibility. Never, until quite recently, have the Kafirs accused us of injustice in insisting on this rule. It is significant to notice who it is that raises the objection. It is the educated Kafir, who has renounced his connection with his clan, who has lost, through our teaching, his sense of solidarity with his fellows, who shirks his obligations, who demands his rights, and who has become an intensely self-centred individualist. From time to time sentimentalists in England have described this law as tyrannical and unjust, for it does not look like British justice. But it has worked with extraordinary smoothness and success; it has found a congenial soil in Kafir thought and senti-

* Mr. Theal says: "This is the ordinary Kafir law, which makes a community responsible for the acts of the individuals composing it." —"History of South Africa," vol. 1795–1834, p. 200.

ment; and is now often regarded by the Kafirs as one of their own laws.

When we reflect that, in our own evolution of legal institutions, we have slowly and with great difficulty passed, during the last thousand years, from semi-primitive conceptions of law through such systems as Legal Fictions, and Equity, to Legislation, we see that we might well be patient with the people that we found but yesterday in a more primitive state than we ourselves were in a thousand years ago. But no; we would fain force the natives into our highly developed Conception of Contract, and in the course of a single generation or two would rush them through all the stages of a legal development that has taken us more than a thousand years to accomplish. We press on them the Canons of Conduct that suit some advanced European State in the midst of complicated world-politics; and when a luckless Kafir of the veld, who does not clearly understand his share in some transaction he has entered into, fails to fulfil his part, we call him bad names; and should the native happen to be a Mission boy we cry out in horror at his hypocrisy. We take a man out of his condition of Status and plunge him headlong into the most advanced conditions of Contract, and then abuse him if, through defective imaginative apprehension, he fails to take the same view as we do of the obligations he has undertaken in ignorance of the full meaning of his action. As Maine would say, the Kafirs "do not possess the faculty of forming a judgment on their own interests: in other words, they are wanting in the first essential of an engagement by Contract."* Is it a cause for wonder that

* "Ancient Law," p. 173.

a miner or a storekeeper in the Colonies, ignorant of the slow development of law, should feel that he has all the right on his side when he condemns a native for breach of engagement?

"Ancient law knows next to nothing of individuals, it is concerned not with individuals but with families, not with single human beings but with groups. Even when the law of the State has succeeded in penetrating the small circles of kindred into which it had originally no means of penetrating, the view it takes of individuals is curiously different from that taken by jurisprudence in its maturest stage. The life of each citizen is not regarded as limited by birth and death; it is but a continuation of the existence of its forefathers, and it will be prolonged in the existence of his descendants." * Our profound belief in the individual and the Kafirs' equally profound belief in the community tinge all our several thoughts, both in the administration of justice and in political life. The Kafirs carry their idea of group-association to such an extent that they regard a debt as a family concern. A man's debts succeed to his nearest relations. We take the Kafir out of this group-system to which he is accustomed, and then wonder that the man does not consider it dishonest to run into debt and die without paying it. We cannot have it both ways: if we elect to insist on importing our own changes into Kafir society, we must be prepared to be more intelligent than to blame the native who but dimly grasps the significance of the enormous change we make in his condition. A curious result of our haste is seen in the case of the native convert. A Christian Kafir is, as we have seen, cut off from his clan by the very fact of his change of religion:

* Maine, "Ancient Law," p. 270.

he retains, however, his natural habit of incurring debt, while his children, who have been brought up outside the clan, do not see the fun of paying the debts he leaves at death, for their sense of corporate union with others has been destroyed by the missionary's teaching of individual responsibility.

I can imagine some objector still persisting in saying that all this is mere theory, and entirely remote from daily practice. I will therefore point out a case in which our conflicting views of justice led directly to a serious war which the Kafirs still regard as the most unjust one the white man has ever waged against the black—though the British were entirely justified from their point of view. I refer to what is known as the War of the Axe. In 1846 a Kafir named Kleintje was caught stealing an axe, and was sent to be tried by a magistrate at Grahamstown. He was handcuffed to a Hottentot offender, and was accompanied by four armed Hottentots who were sent with them as a guard. On the road the guard was surprised by members of Kleintje's clan, who seized two of the guns. One of the Hottentot guards, seeing a companion beneath a Kafir, fired at the native and killed him on the spot. The man who was slain happened to be Kleintje's brother. The guards escaped in safety, while the Kafirs murdered the Hottentot to whom Kleintje was manacled. Now Kleintje's crime had been committed on colonial ground, and the murdered Hottentot was a British subject; the matter therefore could not be overlooked. The British demanded the surrender of the rescued prisoner as well as the murderer of the Hottentot. The head-man declined to give him up, though he sent back the guns. The chief of the clan was then appealed to, but he refused to deliver them up, explaining that in his view of the case the death of the Hottentot was compensated by the death of Kleintje's brother; he added that if the governor was grieving for the Hottentot he himself was grieving for his own man. Sandile, with whose people the criminals were known to be, was then called on to surrender the two men, but acted in the same manner as the others.*

I think that in this case the natives were not bluffing; they were truthfully stating the case as it appeared to them. They believe in the justice of retaliation against people outside their clan, and think that in a case like this blood washes out blood. Justice, they think, is corporate rather than individualistic. A member of the clan was killed, and the matter could never be levelled up till a member belonging to the other party was killed. As a result of this clashing of conceptions of justice, a long and tedious war ensued. So far, then, from these considerations as to differences in the conception of justice being academic, they are intensely practical, and a failure to understand them has led, and I fear will lead again, to widespread bloodshed in South Africa.

(4) With regard to the subject of individual liberty, the Kafirs, on account of their socialistic tendencies, differ widely from us, and, "barbarians" though they be, do not think "a man may do what he likes with his own." They are not obsessed with the European idea of personal liberty, but believe strongly that individuals belong to the chief, and that they are his property. They find their self-realisation in their constituted head, for the tribe comes to self-consciousness in the person of the chief.

* The above account is condensed from Theal's "History of South Africa," vol. 1834–1854, pp. 258–260.

Offences are divided into two classes, criminal and civil: an offence against the person is a "case of blood," and is criminal, because an injury to a person is an injury done to the chief's property, and is a loss not so much to the person hurt as to the chief, to whom the fine is paid. The tribe cannot afford to have its fighting power weakened, and therefore any damage done to an able-bodied person is a damage done to the fighting power of the tribe, and therefore to the chief, who is regarded by the people as the embodiment of the tribe. All offences committed against private property are civil cases, and are regarded as of a less serious nature than those committed against the chief's property.

We may feel that a man who has had his leg broken by another should have the right to claim personal damages; but the Kafir thinks that it is the chief who suffers loss; for the injured man is the chief's property. That a fine, paid by a native, should go, not to his chief or clan, but to an alien Government, is well-nigh inconceivable injustice in the eyes of a Kafir.

There was quoted in the previous chapter the statement of a Zulu with regard to the chief's right to forbid people to eat the produce of their own gardens until the Feast of First Fruits. The passage was quoted to illustrate the native's conception of the relation of the individual to the chief. It also throws much light on the Kafir's conception of justice, and gives proof, if that were needed, how useless it is to think that British justice with regard to the rights of the individual can appeal to the Kafirs.

(5) According to Kafir law a man is guilty until he proves he is innocent; the plaintiff therefore feels aggrieved when

he comes into our courts and finds the onus of proof shifted on to his own shoulders. "This is a strange thing!" thinks the injured Kafir in school-boy fashion. "That rascal of the dirty Jama clan has not only taken three of my oxen which he has got all snug in his own cattle-kraal, but here I come to the white man of the law for redress, and he actually takes the side of that scoundrel of a fellow, and tells me—*me!* the man who is grieving for his stolen cattle!—that it is I, forsooth, who must prove this fellow guilty; though there are the cattle actually in the cattle-kraal of that thief, and anybody with eyes in his head can see the fact for himself!"

It need not surprise us that the Kafirs take this point of view, for it is a principle well known in Europe. But there are special reasons why this custom should be found amongst the Kafirs. It is very difficult to procure evidence to incriminate a man; the people are too clannish to give evidence voluntarily against one another, unless it be for the common good of the tribe. There is no judicial oath required of witnesses, who may, however, volunteer an oath if they wish; in such cases the evidence gains in value; but no one can be subpœnaed to give evidence: there is thus no offence of perjury, and no compulsion to appear as a witness. Under such conditions it is but natural that a man should be considered guilty until he proves his innocence, for it is extremely difficult for the prosecution to make out a case.

(6) Kafir conceptions about responsibility often seem very humorous to Europeans. A Kafir lends a knife or a hoe to a friend who injures himself while using the implement; the injured man will argue that if his friend had

never lent him the article in question there could have been no injury done: the responsibility for the damage is therefore said to rest with the man who lent the instrument.* In such matters the Kafirs are very like European children. They sometimes make the most unexpected demands of this nature, and the decisions of the magistrate may seem obviously right to us and yet obviously wrong to the Kafirs. Mr. Carl Jeppe, in his book on the Transvaal, has given an example of this sort of difficulty which he met with in his official life; he does not seem to appreciate the point of view of the Kafir, but seems to regard such a demand as something utterly inconsequent and absurd. It is evidently very difficult for a European to divest himself, even for a moment, of his European cast of thought.

Here is another Kafir conception that is somewhat akin to the previous one. When a Kafir is on a journey and receives hospitality for the night at some hut he is passing, he leaves his possessions on the floor of the hut and troubles no more about them until he is leaving. He holds the host responsible for taking care of such property while he is under his roof; and a Kafir court of law in olden days would certainly have maintained the man's case.

(7) With regard to the question of theft, it may be pointed out that it is not an offence to steal from people of a hostile or rival tribe. All tribes are, in primitive races, at least potential, if not actual, enemies of one another. Europeans still rob from their enemies during war, and justify the

* Such a case is not very far removed from some unexpected side-results of recent legislation in England with regard to the liability of employers of labour.

action. The Kafirs rob from their rivals in times of peace, and advance similar arguments. In olden days, to punish a Zulu for robbing or injuring a Pondo or a Basuto would have appeared absurd to all parties. Is it thus that a man's meritorious action, in advancing the interests of his own clan by spoiling the Egyptians, is rewarded? A man who is injured by a person of another tribe is, in the eyes of the Kafirs, entirely right in taking his revenge on any member of that rival tribe. If a Zulu had an ox stolen by a Tonga, he would feel it essentially just—so strong is the sense of corporate responsibility—that he should recoup himself by taking an ox from any Tonga that came in his way.

There is no one who has any judicial power to interfere in such inter-tribal affairs. There is no such thing as international or inter-tribal law among the Kafirs, and so force is the prime and final arbiter in all such quarrels. The individual who has suffered loss at the hands of a member of a rival tribe must either overlook the insult and loss or resort to retaliation. The Kafirs believe more than we do in the intrinsic justice of retaliation. In this they are like the English school-boy, but they show a sweet reasonableness, as has already been pointed out. It is only in certain offences that they may take the law into their own hands. Theoretically a man has no right to judge his own case and to take redress, but in certain cases custom allows him to do so. The question as to retaliation is left in some directions undefined, and it has worked well to trust the uncommon good sense of the people in this matter.

(8) With regard to the question of punishment, the Kafirs display a very characteristic mildness in ordinary cases,

and a corresponding severity in other cases. If a man should have his cattle stolen, there is no idea in his head of punishing the thief; all he wants is to get his cattle back, and to be allowed to be left unmolested. Should the cattle be returned without any trouble, then recourse is not had to the chief. All that the aggrieved man seeks, and all that Kafir law gives him, is redress when the cattle cannot be discovered. The theft is not punished.

The natives do not as a rule recognise any one's right to administer corporal punishment, for such a procedure would appear to them indecorous and undignified. There are, however, the inevitable exceptions. When boys are being initiated into manhood, they are subjected to an extremely severe course of thrashing; and in olden days it was not uncommon for boys to die under such treatment. A father, also, sometimes administers corporal punishment to his son; he very rarely nags at his boy, but leaves him alone to his own good sense: but should the boy do anything worthy of thrashing, the father administers it with a vigour and fury that are simply astonishing.

There are certain occasions in which a Kafir will beat a man. In this he is like an English school-boy smarting under the injury done to him by another boy. The immediate personal chastisement of the offending boy is the only form of redress that will satisfy this temporary little Shylock. The Kafir may sometimes find his heart seething with fury, and may deal with his opponent in this schoolboy fashion so as to get rid of the perilous stuff from off his chest: in five minutes' time he will be as calm as the placidest cow.

Professor Westermarck has said that punishment in all its forms is essentially an expression of indignation in the society which inflicts it.* If that is so, the Kafirs must be a people signally deficient in moral feeling. If we contrast with their procedure the severity of punishment which obtained in England during the early part of the nineteenth century, we shall be forced to admit that we are a very indignant people. "When, in 1837, the punishment of death was removed from about 200 crimes, it was still left applicable to exactly the same offences as were capital at the end of the thirteenth century. Pocket-picking was punishable with death until the year 1808; horse-stealing, cattle-stealing, sheep-stealing, stealing from a dwelling-house and forgery, until 1832; letter-stealing and sacrilege, until 1835; rape, until 1841; robbery with violence, arson of dwelling-houses and sodomy, until 1861."† Such a list would simply shock the mind of a Kafir, who would regard us as monsters of cruelty for such needless severity.

There is only one type of offence for which a Kafir inflicts a very heavy punishment: any kind of action that he regards as anti-social, he punishes in the extremest fashion. There is, of course, a reason for this, for such an action weakens the tribe and must be prevented in self-defence. It shocks the European to find that the one offence which is punished by a death of torture is such a seemingly harmless thing as the use of witchcraft. Missionaries are apt to describe some punishment for such an offence, and then to add, "The dark places of the earth are full of the habitations of cruelty," altogether forgetting the

* "Origin of the Moral Ideas," vol. i. p. 169.

† *Ibid.* p. 188.

severity of punishment meted out in Europe. It is too little understood by people who condemn the Kafirs for such severity that the crime of witchcraft is thought to sap the very foundation of social life. The Kafir therefore shows his utter indignation at such base proceedings by inflicting the severest penalty he can devise. It is only fair to own that the cruelty in such cases which so shocks our sentiment is the expression of their hatred of the criminal selfishness they are punishing, and is therefore due to injured moral feeling. Distorted thought, it may show, but not callous cruelty.

(9) When the methods employed to ascertain the truth and to test accusations are concerned, the matter becomes more complicated. To the Kafir, trial by ordeal, whether by poison or any other similar method, seems absolutely just and infallible—much more so than a trial by a white magistrate could ever be. When the Kafirs come into our courts, they find themselves lost in what is to them a maze of forms and ceremonies, which they do not understand, and which are alien to their whole type of thought. They find their own ideals and customs overridden rough-shod. Furthermore, the white man is so easily duped by sly Kafirs that it is very difficult for him to sift false evidence from true. A native chief, just because he is a Kafir, can see through the imposture in a moment. The result of all this is that the Kafirs go back to their kraals and say that "The white man does not go by the truth," and that "Lies go down better and pay better than truth." The next time they have to give evidence, the temptation to tell deliberate untruths is very great. But an ordeal instituted by the native diviner is infallible in all cases. "There is no

shuffling, there the action lies in his true nature." It is astonishing to the European who sees through the tricks of some of these diviners to note how even the man accused of witchcraft comes finally to admit the entire justice of his own punishment. For example, here is a sick person who is supposed to be the subject of secret bewitchment by some enemy. A doctor declares the illness is caused by a lizard which some witch or wizard has placed in the patient's stomach. The diviner hides a lizard about his person, and then, after impressing the audience as to the charms he is working, by mere sleight of hand produces the lizard out of the patient's mouth. Every one is so impressed by the production of the lizard that there is not a grain of doubt left in any mind. Then follows the smelling out—generally performed by another type of doctor—of the witch or wizard. The man finally settled on as the culprit is amazed at the accusation, but cannot gainsay the evidence. He is told that he committed his crime in the following way. In his body there lives a kind of "beast,"* very largely independent of his personality and will. When the culprit was sleeping, this beast left the body of the man lying on the mat in the hut, and went and placed the lizard in the stomach of the person who is ill. Having done this, the beast hastened back to the hut, and re-entered the sleeping body. When the man awoke in the morning, he was entirely ignorant of what he (or his "beast") had done during the night. But when the diviner actually produces the lizard, the man is dumbfounded and exclaims:

* I describe the affair as natives have described it to me. The account given above is not nearly so full as that given in the admirable paper by M. Junod referred to in the previous chapter.

"Eh! sirs, but I admit I must have done this thing; I remember nothing about it, but indeed I own that I deserve to be punished for doing this evil thing." And what is more, the man's best friends will leave him in horror, and will say in the name of justice that such a wretch should not be allowed to live, for he has been secretly working evil against the clan.

The Kafirs also differ from us fundamentally as to what constitutes sufficient evidence to condemn a person; and this difference sometimes works to our serious disadvantage. A native chief will not hesitate for a moment to condemn a man of whose guilt he has no doubt, even though nothing in the shape of what we regard as formal proof of the man's guilt has been adduced. Our magistrates may be assured of a man's guilt, but unless the evidence is technically complete, the man is given the benefit of the doubt. For example, a chief is accused of fomenting rebellion: we may be morally certain that he is guilty, but unless we can bring formal proof that will be accepted in our own courts of law, the man will be discharged with his character cleared, and with added power to do mischief. And more than that: the Kafirs who look on laugh at our weakness and divine in a moment that they have the whip-hand of us. It is not so they would treat us if we fell into their hands: they would give us summary Kafir justice.

The natives know how to take advantage of the curious ideas of the white men better than the white men know how to take advantage of the ideas of the Kafirs. It would be difficult to beat the "applied ethnological knowledge" which led a whole army of Kafirs, when caught in a bad strategic position in one of our old Border Wars, to sit down unarmed in front of our soldiers. They knew we would not shoot down unresisting people, and took advantage of their knowledge. It is hard to decide whether this incident showed more shrewdness or a greater sense of humour.

(10) Then come the law's delays. The Kafirs like to have justice meted out to them while the blood is hot: half the zest of the "justice" evaporates if the delay be prolonged. If it be said that we are confusing two things, namely, the nature of justice and the method of its administration, the reply must be that this is precisely what the Kafir, in keeping with every English school-boy, does. To tell the school-boy that, if he will but wait, he may get abstract justice from some "just beast" of a headmaster, is to talk nonsense to him. He would rather not have that sort of justice; for to have to wait while the headmaster pries into things would be very awkward and very unsatisfactory. By the time the master had examined the case, the whole desire for redress would have vanished. In addition to this, every Kafir winces at the thought of encountering the schoolmaster of a magistrate, just as every school-boy winces at the idea of encountering the magistrate of a schoolmaster. Both Kafir and school-boy expect that all sorts of awkward questions will be asked; and the very witnesses fear that the magistrate or schoolmaster may bring up some past actions of the witnesses themselves, even though such things have no connection with the matter in hand. There is probably neither a native nor a school-boy who is not conscious that he has done things that his judges would condemn, if only they knew about them: and the longer the delay in settling the question, the longer is the

victim kept on tenter-hooks. So while the Kafir is kept waiting for the judgment of the white magistrate, he is all the time kept in an uncomfortable condition of anxiety as to which of his misdeeds the magistrate will refer; for if every man got his desert few of us would escape whipping.

The Kafirs think that judgment should be carried out immediately after the verdict has been given. They really cannot take the white man seriously when, with much pomp and seriousness, he inflicts the death penalty and then grants a reprieve. In the eyes of the Kafir that is not justice; it is mere folly. We may think it important to delay an execution lest there might possibly have been some miscarriage of justice. But that is not what the Kafir is thinking about. If, while our blood was hot, we were even to shoot down the man suspected of rebellion, the Kafir would quite understand our action even though he pretended he did not: it is just what the Kafir himself would do if he were in our place.

Our final insult consists in the employment of Kafir policemen, who are, as a rule, men of mean extraction. These "dogs of the Government," as they are called by the Kafirs, are universally hated; they are nearly always tyrannical, and not infrequently grossly immoral, abusing the moral support they get from the white man to ride a high horse when they enter a native kraal. When a Kafir is given unlimited power to lord it over men who would look down upon him in the ordinary tribal life, he becomes ten times more cruel and callous than the very worst white man. The supervision of these native policemen by white men is necessarily inadequate. It is less so in the towns, no doubt; though the place where the white supervision is most wanted is the districts far away from civilisation. But that is just where the native policeman, on account of the expense, cannot be adequately supervised. Moreover, it would be useless and superfluous to have native police at all if they were invariably accompanied by white men. We are periodically informed on official authority that the native police do not abuse their power. It rarely occurs to us to note that the white Government official who makes such a statement naturally never sees the evil complained of, and is the worst possible judge of the subject, for the native policeman is on his good behaviour when the white official is at hand. I have frequently seen these native policemen entering kraals far away from civilisation; I say nothing about the way the women fly in terror to the bush; but the overbearing manner put on by these men when swaggering about a kraal is peculiarly galling to a self-respecting Kafir. It is bad enough to be roughly handled by men of an alien race, but to be so treated by inferior members of their own race is regarded by the Kafirs as atrocious.

When this subject of the differences in the sense of justice is considered in all its bearings, we cease to wonder that the Kafir dislikes our impartial British justice. It is the irony of fate that the very love of justice—that quality on which every Briton prides himself, and which is the one thing he thinks is alone necessary for the successful management of backward races—should be the very thing of all others to aggravate and complicate the native problem.

"The philosophic administrator of a native district," says Mr. Scully, a Cape magistrate well known for his patient study of Kafir thought, "may draw comfort from the reflection that in the more difficult future other hands than his will hold the plough. Problems ahead make one almost afraid to think. When one considers the tremendous increase of population, and remembers there is no room for expansion in any direction, the prospect looks dark indeed. What will become of these inarticulate myriads whose standards of righteousness we are so rapidly destroying, and to whom our standard of righteousness is so unintelligible?"

Unable ourselves to recognise any good in customs and modes of thought which were not familiar to us, we expected the Kafirs instantly to divine the value and beauty of our customs and modes of thought with which they were not familiar. We expected the savage to be broader-minded than ourselves. The old standards of righteousness familiar, and in many directions extremely effective, in Kafir society scandalised our moral sense—partly on account of our taking but little pains to understand the Kafir point of view, and partly because we are so slow to see anything good in customs that are unfamiliar to us. These standards of righteousness, such as they were, were rooted in the Clan-System. With the best intentions we set to work to destroy this system, and we have as yet supplied no adequate substitutes that a primitive people can understand. Our moral sense or our soft sentiment, it matters not which, made it impossible for us to place severe and effective restraints in the place of those we removed: as a consequence we have bred lawlessness and crime, and have undermined the morality of the people. It is time we brought to bear on this difficult problem less sentiment and more intelligence, lest our moral impulses bring disaster on South Africa.

It should be plain, at this stage of our study, that the mode of organisation of society produces far-reaching effects in the fundamental conceptions of people and races. Laws and privileges that are excellently well adapted to a nation of individualists are inadequate or pernicious in a socialistic community. A race must grow its own laws, just as an animal must grow its skeleton, so as to meet its own special requirements. All organisms are such delicate things that if we upset the balance in one direction we produce many unlooked-for consequences in other directions. With this idea in our minds, let us proceed to examine the question as to whether political ideals that are suited to individualistic Europe are helpful or baneful to the socialistic Kafirs.

## CHAPTER III

### THE NATIVE FRANCHISE

THERE are but two possible types of theory with regard to the political status of the Kafir, though each of these is divided into endless sub-groups. On the one hand, it is proposed that we should fuse the Kafirs into our democratic, individualistic, political life, giving them a voice in South African affairs; on the other hand, it is suggested that we should keep the Europeans and Kafirs politically separate, ruling the natives in a parental fashion and leaving them more or less to cherish socialistic ideals. At present we are trying to combine both methods—with unfortunate results. Politicians find the problem a most difficult one to argue upon, largely owing to their very slight acquaintance with the Kafir of the kraal, who, in spite of Native Commissions, remains much of an unknown quantity: it is not surprising, therefore, to find political publicists taking refuge in the vaguest of terms. But surely we must be getting a little tired of being told that our methods must be founded on "justice and humanity," as Sir R. Solomon sagely tells us, or that "the natives must not be kept in a state of virtual slavery," as Dr. Jameson, catching the popular cry of the hour and wishing to make party capital at the expense of Natal and the Transvaal, adroitly says; or that we should adopt "a humane and just native policy, removed alike from the impracticabilities of uninformed sentiment and from the spirit of uneducative repression," as we were grandiloquently told in the colonial address presented to Lord Milner; or, again, that it is to be hoped that the new Transvaal Government will show a proper recognition of the principle, "equal rights for all civilised men," as the Under-Secretary of the Colonies, quoting Cecil Rhodes, said in answer to a very awkward question asked in the House of Commons. We are all of us agreed as to the excellence of all these platitudes, for who imagines the policy he favours to be unjust, deficient in humanity, tainted with slavery, impracticable, uninformed, sentimental, uneducative, repressive or neglectful of every human "right"? We differ as to the blessedness of such abstract and vague catchwords no more than we do as to the truths of the multiplication table; but we need some one to explain clearly to us precisely what, in the case of the Kafirs, is just, unrepressive, practicable, humane, educative and civilised; for it is on these points that we all differ. Take, for example, the expression, "equal rights for all civilised men": the phrase seems irreproachable, and yet no less than five out of the six words, when used in connection with the Native Problem, are vague and inexact in their connotation, as the following brief examination will show.*

*Equal.*—Apart from the fact that no system of franchise has yet been devised that, even in theory, gives one vote

* This vagueness of expression is accountable for more trouble than is generally imagined. Leaving South Africa, let us take an example from India, where racial problems are perhaps more intricate than they are in South Africa. Holland, in his "Jurisprudence," says: "The commissioners for preparing a body of substantive law for India recommended that the judges should decide such cases 'in the manner they

one value, black and white will never agree in such a simple thing as taxation. But equality in taxation is one of the most essential aspects of equality in political rights. The white men say that indirect taxation is not "equal" because black men do not thus pay a fair proportion of the national expenses: the natives say that all systems of hut tax are unequal because white men do not pay their share; when the Kafir has to pay ten hut taxes, simply because he has ten wives, he complains of the inequality, and feels that he should be rewarded and not penalised for doing his duty and strengthening the State—or should at least be given ten votes: when a poll-tax is applied without respect to colour, the educated natives are up in arms at once, and say the tax is unequal because white men earn five times the wages that Kafirs receive. Whatever aspect of political life we touch, similar invincible differences of opinion as to *equality* of rights are found.

*Rights.*—But what are to be regarded as "rights"? The white man maintains that he has a right to the land he buys and improves, but the Kafir regards such ownership as usurpation, for he thinks the land belongs to the natives on account of priority of possession. The white man retorts that on that theory the Kafirs should be dispossessed and the land given to the Bushmen, for they were in the country before them. The white man also says that the Kafirs have no right to carry arms or to buy liquor, but the

deem most convenient with the principles of justice, equity, and good conscience.'" These words are considerably more definite than the words "Equal rights for all civilised men," and yet, in a foot-note, Holland says: "Sir Fitzjames Stephen seems to have maintained that such attractive phrases mean 'little more than an imperfect understanding of imperfect collections of not very recent editions of English text-books'" (p. 37).

educated natives agitate for both these "rights." Again, Europeans and Kafirs differ radically as to the relative rights of the individual and of the corporate community or clan. It is quite impossible to define "rights" in a way that will please all parties concerned.

*All.*—And how shall we determine the meaning of this simple word? Shall it include Randlords who spend three months, six months, a year, three years, out of the country? Shall it include Kafirs who do the same? Shall it cover natives who migrate from the kraal to the Rand, or from one colony to another? Shall it include British soldiers and Government servants (who form a very large class in South Africa)? After giving expression to the ambiguity I am discussing, the Under-Secretary for the Colonies wrote to Mr. R. Bell, M.P. (*see* the *Times*, January 18, 1907), justifying a circular "to restrain the servants of the Central South African Railways from taking an active part in political agitation arising out of the approaching elections." He remarked: "Wherever State servants take an active part in the warfare of political parties there is always the danger that triumphant political parties"—was he here thinking of the agitation to increase the number of Liberal Justices of the Peace in England?—"will try to job their own supporters into positions of profit and trust and to exclude their opponents. Such a system has been found everywhere to be fatal to good Government, and we should certainly not be justified in doing anything to introduce it into those new colonies for whose fair start we are responsible." So it was decided that these men should be allowed to join any political association, and even to sign requisitions to candidates: but "prominent political activities" were denied them. It is difficult to decide whether this arrangement throws light on the meaning of the word "equal," or "rights," or "all," or "civilised," or "men." The chief fact of importance seems to be that Mr. Winston, wishing to favour the Dutch at the expense of the British, would adopt one definition of—shall we say?—the word "all," and later on Mr. Churchill would use the word in a different sense when the exigencies of Party required a catchword in the House of Commons. The word is thus seen to be a most inexact and accommodating one; an election might be won on the adroit usage of the word.

*Civilised.*—But who would venture to define the word, seeing we have to deal with a very slow progression that vignettes off from absolute savagery on the one hand up to, let us say, Government Ministers on the other? Who could possibly draw a line to please all parties? The word is too inexact and artificial to be of any service when used in the above connection.

*Men.*—Finally, what constitutes a man? Shall we say a male human being above the age of twenty-one? There are well-known racial differences as to the age at which people reach manhood, and the Malays, Indians, Chinese and Kafirs would all have to be consulted in this matter. The Kafirs always contend that a male reaches manhood at the circumcision rite, or at the initiation into the clan, which usually takes place between the ages of sixteen and eighteen. It would be a great insult to refuse to such a lad the name of "man," for he is very proud, not only of the adult clan-privileges he receives at such a time, but also of the much-coveted name of man, which he may then use for the first time; and, indeed, in many ways a

Kafir lad of eighteen is as much grown up as a white man of twenty-one.

I have but pointed out a few of the most obvious and superficial differences of meaning in the above five words; the moment the politician got to constructive work, he would find many other differences awaiting solution. None of the terms used can for one moment be regarded as the exclusive property of any person or party, though many politicians seem anxious to annex them for their own exclusive use.

Thus it comes about that we are asked to choose between two diametrically opposed policies, each of which is expressed in irreproachable Pecksniffian language, and each of which threatens us with the most dire alternatives. When asked to state which we like the better, we can only reply with the children that we like both best. Our politicians play with fictions, and because their painted ship is making rapid progress on their painted ocean, they imagine that South African problems are being solved. If it is sound rather than sense, appearance rather than reality, that we want, then we should be charmed with the terminological ambiguities offered to us.

Our national progress has been so intimately connected with our political development that we are apt to assume, not only that the former was the result of the latter, but also that no other race can hope to advance unless it follows in the same path. We feel in a dim way that political methods, which more or less satisfy our sense of expediency, must of necessity satisfy a similar feeling in all other races. We forget how slow has been our own political development, and we ignore the fact that there are not wanting symptoms to indicate that our own custom needs a change. Even our democratic newspapers to-day are discussing the causes of the smallness of the number of men who exercise their right of voting; and in the most democratic of our colonies, so difficult is it to get people to take an interest in politics that it is even proposed—not in the comic papers, as one might have expected—to penalise people who do not use their vote by refusing them the suffrage.

Every nation that is substantially contented with its form of government virtually enjoys self-government: and conversely, a race that has an alien form of government forced on it, even though that form of government be accompanied with universal suffrage, is not free. It has been well said that "every nation is free whose institutions are adequate to its needs." A people that is content to sit down quietly under a form of government which we regard as a tyranny has clearly not yet arrived at that stage of development at which it can make good use of democratic rule.

We know that there is "Nationality in Drinks": for there is Claret, there is Tokay, and there is British Beer: we scarcely need a Browning Society to explain to us the meaning of the particular poem to which I refer. But apparently we *do* need an Ethnological Society to prove to us that if there be nationality in drinks much more must there be nationality in methods of government. Ethnology is bound ultimately to destroy our insular idea that there is in the supernal heights of the British heavens a platonic pattern of perfect government suited to all races of mankind.

There would seem to be two axioms with regard to the political development of the Kafirs. The first is that, while we should give them every privilege they can use wisely for their own good and for the good of the country, we should force on them no privilege that will lead to more harm than good; the second is that the people should not be given what Mr. Bryce calls the "doubtful boon" of the franchise before they feel the need of it. In deciding a question of this nature the argument from analogy is apt to lead us astray, and to confuse the issues. It does not follow because some backward race, whose condition and environment in no sense resemble those of the South African natives, has made good use of the franchise, that the system would suit the Kafirs. Nothing therefore is proved in favour of granting the franchise when it is argued that the system has worked well amongst negroes of a different type in a different land. Analogy, however, may prove helpful in a negative way, for if it can be shown that the granting of the franchise has proved a failure amongst negroes more advanced than the Kafirs, then at least we have cause for walking warily. The case of the Kafirs can be argued on its own merits, and I now proceed to give some reasons why I think the franchise should not be granted to the natives.

(1) The Kafirs will never fuse with us politically, and any attempt to bring them into our political system will lead to far more loss than gain both to them and to us. I have pointed out above how loose is the language employed when politicians discuss the Native Problem. Now looseness of expression is not only frequently the result, it is also the cause, of looseness of thought. So long ago as 1842, we find Lord Stanley instructing Sir George Napier, when bargaining with the emigrant Boers of Natal, to insist on

a clause to the effect that "there should not be, in the eye of the law, any distinction or any disqualification whatever founded on mere difference of colour, origin, language, or creed; but that the protection of the law, in letter and in substance, should be extended impartially to all alike."* Quite recently an educated native in Natal, the Rev. J. L. Dube, has taken up his parable, and in an inflammatory letter has asked: "Why should the colour of a man make a difference as to his obtaining his rights † any more than the colour of his hair or his eyes?" What are we to say to this question that is often echoed in England? There are, amongst others, two main answers; and the first is that we do *not* propose to withhold the franchise from any one because of his "mere colour," but because, when a Kafir is brought into contact with white men on equal terms, any form of competition leads to the hopeless defeat of the black man, who invariably loses more than he gains by his "privilege"; and the second reason is that we wish to give the educated Kafir (who is the only person who wants the franchise) something that is very much better for his race than the thing he clamours for.

With regard to Dube's question, the colour of the eyes and of the hair is accompanied with but a very trifling

* Theal's "History of South Africa," vol. 1834–1854, p. 353.

† It is just this question of "rights" that has to be settled. It is a cavalier procedure for one of the disputants to assume the necessary truth of his view of the problem under discussion. The inquiry is, What are the "rights" of Kafirs in contact with a civilised race that is immeasurably superior in knowledge? That question cannot be solved by insisting on the assumptions of one of the disputants. Let us suppose but for a moment that the existence of these "rights" depends on the performance of certain duties that all civilised nations recognise—and where do Kafir "rights" come in then?

difference in the underlying nature: * but the difference in the colour of the skin is correlated with far vaster temperamental differences. That Dube does not see through his verbal fallacy is proved by his further statement: "Let us compare our status with other subjects of the English. How is it in New Zealand? In that land there are of the aborigines about 50,000 people called Maoris. They are as black as we are. White men only came there about twenty years before they came to us; but for more than twenty years those people have had representatives in the government—four of their own men chosen by themselves to stand for them in Parliament." Because Maoris are black (*sic*), *therefore* they are on all fours with Kafirs! But what about the relative mental capacity and temperamental differences? "Colour" is not even skin-deep, as any one who examines a microscopical section of a Kafir's skin will see; the coloration is confined to the single layer of the superficial cells of the thick skin. *It is not the colour of the skin that makes the Kafir;* and the difficulty does not lie in the superficial, but in the deep-seated differences, physiological, psychical and temperamental, that for some reason or other are integrally correlated with the colour of the skin. The question as to why we should make "colour" the occasion of discrimination seems to be so simple and answer-compelling that people get flurried and forget that the question derives what little plausibility it possesses from looseness of expression and from the superficiality of popular thought

* I speak comparatively. It seems to have been proved that the blonde type of European with blue eyes is considerably less fertile in town life than the dark type with brown eyes.

on racial problems. It is forgotten that the real question is concerned with almost everything but colour; consequently few people seem to detect the fallacy that lurks in the misuse of a word that has two connotations, one direct and the other metaphorical; for the word "colour" may refer either to the tint of the skin or else to constitutional differences of character, outlook on life, and racial characteristics. Just as the expressions Eastern and Western, when applied to an individual, refer, not to his actual place of abode at the moment, but to his heredity and temperament, so the word "colour" may refer to a man's nature rather than to the colour of his skin. Coleridge has said: "I for one do not call the sod under my feet my country; but language, religion, laws, government, blood; identity in these makes men of one country." He might also have said that identity in these things makes men of one "colour."

It is a "mere" accident that the sense of sight rather than that of, let us say, smell, should be the first to acquaint us with the profound hidden differences I have spoken of; otherwise we should be speaking popularly of questions of odour rather than of colour. A sailor at a fashionable sea-side resort recently complained of the inadequacy of an excellent photograph of the local harbour, and justified his criticism by the remark that the photograph entirely failed to convey any impression of the characteristic and evil smell. People in England, who get most of their knowledge of the Kafir from picture-books or the illustrated papers, are apt to think unduly of the Kafirs in terms of colour, and wonder why there should be such a social and political cleavage on account of it. Were the photographs but duly scented, they would learn a very valuable lesson. Not only do the white men object to the smell of the natives; the Kafirs also complain of the sickly and unpleasant odour of the white man. Sir Ian Hamilton has told us that the Japanese say the very same thing about an Englishman fresh from his morning tub. Now a man might live very comfortably with a woman whose skin was any colour of the rainbow, so long as she was a companionable sort of person; but he would find it difficult to live happily in the constant society of a person whose odour was offensive. Speaking for myself, I think the colour of a Kafir's skin, especially when he has well greased himself, is extremely fine: in almost every way it is superior to the sickly colour of the average European. One has only to see a white man bathing alongside of Kafirs to be convinced that he is but a bleached specimen of humanity. Mr. Bryce has said: "Nothing really arrests intermarriage except physical repulsion, and physical repulsion exists only where there is a marked difference in physical aspect, and especially in colour." If the word colour be expanded so as to cover odour, the statement may be accepted. One cannot argue with a dislike that is so profound and instinctive. "It needs something more than the virtue of a philosopher—it needs the tenderness of the saint—to preserve the same courtesy toward the members of a backward race as is naturally extended to equals." * The social fusion of the races of South Africa is impossible. Where the difficulty of social intercourse is felt on one side only, there may be some chance of an ultimate blending of the races, but when the barrier is acutely felt

* Bryce, "Romanes Lecture," p. 40.

by both parties, as it is in South Africa, a *rapprochement* is impossible.

Religion also seems powerless to uproot these deep-seated prejudices. The Dutch, who are by far the most religious people in South Africa, will not allow coloured persons into their churches. The English churches are not so exclusive in this respect,—anyhow in theory ; yet they cannot be said to have begun to break down the barrier. If religion is powerless to unite two peoples, it is not likely that politics will prove effective. When one race says to another : " I will buy with you, sell with you, talk with you, walk with you, and so following, but I will not eat with you, drink with you, nor play with you," there is no chance of their fusing in political life. The races will remain distinct, and will cherish antagonistic ideals. It is therefore better for the Kafirs that they should be brought into contact with white men as little as possible, and *vice versa ;* for the entire separation of the races, with mutual contentment, is better than intermingling with constant exhibition of ill-will. Tolerance is easier to cultivate when occasions for the clashings of interests are reduced to a minimum.

The question we are discussing is far more important than many people imagine. The idea that discrimination in legislation is inherently unjust has ever appealed to theorists, who object to it, not because it does not tend to the greatest happiness of the people ruled, but because it offends their sentiment with regard to the abstract equality of all human beings. They will continue to ask, no matter how much the fallacy is exposed, why a mere difference of colour should make it necessary to treat people differently. Their argument seems to be that because all human beings are men, therefore all human beings are equal and should be treated as equals. Without going into the logic of such an argument, it is not difficult to see that the facts on which it is based are at fault. The truth is—and all the facts at the base of the doctrine of evolution can be called in as witness—that all men are *not* equal. It is a suggestive fact that the ignorant Boer farmers of Natal were able to see through the fallacy that deceived Lord Stanley and Sir George Napier. They pointed out, in reply to the British demands which have been referred to above, that even if nature had not made a great constitutional difference between white men and black, the training of the two races during countless generations had been so unlike that it was impossible they should live harmoniously together under exactly the same laws. They remarked that one might as well try to put a horse and an ox in the same yoke. They looked beneath the skin and thus saw that what actually was in question was, not the colour of the skin, but the entire difference of conception as to what the two races considered just and desirable. To be fair to one was to be unfair to the other and *vice versa*. Taught by the hard logic of facts, we have had to abandon our doctrinaire attitude, and have had to govern the natives under a discriminating native code. This necessity should have been obvious to the most superficial observer. Take, for example, such a subject as polygamy: if we have one law for black and white, then we must either commit folly in sanctioning polygamy among white men, or else we must most unjustly drive all the native races of South Africa into violent opposition. There are many similar points that might be pointed out, but it is striking that such an obvious thing as this did not occur to our statesmen in England. Now the moment we allow *any* discrimination whatever, no matter on what subject, we give away the entire case for "no discrimination"; for the whole theory of the policy is based on the supposed equality of all men. As the Kafirs say, it is the chip that killed the elephant. Admit that the races differ as to equality in but one direction, and the whole theory goes by the board. If the theory is to be accepted, then we can allow *no* discriminating privileges with regard to, let us say, land; *no* discrimination as to civic obligations; *no* discrimination as to taxation; and *no* discrimination as to liquor laws, and so forth. But under such conditions it would obviously be impossible to rule a backward race that is in contact with a forward one. So long as nature makes profound discrimination in the character of races so long must the statesman do the same in politics.

We had better frankly admit that when two races differ so much that they require discriminating legislation (and moreover cannot fuse either in social or religious life), it is better to keep them politically distinct. The love of maintaining an abstract unity on paper must not be allowed to hide from us the immense temperamental differences—differences, amongst other things, as to individualism and collectivism—that lie behind colour. What we need to do is to consider the government of the whites on its own merits, and that of the Kafirs also on its own merits: if we separate entirely these two functions, we give each race a chance to work out its own ideal, and we reduce to a minimum the conflict arising from different racial aspirations. Where these functions are separated, as, for example, in the Crown Colony of Basutoland, we find that a *modus vivendi* has become established, and we note that the system works well, though of course there is room for improvement even in that district.

(2) The franchise is not in keeping with the genius of the people, and would not be a form of true self-government. The Kafirs have given expression of their own ideas on self-government in the formation of the Clan-System, which has given the people great satisfaction. The people have been amazingly patient and content under the rule of their chiefs, even when these men abused their power: how much more content would they be under the rule of their chiefs if we simply guaranteed that such abuses should never again occur? To say the least, it is doubtful whether the natives will ever be as happy under the franchise as they have been under their chiefs. And the vast bulk of the people would rather bear the ills they have than fly to others that they know not of.

There are no doubt many things about which the Kafirs are uneasy. They are conscious of the workings of race-hatred; they dislike our system of taxation; they dread our administration of justice; they are extremely suspicious of our Missions and of our schools; they dislike being hustled on along the path of civilisation; they abhor change of all sorts: it is not any one of these things, however, that is really at the bottom of their unrest, though once their minds are disturbed from a state of stable equilibrium they gather these, and a dozen similar suspicions, in their progress towards revolt. The thing that is the *fons et origo mali* is the constant dread that we are going to "eat" up their land. If a Kafir could give expression to his fears he would say, the land's the thing; that is the touchstone that shows the real attitude of the white man towards the black. If all the States of South Africa could but put the native mind at rest on this point, the trouble that is fermenting everywhere would soon disappear: but somehow or other our assurances do not assure the Kafirs.

(3) The natives as a whole have not asked for the franchise. To tinker at the constitution is about the last thing a Kafir would think of doing. The native imagines that whatever is, is right: this is his basal thought in politics. With regard to the franchise, we may use the words of the native already quoted: "The black man is not wondering about that." The average Kafir, if left to himself, would as soon think of asking for a vote for his cows as for himself. It is only a very small section of educated natives that makes such a noise and pother about the subject; while most of these agitators have been artificially inoculated from America. The great majority of the natives have never so much as heard that there is such a thing as the franchise, nor would they be able readily to understand what it is even if it were explained to them.

There are not many things about the Kafir on which all white men who have had much dealings with them are agreed: but there *is* one thing, and it is that it is never wise to give a native a thing he has *not* asked for, because such an action immediately leads to a demand for something else. Newcomers, who scorn to learn from the experience of every white man who made the mistake before them, are always falling into this trap. It is commonly said in South Africa that the Kafir has no sense of gratitude, but is a confirmed and hopeless beggar; whereas the very demand for something more *is* the exhibition of the man's gratitude. The Kafir mode of giving thanks consists in saying: "Don't be tired of giving to-morrow." This remark is meant to imply that the recipient believes the donor is so very liberal that he can never be tired of giving. That is not a British way of returning thanks, and so the average colonist is unable to believe that the Kafir is thankful when he uses such language. In keeping with this idea of thanking a man by begging and by showing belief in his liberality, a native always holds out two hands to receive the smallest gift. The Briton has such a love of independence that he cannot understand any one acting in this way. But the Kafir is a beggar partly because he is grateful. So it happens that when a man gives a raw Kafir a sixpence, the fellow holds out both his hands with which to take it, and promptly asks for a shilling, though he has not the least desire to have the money. He would entirely understand the Arab Sheik who gave money to a necessitous friend with the words, "Ennoble me by accepting these two piastres." As a result of this racial mode of giving thanks, it comes about that no sooner does the most ephemeral whim cross the mind of a native than he asks for the boon. A native once noticed something desirable about my boots and gaiters, and unblushingly asked me to take them off and give them to him. He saw nothing strange in the request. The Englishman feels it a sort of degradation to act thus: to beg he is ashamed. In the case of the Kafir such an emotion simply does not exist: to beg well is one of the graces of life, and who is ashamed of his graces? If the Kafir feels the least desire for the franchise he will ask promptly for two franchises so as to ensure getting one. To press political boons on the natives as though they were shamefacedly disinclined to demean themselves by begging for a gift, is the sheerest folly and shows a radical misunderstanding of native character. The Kafir never suffers in silence for the loss of a thing he passionately desires: his conscious wants are never inarticulate. However, sentimental friends of the Kafirs are never tired of harrowing our feelings with regard to the sufferings of the natives. I quote a typical passage from a recent book written to accuse the Europeans in South Africa of tyrannising over the natives. The indictment runs as follows:

"You have seen a little child who has cried for something till in sheer weariness and despair he has cried himself to sleep. By-and-by the mother will come and take the child into her arms, and kiss his tear-stained cheek, and when he awakes his tears will change to smiles; for to the mother-heart the silence that has sobbed out its grief is a more pitiful appeal than any sound—and the silent cry of Africa will be heard at last."

Where amongst the actual Kafirs do we find tear-stained cheeks? Where the silence that has sobbed out its grief? Where the silent crying in sheer weariness and despair? Where the Kafir who cries himself to sleep? Nay, rather, where do we find the Kafir who does not without the slightest embarrassment ask for all, and far more than all, he wants? The fact that the natives do not ask for the franchise may be regarded therefore as the surest of all proofs that they do not really want it.

When it is said that the Kafirs have not asked for the franchise, reference is only made to the raw natives. In recent years the civilised Kafirs, who have broken entirely with all clan-relationships, and who have now become a small and exclusive party of their own, have been agitating on the subject of the franchise. If we may judge by the violence and intemperance of their language, this handful of educated Kafirs wants the franchise very badly. It would, however, be folly to listen to the clamour of these men who make extravagant demands, for they do not quite know what they want, and would soon be more discontented than ever if they got what they demanded. Our difficulties would be enormously increased if we were to exploit the interests of a clique to the detriment of the whole community. A nation must rise as a whole, and those who form the vanguard must not lose touch with the main body. That cannot be a racial demand which is unknown even in name to the majority of the people. The question can be reduced to its true proportions by asking whether in England we should alter our entire constitution because *half a member* kept creating a continual disturbance in the House of Commons.

(4) The Kafirs are not fitted to profit by the franchise even if it were granted to them, for democracy is a conception alien to their past thought. The natives have a sententious proverb, which says that height is not reached in a hurry. This is their own shrewd remark that is addressed to all young men who are in great haste. I have more hope than many have with regard to the future of the Kafir, and for that reason I feel anxious that the natives should not be led into a *cul-de-sac*. If they are

left to follow their own natural political development, the result arrived at will be more stable and will have a more permanent value than the outcome of any impatient patchwork of our own. It is of the utmost importance that the Kafirs should not get their attention artificially turned to futile topics. There are far more important things than the franchise for the educated natives to think about. At present it is largely the bizarre and the fantastic that appeal to them, and every crack-brained idea that is mooted is apt to occupy their thoughts unduly. They are not yet capable of taking long views on the problems that arise from the contact of the races, and, like children, would gaily sacrifice the future for the present. The natives are quite capable, so long as they are not in contact with Europeans, of managing their own affairs: but they cannot steer their course aright when they are brought into contact or competition with white races. It is agreed on all sides, on the side of the Kafir no less than on that of the European, that a social fusion of the races is impossible: why then should we seek to bring the Kafirs into the stress and turmoil of our political life? It is difficult to conceive a more risky thing for the future of South Africa than to throw two races, which are entirely distinct socially, into violent conflict on political matters. Even the educated natives are better off attending to the things that concern their own progress than they would be in meddling with matters that do not concern them by carrying on a race-warfare at the Polls. They have more than sufficient work before them in attending to education, industry, and the evolution of their race. The granting of the franchise would not only distract the attention of the natives from urgent to trivial matters, but it would certainly lead to accentuated race-animosity: it would throw the respective interests of the races into conflict, and it would make racial problems perennial. If only this question could be settled once and for all, then the various parties would recognise the fact that it was useless to pit race against race; they would then bury the subject of their differences and turn their attention to the next thing. If we insist on keeping alive racial conflict by endless conflict at the hustings, we must be prepared for the inevitable consequence; racial problems will then remain an open sore, for as long as a man looks at a grievance it worries and chafes him. The very machinery of political life would stir up race-hatred owing to a great increase of racial contact; and it would do this at a time when both the parties had their passions inflamed by frothy eloquence. At present the white men are, on the whole, well disposed towards the natives; but any granting of the franchise would be certain to stir up slumbering fires. There are plenty of white men keen on the welfare of the Kafirs, and who will see that no injustice is done to them. And as for the natives, they are happier, more contented, and generally better off under parental government than they would be when frittering away their time in fighting the white man on the political platform.

Mr. Bryce has summed up admirably the relative advantages and disadvantages of such a situation, thus:

"If one race enjoys privileges denied to the other, it is likely to abuse its power to the prejudice of the backward people, placing them, it may be, under civil as well as political disabilities, or imposing heavier taxes upon them, or refusing them their fair share of benefits from the public revenue. If, on the other hand, both races are treated alike, granted the same suffrage, made eligible for the same offices, each will be disposed to organise itself separately for political purposes, so that a permanent separation of parties will be created, which, because irrespective of the issues that naturally arise from time to time, may prevent those issues from being dealt with on their merits, and may check the natural ebbs and flows of political life. The nation will, in fact, be rather two nations than one, may waste its force on internal dissensions, may lose its unity of action at moments of public danger. Evils of this sort tend to become more acute the more democratic a government becomes." *

The Kafirs have been accustomed from time immemorial to fixed and stable rule, and changes of Party would certainly worry them. The one thing necessary for the Kafirs, if they are to rise out of barbarism, is that their minds should be left at peace for many a long year to come. Continuity in government is therefore essential. In this connection reference must be made to the evidence of Dr. Addison given before the Native Commission. He stated most clearly that the natives are mystified by our frequent changes of Ministry, and by our lack of a fixed policy: the result is that the natives say we are always "prodding" them. If it is unfortunate for us to bring the Kafirs partly under our party system, it surely will not mend matters to bring them wholly under it, for then the last vestige of fixed policy will vanish, and the "prodding" would be incessant. The

* "Romanes Lecture," pp. 30, 31.

raw natives would be bewildered for many a long day to come, for they would be mere pawns in the party game: the educated natives would, for their own purposes, at first exploit the raw Kafir, who is quite as good a fellow, if not better, than his educated brothers; for these half-educated natives think only of their own personal interests, and would without a pang of regret let the devil take the unlucky black man who was hindmost. But even the educated natives would soon find out that as they had treated the raw Kafir so would the white men treat them; for anything, apparently, is fair in British political warfare. It is strange that the educated natives are unable to see that they cannot have it both ways. They want all the advantages of political "rights" that are given only to mature adults, and yet, as all who follow the speeches of the educated Kafirs know, they want also to have at the same time all the discriminating privileges that are given only to children or minors. But the moment they get their political "rights" they will lose their children's privileges. Because they are backward and immature, they ask us to protect them from competition with keen and smart white men, and piteously appeal for discriminating legislation on such a subject as the high rates of usury demanded by shady European money-lenders; they expect us to secure to them enormous tracts of land—and they insist on having the most fertile land—though thousands of white men are anxious that this land should be thrown into the market. At present we decline to listen to the white people, even though we know they would exploit the land to better purpose than the Kafirs do; and we base our refusal to listen to the white men simply on the fact that we adopt a parental relation to the native, and therefore protect him from the fierce competition of civilisation. The moment we really grant an honest franchise, the Kafirs will find the white man "eating up" the land. In a dozen different ways we protect and shield the natives because of their political immaturity. The educated Kafirs may now clamour for the rights of fully civilised men, but they would be the very first people to cry out when they found that the privileges, granted merely because of their immaturity, were vanishing one by one. The educated natives therefore could not be more short-sighted than to seek to be placed on an absolute equality with white men. They may not now fully realise their immeasurable inferiority to the Europeans; let them but receive a real franchise and they would find it out with a vengeance.

They are insistent on the curtailment of the powers of the chiefs, who do not take them at their own valuation. They may chafe at that now, but they would chafe still more if they were brought into inexorable competition with white men, who would value them even less than do their chiefs.

There may be no objection in the abstract to allowing natives who are really sufficiently educated and civilised to appreciate the bearing of South African politics to exercise a vote; but when we ask how many natives show even an intellectual appreciation of such problems, we must admit that there are very few who are qualified in this respect, though there are probably fifty thousand natives who fancy themselves quite competent to exercise the vote wisely. A character-test would be essential, and I, for one, am not surprised that, though Natal theoretically grants the franchise to Kafirs of a certain state of civilisation, yet she has added the proviso that the consent of the Governor must be obtained in each individual case before the privilege is granted.

(5) The native franchise would almost certainly prove either a sham or a calamity to South Africa. To offer the native even the instalment of a limited franchise would make it inevitable that he would ultimately demand the full gift of manhood suffrage; it is indeed possible that we should receive ever-increasing demands for fuller and yet fuller representations until in every kraal of the country there was raised the cry, Votes for Women! It is difficult to see how—unless they threw their hearts into the scales—the recent Native Commissioners failed to perceive that the very cautious scheme they proposed could but end in a demand for manhood suffrage, for the small dole of representation that they propose would but serve as *hors-d'œuvres* to the appetite.

It is almost certain that if a real franchise were given to the Kafirs, the white men would find means, as in America, of rendering the gift illusive. Mr. Bryce admits that in America it was impossible to give the negroes effective protection in the exercise of the suffrage. The same is undoubtedly true of South Africa. There is one thing the white men in South Africa are determined on, and that is that the whites and not the blacks must be what the Kafirs call the "Bull in the Kraal." Even Mr. Bryce, who seems to be in favour of a limited native franchise, says: "It is easy for people in Europe, who have had no experience of the presence among them of a semi-civilised race, destitute of the ideas and habits which lie at the basis of a free government, to condemn the action of these colonies, in seeking to preserve a decisive electoral majority for the whites. But any one who has studied the question on the spot, especially any one who has seen the evils which in America have followed the granting of the suffrage to persons unfit for it, will form a more charitable judgment." *

It is not necessary to enter into a lengthy description of the various schemes of native representation that have been suggested. These range from the formation of a Council or Debating Society of Hereditary Chiefs—with no executive power—with which the white Government might consult, up to a representation of black men by their full numerical proportion of Kafirs who should actually sit in Parliament. Every conceivable compromise between these extremes has been suggested, though no one seems to have sought to show that the movement could be stayed anywhere short of the logical conclusion in which there would be at least five black men to every white man in Parliament. Neither representation of black men by white men, nor representation by two or three black men, nor representation by men chosen by the Governor to watch native interests, would have the remotest chance of satisfying any sense of need such schemes might awaken. We do not usually give children just a little taste of a thing we know they will eat to excess. And the worst of experimenting in a subject of this sort is that, should the scheme prove impracticable, the recall of such a privilege would stir up every evil passion.

* "Impressions of South Africa," p. 452.

There are those who reply to my line of argument by pointing to the Cape franchise; they will say that as a matter of fact the evil consequences I have prophesied have not been found to arise. The reply to such a rejoinder is very simple. The rake's progress is notoriously easy and pleasant in its first stages. In Cape Colony only eight thousand natives out of a quarter of a million adult male Kafirs have a vote: and this pitiful handful of men is broken up into a number of ineffective groups owing to our electoral system. The "blanket" vote is just big enough to cause at times serious complication in questions that have nothing whatever to do with the natives, but it is not large enough to gain for the natives a single thing they want. Regarded as a means of making the will of the people effective, it is a delusion; for if a franchise be a democratic instrument designed for the practical obtaining of what men want, namely, a voice in the management of their own affairs, then the Cape native franchise is mere tinsel and pinchbeck. Indeed, it is something worse than this, for while it is no good to the Kafirs, it keeps up the illusion that the natives are in some sense "represented" and given self-government. Those who know anything of party devices in politics will readily see that the Cape franchise is of but little good to the Kafirs. If white men are determined that black men shall not capture the political machine, and with it the country, had they better not say so frankly once and for all? And can any one believe that we mean to let the quintuple majority of the Kafirs ever become politically effective?

Let us suppose for a moment that an honest franchise is granted to the natives, and that, in the favourite catchword of the hour, Colour is not made any test of political rights: what would be the result? The Kafirs would at once set to work in real earnest to wrest the country from the white man. It is often said that the natives would never unite; but it is one thing to unite on the field of battle, where fierce and clashing clan-instincts would be sure to arise, but it is quite another—and easier thing—to combine at the polls. Furthermore, it must be remembered that the very granting of such a franchise would not only force on the Kafirs the fact of their immense numerical superiority over us, but would also teach them the value of combination. Indeed it would do more; such an action would be the one thing to break down the very last remains of the Clan-System, which alone keeps Kafirs from combining.

But long before things came to such a pass as this, the country would be wrecked by misrule. "Equality of rights," says Mr. Bryce, speaking of the abstract problem, "might seem to be here (in the sphere of politics) also that which is fairest and most likely to make for unity and peace. But the backward race may be really unfit to exercise political power, whether from ignorance, or from an indifference that would dispose it to sell its votes, or from a propensity to sudden and unreasonable impulses. The familiar illustration of a boy put to drive a locomotive engine might in some communities be no extreme way of describing the risks a democracy runs when a suffrage is granted to a large mass of half-civilised men." *

(6) The granting of the franchise would immensely complicate colonial politics. Apart from the fact that the

* "Romanes Lecture," p. 38.

natives might quite conceivably legislate by sheer force of numbers with regard to polygamy and other moral problems in a way that would stagger the world, they would certainly ask for two things that can never be granted them. I refer to Drink and Arms. In saying this one is in no sense drawing on the imagination; for the educated natives have already in speech and in print demanded the right to carry guns, and have insisted on the removal of the existing liquor restrictions.* I do not think it is necessary to waste time in arguing that the liquor restrictions cannot be removed on any pretext whatever: if they were withdrawn, the country would be turned into a pandemonium in six months. It may be well, in passing, to point out the bearing of this fact: if a people is fit to receive the franchise it is, *ex hypothesi*, fit to legislate for itself on a topic like this; and conversely, if it is fit to legislate for itself then it is impossible for us permanently to maintain a restriction on drink against the wish of such enlightened and responsible people.

With regard to the demand for the right to carry guns, we must ask for what conceivable object, other than a native rising, could such a request be made? The educated Kafirs say guns are required for protection and hunting; but for protection from what? And for hunting what kind of animal? Most of the native territories are well-nigh denuded of game and wild animals; and Natal, from whence the proposal emanates, may be said to be practically free from such things. The only places where guns could be required for shooting game are a few isolated fever

* I refer to Dube's letter referred to above, in which both these demands were made.

districts, where, however, the natives are not asking for this privilege. With regard to protection, the natives cannot require guns for this purpose, for we do not allow inter-tribal wars, and so there is no one—shall we say, except the white man?—from whom the natives need to be protected. The barefacedness of the demand at a time when the native franchise is in dispute shows us what we may expect when the Kafir suffrage will be in full swing. If they do these things in a green tree, what will they do in a dry?

The native franchise would also have bearings upon Imperial problems. In the Colonial Parliaments, Imperial problems are for ever cropping up. If the natives enjoyed the franchise, they would make their will felt in such matters; and how can people who have lived all their lives in a tea-cup understand problems of finance, commerce, and world-politics that have their roots across an ocean? At present the average Kafir thinks that the white man gets his goods ready-made out of the sea; yet when granted the suffrage he will give his vote, forsooth, on questions that affect the commerce and politics of nations and continents. If England were embroiled in war, it would be a pretty pass if the action of a native editor of a certain Kafir paper during the Boer War were to be repeated: and repeated it most assuredly would be. That would be bad enough, but it would be as nothing to the asking of awkward questions, and still more awkward voting, by native representatives in the Colonial Parliament. We have sufficient burden of Empire already without going out of our way to add to it. The natives would at one moment vote with sententious wisdom, and would the next, owing to their natural instability of nature and limited knowledge, vote with the most egregious folly: nor could we hope to educate the Kafir to take a place in our political life without passing him through a preliminary stage which would be accompanied with the gravest risk. At the present moment, the few Cape Kafirs who have a vote are on their good behaviour, and have as yet not come to full self-consciousness. Consequently they do not quite know what they want. They are few in number, and are but at the top of the hill; let them gain impetus through an extension of the franchise, and there is no telling what they may do when obsessed by some silly whim. They are such an uncertain quantity that it would be indeed risky to give them a voice in Imperial or Colonial matters.

(7) The experiment of granting the franchise to a backward race, *that is in close contact with a forward one*, has been tried on a large scale in America, and it has proved a colossal failure. As has been pointed out above, this analogy might not have much weight unless there were a number of other reasons pointing in the same direction. An argument drawn from the West Indies or from Jamaica, where the interests concerned are not so great or so clashing, and where the conditions of environment are totally dissimilar, has really no force. But the analogy of America, where the negroes are far more civilised and more intellectually developed than the Kafirs, is at least suggestive. The humanitarian sentiment of the North imposed its infallibility on the practical instincts of the South, and the infallibility of sentiment has gone the way of all its kind. The "intuition" which the North felt sure would lead

to race-friendship has led to the race-hatred it sought to avoid. It were better never to grant a franchise than, having granted it, to be forced to prevent the recipients availing themselves of the "doubtful boon." If the comparatively advanced American negroes could not be trusted to use the gift, how much less can we expect the backward Kafirs to use it wisely? In America the relative proportion of blacks to whites is roughly one to ten: in South Africa it is as ten to one.* To prevent the danger of overcolouring the matter, I quote from Mr. Bryce, who, owing to his knowledge of American politics and to his sympathy to backward races, is above suspicion of taking a gloomy view of the matter.

Speaking of the granting of the franchise to the American negroes, Mr. Bryce says: "The moral to be drawn from the case of the Southern States seems to be that you must not, however excellent your intentions, and however admirable your sentiments, legislate in the teeth of facts. The great bulk of the negroes were not fit for the suffrage; nor under the American Federal system was it possible (without incurring other grave evils) to give them effective protection in the exercise of the suffrage. It would, therefore, have been better to postpone the bestowal of this dangerous boon. True it is that rocks and shoals were set thick round every course; true that it is easier to perceive the evils of a course actually taken than to realise other evils that might have followed some other course. Nevertheless, the general opinion of dispassionate men

* In this latter figure the natives in German and Portuguese territory south of the Zambesi are included. The general granting of a native franchise in British territory would have far-reaching consequences in German and Portuguese territory.

has come to deem the action taken in 1879 A.D. a mistake." *

In the face of the admissions made by Mr. Bryce the philosopher, when speaking on abstract racial problems, it is somewhat surprising to read the conclusions of Mr. Bryce the politician, with regard to the problem of the native franchise in South Africa. "The tremendous problems," says Mr. Bryce, "presented by the Southern States of America, and the likelihood that similar problems will have to be solved elsewhere, as for instance, in South Africa and the Philippine Isles, bid us ask, What should be the duty and the policy of a dominant race where it cannot fuse with a backward race? Duty and policy are one, for it is equally to the interest of both races that their relations should be friendly.

"The answer seems to be that, as regards political rights, race and blood should not be made the ground of discrimination. Where the bulk of the coloured race are obviously unfit for political power, a qualification based on property and education might be established which should permit the upper section of that race to enjoy the suffrage. Such a qualification would, doubtless, exclude some of the poorest and most ignorant whites, and might on that ground be resisted. But it is better to face this difficulty than to wound and alienate the whole of the coloured race by placing them without the pale of civic functions and duties." †

Mr. Bryce evidently sees grave difficulties in connection with his own conclusion, which does not seem to rise

* "Romanes Lecture," pp. 39, 40.

† *Ibid.* pp. 42, 43.

logically out of the facts and metaphors that form his data. In the first place there is no question about "wounding and alienating the whole of the coloured race" in South Africa, because the majority of those people have not the least glimmering idea about our "civic functions and duties." It would therefore be gratuitous folly, for the sake of mere theory, to exclude a large mass of "the poorest and most ignorant whites" from political activity, and so to ensure a certain difficulty, for, at best, a doubtful gain. Such a test as Mr. Bryce proposes, if made at all stringent and effective, would exclude about half the Boer population, a state of affairs that Mr. Bryce's party would never listen to. The plan would lead to endless heart-burnings amongst the white men who were denied a privilege granted to some of the natives. Such men would never consent to remain voiceless and voteless when some Kafirs, centuries behind them in imaginative grasp of world-problems, were allowed to propose, or vote on, a policy that might be destructive of civilisation. But apart from such considerations, even those who think Mr. Bryce wise in placing school-boys—for that is what educated Kafirs are at the best—on the engine of South African progress, must admit that the policy is what medical men call an heroic remedy. Moreover, such a proposal cannot be regarded for one moment, even in theory, as a final solution of the problem; for by introducing arbitrary tests and standards it is lacking in all the essential elements of permanence, and is, at the best, heroic though it be, a mere palliative designed to give relief to one symptom of the trouble. It must fail to solve the problem, if for no other reason, because the politically excited Kafirs would not rest content with the sweet reasonableness expected by the philosophical Englishman. We should remember the Kafir proverb—it is easier to turn back the enemy from the hill than to drive him out of the village.

* * * * *

What then is the conclusion of the matter, and what should we do? In the first place, we should, I think, as far as possible leave things exactly as they are, altering as little as possible, for amongst primitive races all violent changes are bad. We must accept whole-heartedly the burden of maintaining parental rule, and must own that the Kafirs are not a democratic people. We might inquire into and remove all real grievances, explaining to the natives how unreal are some of the trumped-up ones. This would not be difficult, for the Kafirs are above all things a shrewd people. We should retain every relic we can of the Clan-System, even giving back to the chiefs little by little some of their lost power. This should be done with a clear proviso that any breach of trust on the part of the chiefs, who would, of course, be under white supervision, would be followed by a withdrawal of privilege. Even though this policy might put back the clock in some districts, it would do but little harm, for the hands of the clock have been jerked forward artificially by civilisation and by the Ethiopians. In this way we should give to the Kafirs a larger amount of honest and straightforward self-government, and since the position of all missionaries and traders would naturally be respected, the seeds of progress would still be present. We might extend the experiment tried by the Cape Colony, and develop the idea that led to the formation of the Transkeian District Council. We should interfere as little as possible with the "domestic" affairs of the natives, simply restraining such abuses as the condemning of people on charges of witchcraft, glaring miscarriage of justice, persecution of Christian natives, &c.

We should seek to persuade the educated Kafir to stop fostering an artificial demand for the franchise, and should get him to imitate Brooker Washington, and to turn his thought to the moral, intellectual and social improvement of his fellows and of himself.

Finally, we should be very chary of seeking to draw up any uniform paper-policy, to be applied with undiscriminating energy to all the different tribes of the various colonies. I think it so important that we should refuse to be hustled into an artificial and rigid uniformity in this matter, that I must explain my reasons. There is a general movement in South Africa to hasten on federation by devising a solution of the Native Problem to be accepted by all the various colonies. The idea is most tempting, but I fear it is Utopian and will lead to great disappointment; the most we can do is to have a common goal toward which to aim: it is too late in the day—or too early—for uniformity in methods.

It is sometimes thought that the proposal is a new one, due to the recent Native Commissioners; but the idea is very old. The Earl of Carnarvon, writing to Sir H. Barkley on May 4, 1875, said officially: "While I believe the policy of each Government (in South Africa) to present features which may be studied with advantage, there is a real and serious inconvenience containing the germs of great danger, in the continued maintenance, in close proximity, of widely differing systems of native treatment.

"As long as the natives, who are shrewd observers in such matters, perceive that the comparatively small population of South Africa is divided under a number of Governments, which not only are not in close and cordial relations with each other in regard either to native questions or to any other matters, but are in some cases estranged by controversies which are sometimes sustained with only too much warmth, they must continue restless and unsettled; they are at the mercy of factious intrigues, and are ready to listen to suggestions as to their power of combining successfully against the disunited European Governments.

The opinion advanced by the Earl is endorsed by some of the men who are engaged in the administration of native affairs. The Civil Commissioner of Zululand has stated that since the natives travel from one State to another so very much, they are getting bewildered with the differences of our various systems of native law. But the things that puzzle the natives are mainly such things as differences as to the amount of taxation. We can easily perceive that a Kafir must be puzzled why a native should be charged £2 hut tax in one district and only 14*s*. in another. The natives say: "We are all under the British Government"; they wonder, in consequence, why the amount of taxation should vary.

The real difficulty does not consist in differences of native taxation but in differences of economic condition

South African Blue Book. Proposal for a Conference of Delegates from the Colonies and States of South Africa, May 1875.

in various parts of South Africa; and until that (which is the cause) can be remedied, it is difficult to see how the other matters (the symptoms) arising out of such economic disturbances can be remedied. It will not do to rest satisfied with treating symptoms: we shall not get much help from such a line of treatment. And until the *causes* of the trouble can be dealt with radically, we shall gain but little from tinkering at the symptoms. A hasty institution of uniformity might possibly introduce far greater difficulties than it would remove. So long as a native on the Zambesi gets a wage of but three shillings a month, while a native in domestic service at the Rand gets three shillings a day, it is idle to set up an artificial and uniform standard of taxation. The natives, of course, cannot see this, and that is where so many of our difficulties come in. We insist on civilising the natives, and on urging them to enter into economic relationships with us, and then complain because the consequences are awkward.

To legislate in favour of the natives who travel, we must legislate to the disadvantage of those who do not. Under these conditions it is safer not to press for uniformity; for though the matter may be awkward, it is in no sense serious. We should lose more than we should gain if we were to sacrifice vital needs for our love of symmetry and order. Our policy should be elastic if it is to meet the real, rather than the paper, requirements of the case. Just when we think we have all the wheels of the mechanism adjusted, one wheel will insist on jumping out of its bearings, and so spoils the working of the machine. The natives in one district should not be put under a certain law because it suited the Kafirs in another district.

It is not a cast-iron plan we need, but a master-conception that might be developed differently in every district. If our policy is to succeed in a rough-and-ready workaday world, then it should have many seemingly illogical turns and twists—and great capacity for adaptation—about it. We shall never solve a Kafir problem by geometry.

There is a rage nowadays for monism. The politician with his dream of the Federation of the World is moved by the same impulse as is the philosophical or scientific monist. We seem forced, by some hidden spring of compulsion deep in our nature, to reduce all things to unity, if not to uniformity. If we cannot explain matter in terms of spirit, let us try to explain spirit in terms of matter: if we cannot succeed in that, then let us try to explain both matter and spirit in terms of some common *tertium quid*, of which both matter and spirit are but manifestations or "aspects." But of all forms of monism the political is the most apt to lead us to an *impasse.* To this desire of reducing all things to one principle is probably due the effort to reduce the Native Problem to some one single question, such as the labour-supply, or land-tenure, or the franchise, or the administration of British justice, or education, or missionary work. We must attend to a number of things if we would solve the Native Problem, for it has as many roots as a man has fingers.

One reason why we are asked to adopt a uniform native policy would seem to be based in the idea that since all Kafirs are black men therefore all Kafirs need a similar mode of treatment. But the various Kafir tribes, in common with European nations, differ amongst themselves, and are found to be at very different stages of development and culture. Our civilising process has been carried on vigorously in one district for a century, while in others, especially in fever districts, very little or nothing has been done.

If any one will start from, let us say, King Williamstown, and will travel up the country to the Zambesi, spending several months in each tribe, he will see how impossible it is to suit all the various tribes with a hard-and-fast policy on any subject whatever. Let us confine ourselves to a single question—say, land-tenure, and see how the matter would work out. Starting at King Williamstown we find the natives quite ready for the Glen Grey Act. On crossing the Kei we find the natives much less ready for it, though the Fingos are an intelligent and industrious people. Crossing the Bashee, we find the Tembus and Bomvanas still less ready for the Act. If we pay a hurried visit to Basutoland before crossing the Umtata River, we find the Basutos advanced in quite a different manner; the Act would not suit them: they want something quite different. Coming down towards the coast, we cross the Umtata River and find the Pondos so backward that the Act would be neither welcome nor useful. Crossing into Natal, we find the conditions of native life amongst white men so different that something quite unlike a Glen Grey Act is required to meet the needs of the case. Crossing the Tugela, we find the Zulus wedded to tribal land-tenure and not at all ready for the Glen Grey Act. Swaziland, Gazaland, Matabeleland, Mashonaland and the Gorongoza country are all in different stages of development. Uniformity of legislation is impossible. Thus the Act would be a progressive measure in Bomvanaland, but a retrogressive one in the centre of Natal. Not only is uniformity inadvisable, it is impossible.

A similar result would be arrived at if we took up any other important detail of our policy; and when we came to examine the opinion of the Europeans in these different districts, we should find that the Cape Colony and Natal, for example, would never consent to a uniform policy on such a subject as the franchise. Political monism may be attractive, but it is impracticable, because the various Kafir tribes are not political counters each of a conveniently equivalent value.

The reason why certain officials press uniformity of detail upon us is doubtless due to the fact that their vision is keenly and laudably focussed on the natives in the district in which they work. They thus become somewhat provincial in their view of a very broad problem. As I have travelled for years in various districts and amongst many tribes, I have been astonished to find how very little the officials in one district knew about the natives of the adjoining tribes: yet they seem to think that their very local experience of one set of natives entitled them to argue from the particular to the universal.

There are, of course, many directions in which we might simplify our Native Administration. We might do much to centralise our organisation, and not a few anomalies in our procedure might be altered. In several departments we might bring about a much greater uniformity. But for all that, each tribe should be treated on its own merits, and we should do well to refuse to sacrifice the actual needs of any group of natives to our love of uniformity. . . .

It has been said that the justification of democracy consists in the fact that it clears the way for superiority. The justification of Socialism, at least in primitive peoples, consists in the fact that it clears the way for inferiority, and so gives the laggards in the race a chance. Democracy is fiercely individualistic when it first arises, and, if introduced, will surely break up Kafir Socialism and altruism. The fundamental conceptions of a race should be altered slowly; and I do not think that South Africa is in a sufficiently stable state of equilibrium to justify us in making an experiment that must of necessity let loose vast forces of discontent.

It should be clear by now that a political individualism, suited to Europe, cannot be regarded as a wise policy for a socialistic race. If the essential spirit and genius of the Kafirs consist in the negation of individualism, and if it is *self*-government that the Kafirs need, then to give them the franchise is but to offer stones to hungry men.

# PART II

# THE DAWN OF INDIVIDUALISM

# CHAPTER IV

## THE EDUCATION OF THE KAFIR

THERE have been three forces at work, all tending to awaken the sense of individuality in the Kafir. In the first place, commercial activity has led to the opening of markets for our goods, while the need of cheap labour has attracted the Kafir to our industrial centres. The creation of wants and the demand for labour have united in arousing the natives from their placid life, and in inoculating them with the ferment of economic individualism. In the second place, education has been the means of quickening the intelligence and of directing the mind of the people to their individual, rather than to their corporate, improvement. In the third place, missionaries, by arousing the religious sense of personal responsibility and by holding over the heads of the people the fear of future punishment, have developed the sense of individuality to a considerable degree of intensity in some cases.

It must be admitted that, on the whole, commerce has done, and is doing, its work thoroughly. Philanthropists are never tired of telling us that the evil deeds of the trader are the real cause of the native's suspicion and dislike of white men. Arguing from their own personal point of view, they contend that the Kafirs *ought* to be tremendously shocked when they find themselves deceived by a trader, and that, from the nature of the case, they must nurse a sense of ill-will in consequence. No doubt savages ought to do this: but equally there is no doubt that they do nothing of the kind. Any one who has seen a Kafir, after he has been egregiously cheated, will not readily forget the way the man shows a mixture of amusement at his own stupidity and admiration at the cleverness of the cunning white man. The native is too much of a sportsman to harbour ill-will, for he feels that the white man has but beaten him at his own game of bluff. So far from having his moral sense injured, he is apt to think the better of the white man for his cleverness. *A priori* reasoning is little use in ethnology.

No doubt individual traders have fleeced the natives; such a thing is inevitable since human nature is what it is. No doubt from time to time there have been certain abuses at our mining-centres and on our farms: but commercial white men have avoided, in the main, the gross vices that have marred their contact with primitive peoples in other countries. It is true that in a past generation the Europeans held slaves, but modern industrial South Africa has been free from the vice of using slave labour, of underpaying natives (indeed, we are notorious for the way in which we have overpaid them), or of "sweating." There are spots in every sun; but there have been few backward races in the history of the world that have had so much consideration shown to them, or that have been exploited with so little admixture of abuses. This is all the more creditable to South Africa, on account of the fact that our main industry has been gold-mining, which is notorious for its awakening of fierce passions in the white man. Yet in spite of this, our contact with the native races of South Africa has been comparatively free from the blots—for example, the lynching of negroes—that disgrace the exploitation of primitive races in other parts of the world. It is but the irony of fate that South Africa should be picked out for unmeasured abuse by people who, either owing to their ignorance or their overpowering compassion, are deficient in a sense of proportion. The white man who engages in commerce does not go to South Africa "for his health"—as the Americans say: he frankly admits that he goes there to make money: he does not profess to be impelled by altruistic motives: he does not give it out that he is an apostle of self-denial. His function in the body politic is the creation and exploitation of wants; and though perhaps one cannot agree with Huxley in thinking that the trader does more than the missionary to elevate savages, one cannot deny that if an awakening of the sense of individuality in a backward race be a boon, then the natives have little cause for complaint against trade and commerce. The one great benefit that comes from awakening a race through commerce and industrialism, rather than by politics or missionary work, is that the people awaken slowly, and have time to adjust themselves to their changed condition. We may think the Kafirs would have been better off if they had never come in contact with white men, but that need not cause us to vilify our kith and kin.

When we turn to education and religion, we can be in no doubt as to the altruism of the missionaries. From one point of view they are men "of whom the world is not worthy"; yet for all that we may be strongly tempted to call in question the wisdom of the methods they use.

It is difficult also to maintain that the missionaries have intelligently and wisely anticipated the needs that were bound to arise owing to certain evil consequences of the contact of the natives with white men, or that they have provided a guiding light wholly suited to the changed circumstances.

The Kafirs are the victims, not only of our commercialism, but also of our benevolence and moral impulses. We are bent on educating the Kafirs, and it is too late in the day for the man in the veld to cry out to us to stay our hand. The Kafirs themselves are beginning to demand education; and the missionary naturally asks why he alone should refrain from doing what he considers his part in the civilising process. The trader and the mine-owner are both educating the Kafir in their own way, and why should they expect to be allowed a monopoly of the "education" of the Kafirs? Since the white man has not the slightest intention of ceasing to exploit the native—and such exploitation is a potent form of education—why should the missionary fold his hands and abandon his pet hobby? The spirit of South Africa is fair play all round, and the missionary intends to take advantage of this fact.

The ideal thing would be for the Kafirs to develop a civilisation of their own. Egyptian, Assyrian, Greek, Roman, Indian, Chinese and Japanese ideals of civilisation all differ, though each was suited to the national genius of the people. Why, it may be asked, should not the Kafirs throw up a civilisation of their own, suited to their own nature and environment? There are two answers to this question. The first is, they *have* done so; and the second is, that their Clan-System was unable to stand the disintegrating contact of white civilisation. If we would but leave them alone, they could easily set up a civilisation that would give them unbounded satisfaction. But our industrial requirements, no less than our moral impulses, make that solution of the difficulty impossible. The natives must be helped in the present conditions of affairs because their life is now so interwoven with an alien civilisation that they are bewildered. They have not sufficient originality, spontaneity, intelligence, or ballast to steer their course in the troubled waters in which they find themselves. We have ourselves broken up their own type of civilisation as it expressed itself in the Clan-System. We did this partly because we could not understand it; partly because we did not try to understand it; partly because we were assured that we knew what was good for the Kafirs better than they did themselves; partly because we thought it was to our advantage to break up the system; partly because we did not think about it at all. No doubt we saw some obvious defects in their system, such as their constant tribal wars, their belief in witchcraft, the occasional tyranny of their chiefs, and the "immorality" of some of their customs. These things were so revolting in our eyes that we did not take the trouble to find out whether these abuses were so evil as they were said to be, or whether they were essential elements in the very structure of the Clan-System, or whether they were merely accidental elements which had no organic connection with the system. We thought the Clan-System was a menace to white supremacy, and our moral impulses combined with this belief to urge us to get rid of these evils. In uprooting the Clan-System we made a mistake that has given us the pernicious developments of Ethiopianism (which would never have arisen had we not checked the power of the chiefs); that has introduced questions as to native franchise; that has intensified the evils that arise from intimate race-contact; and that may possibly end in a final undoing of all our work of civilisation in South Africa. The problem before us now is how to awaken the sense of individualism, and how to educate the people, so as to destroy as little as possible of the finer traits in Kafir character that have survived our somewhat unfortunate efforts to uplift the natives.

We may all of us at times feel the Scholar-gipsy mood in which we condemn all Western civilisation with its "sick hurry," its "sick fatigue," its "heads o'ertaxed": and we may listen from time to time to some man as he

> takes dejectedly
> His seat upon the intellectual throne
> And all his store of sad experience he
> Lays bare of wretched days.

But the mood passes; and again "each half lives a hundred different lives" and succumbs to "this strange disease of modern life." Who is there that does not, with Rousseau and the Scholar-gipsy, at times suffer from a nostalgia in which he longs to return to nature, and to wait for the spark to fall from heaven? But the infection of civilisation soon overtakes us, and the dream that held us in its meshes fades into the light of common day. And since we chose the complex and intellectual life for ourselves, we feel bound to give it to those savages who are unlucky enough to fall defenceless into our hands.

"The masters of education," says Leibnitz, "hold in their hands the future of the world." A perilous trust it is. Nothing so complicates the position of a forward race as its attempt to be benevolent to a backward one. It is comparatively easy to recover from the effect of some political mistake, but it is almost hopeless to seek to undo the evils caused by mistaken benevolence. It is our moral impulses that land us in our greatest and most tragic difficulties.

The person who goes through life resolutely abstaining from the attempt to put the world right is saved a thousand heart-aches, for if he behaves but moderately well, he will make no enemies and but few grave mistakes. The moment he sets to work in earnest, and engages in any form of philanthropic or political endeavour, he will make enemies where he expected to make friends; he will do harm where he honestly intended to do good; he will see how seemingly hopeless it is to help people onward; and he will probably discover that his very sentiment and zeal are his most inveterate and subtle enemies. Taking opinion for his guide, he will again and again knock his head against some hard fact, till in moments of despondency he will wonder whether he might not have been better employed at other things. It is so easy to do good, but so difficult not to do harm at the same time.

The philanthropist is apt to think that devotion and good intention will atone for mere technical deficiencies. It is a radical mistake in presuppositions, and it is casting its baneful spell over much of our modern political life. Goethe has made us familiar with the merciful comedy at the heart of things when he made Mephistopheles confess that he was

> Part of that Power, not understood,
> Which always wills the bad, and always works the good.

It was a lesson needed by people who were about to have their moral sense shocked by the theory of natural selection, and it is still needed by sentimentalists who are always shouting about the wicked white man in South Africa. To a certain degree, we have grown accustomed to the ever-pressing struggle for existence in Nature, and yet we are now in the midst of an emotional reaction in which we need to remember Goethe's further words:

> While man's desires and aspirations stir,
> He cannot choose but err.

A nemesis seems to follow hard on the heels of those who, whether in Parliament or out, are for ever calling attention to their benevolent motives. When confronted with some unexpected result caused by their unbalanced sentiment, they are apt to cry out in an aggrieved tone, "But look at our excellent intentions!" They might as well say, with the Mad Hatter, "It was the best butter." Good motives cannot make up for lack of knowledge and sound sense.

The education of a savage is a peculiarly difficult task; and it is pathetic to think how we send out missionaries with the kindest of hearts without giving them any training suited to their requirements. The education of a backward race is as delicate a work as the training of defective or feeble-minded children at home: we educate *them* by means of highly trained teachers, but we let loose upon *the Kafirs* teachers whose sole qualification for the work is their goodness. The ordinary missionary may be an expert in religion, but he rarely even tries to make himself an expert in education. I have seen men and women fresh out from England simply turned loose on the Kafirs. These excellent people knew that there was a thing called education which was thought to elevate people; and without more ado they set to work to experiment on the natives. Again, I have seen native teachers set to work to teach children as though the scholars were automata. The brain of the child seemed to be regarded as a sort of enormously capacious phonographic cylinder, and regulation lessons were hammered in so as to make dents or grooves in the brain, in order that, under suitable conditions, the parrot-lessons might be repeated. The Kafir teacher has too often been utterly ruined by having been put through the process himself; he therefore reproduces and accentuates every vice that has been ground into his composition by a faulty education. The man's development has been stunted, and it seems as if he set to work deliberately to stifle all intelligent progress in his pupils. The fellow could not have done worse if he had tried—though his intentions were faultless. I know nothing so dull as to be taken round some small up-country school and to see the native teacher conducting his lessons. It has often been a puzzle to me what conceivable good could come of the process; the harm was sufficiently obvious. It was weary work to watch the children submitting to their slow torture under the oppression of what Browning would have called "the pig-of-lead pressure of the teaching-man's immense stupidity." No wonder the product of such methods brings discredit on education. The result turned out at Lovedale or Amanzimtoti by trained teachers is of a wholly different order, because the system employed is more rational.

It may seem very ungracious to examine in a cold, dry light the result of years of the self-denying labour of people actuated by the noblest motives. To do so seems as bad as "to peep and botanise upon a mother's grave." Too much honour cannot be given to those who do the thankless work of educating the native; but no criticism need be feared that is intended simply to minimise the monotonous drudgery and to improve the quality of this work. In education everything turns on quality.

### I. The Case against our Present Methods of educating the Kafirs

It is a matter of common knowledge that the average colonist thinks education spoils the native. Let us see what is to be said for this judgment. In actual experience there exists no hard and fast line between the general civilising effect of contact with white men and the effect of formal education; the one vignettes off into the other. In dealing with the drawbacks of our entire civilising process, we will therefore start with the unfortunate consequences of mere civilisation, and will then pass on to a consideration of some of the evil effects of a misguided and formal education, drawing no hard and fast line between these two things.

The first and most obvious result of contact with civilisation is a change in the outward appearance of the Kafir for the worse. The raw native is a fine, big, burly, dignified, merry, courteous, picturesque specimen of humanity. He is one of nature's gentlemen ; he gives himself no airs ; he is frank and natural in his behaviour ; he is unaffected, and yet holds himself in a manner that shows he has plenty of self-respect. He is every inch a man, even if he be somewhat of a savage. There is something about him so free and unconstrained—so perfectly natural and human—that he puts the white man, who sees him in his kraal, in a good humour. He seems conscious neither of superiority nor inferiority (as a matter of fact, however, he thinks himself superior to the white man in all things but knowledge and cunning), but speaks to a white man as if all men were equals. But he does this with such a natural and unaffected grace that no one resents it, for who but a Portuguese * wants the Kafir to debase his manhood by cringing ?

But the moment the Kafir embraces civilisation he gathers a smattering of "knowledge"; he dons dirty, frousy, patched, second-hand clothing ; he looks slovenly and untidy ; he presents either a ridiculous or a sordid appearance ; he looks mean and shabby in the extreme. As he ascends the educational ladder, all the man's natural self-respect vanishes, and in its place there is found an aggressive, unnatural, and unpleasant self-assertion and effrontery. Coupled with this, the fellow wears, for the first time in his life, a hang-dog expression as if he felt the need of apologising for his existence. Instead of feeling

* Englishmen who travel extensively in Portuguese possessions are all disgusted with the way Portuguese officials make the natives *literally* grovel in the dust at their feet.

that nature had made them gentlemen, one can only imagine, with Hamlet, that some of nature's journeymen had made them and not made them well, they imitate humanity so abominably.

The civilised Kafir is taken at his face value, and this by his own request. South Africa is a country where appearance and pretence count for very little, for men are usually taken for what they *are* rather than for what they *seem*; and yet even in South Africa the civilised Kafir cannot escape from the tyranny of his appearance. He thinks he looks excessively grand in his borrowed plumes, and asks to be considered to be all that he looks. The white man does this, and promptly regards the man as a shoddy specimen of mankind, saying: "There can be no kernel in this light nut: the soul of the man is in his clothes." The Kafir has sought to gain a cheap reputation, and is injured to find that the white man accordingly holds him very cheaply. The man is his own enemy, and yet cannot be made to see it. Thus it comes about that the colonist says that civilisation spoils the Kafir. It certainly spoils his appearance.

The next thing that every one notices is that the Kafir is apt to absorb the vices rather than the virtues of the white man. Even in his religion, he borrows the superficial and unlovely elements of modern Christianity more often than its inner and essential spirit. To hear a native evangelist preach on the terrors of hell is enough to make one's hair stand on end. There can be no doubt, I think, that the Colonist has some grounds for maintaining that education at the average Mission school further undermines some of the most valuable elements in the character of a savage, which can resist mere civilisation but not formal education; robs him of some of his original virtues, which are greater than the missionary is usually willing to admit; and gives him instead some very superficial and shoddy accomplishments. A one-sided education at first puffs up the Kafir; it makes him restless and top-heavy; it disturbs his balance and makes him difficult to manage; it perverts his perspective and his sense of proportion; it makes him disinclined for manual labour; it renders him selfish and unduly egoistic; it undermines the safeguards of the old clan-restraints; it leads him to think that he is on an equality with white men in general knowledge and culture; it makes him aggressive in his self-assertion; it prompts him to listen to political agitators; it vastly increases his power to do evil, and generally undermines his character. It is a significant fact that the raw natives are inclined to agree with the colonists in this verdict, for they say that educated Kafirs are feckless and unfortunate people: in their own graphic phrase, they say that these educated natives are unpleasant men to live with, for they always have cockroaches in their ears. (That is to say, they are always grumbling and in trouble.) They add that these men are unfortunate in appearance, and cause endless trouble to their chiefs.

The above list of accusations fairly well exhausts the general colonial condemnation of the education of natives. Where opinion is so united and so intense, there must be some element of truth in the contention; and the colonists, who do not gratuitously go out of their way to condemn things, must see something in the educated Kafir that is both very unpleasant and very unsatisfactory. It should pay the missionary to seek to discover the cause of this opinion, for it will not do to put it down entirely to irreligion or to any other single motive.

When it is said that the foregoing represents the typical colonial attitude with regard to the education of the natives, reference is made neither to the Press nor to the Governments in South Africa. The Press is, on the whole, desirous that the natives should have an industrial education, and the various Governments in South Africa are not slow to make grants for educational purposes. It must be understood therefore that I have been speaking of the opinion of the man in the *veld:* and surely it should not cause us any surprise to find the work of education thus criticised in that quarter. The first effect of education in Europe is notoriously unfortunate; it is difficult to see why we should expect it to be anything else in South Africa. Impatience, all the world over, would often away with all nascent and amorphous kinds of goodness, instead of seeking to cherish the most imperfect and embryonic of beginnings.

From the moment when a native puts on his first shirt right up to the day when he passes his last examination, the whole civilising process forces the attention of the man to himself. He is not slow in finding out that the white man stands up for his own personal "rights"; nor does it take him long to discover that the European is absorbed in the pursuit of his own personal interest, even competing keenly with his fellows for his bread and butter. Hitherto the Kafir had sunk his personality and his individual rights for the good of his clan: to set himself in opposition to, or competition with, his fellows was in his eyes a great offence.

From the white man he learns the new idea—new at least in its intensity—that the individual has inalienable "rights": he consequently determines to have them with a vengeance, and to pay out the clan that has so long trampled on his private interests. The first effect of this change is to make the man intensely self-conscious and selfish, so that he obtrudes his wretched individuality at every angle, and thus appears aggressively conceited. If there were some increase of capacity as a set-off for this self-assertion, the case might be different; but civilisation does not, at least at first, lead to the marked quickening of any capacity, to the substitution of any new restraints, or to the discovery of any new germ of promise. The change is one of external accretion, and not one of absorption and inward growth, for the savage only borrows his new accomplishments. So obvious is this to all but the civilised Kafir, that even the raw natives see through the sham. A young civilised Ethiopian informs an old heathen chief in a superior and pitying tone that the Ethiopians are the coming men; they are going to make a church to embrace and cover all the Kafirs; and are not going to submit any longer to European initiative and control, for they are able, now they are educated, to stand on their own legs. The old chief lets the man have his say and spin ample rope. He then begins to catch the fellow in his own words. He ignores the lofty idea of a universal church, and asks him in an off-hand manner whether the actual building in which the Ethiopians worship was built by civilised natives. The answer is in the negative. Then the chief courteously suggests that possibly civilised Kafirs made the corrugated iron, or cut the timber for the building.

It transpires that they did neither of these things. The chief expresses his astonishment, and chuckles from time to time as, pushing his inquiries, he finds that the civilised Kafirs did not even make the glass of the windows, the nails, the screws, the doors, the paint, the furniture, the books. The Ethiopian has to admit that the civilised Kafirs who worship in the church did not even make their own clothes. The old chief then tells the upstart that he is "big in the mouth," and advises him and his friends first of all to learn how to make some of these things before they boast of getting on without the white man's help.

This hopeless lack of a sense of proportion is not to be wondered at, though it is to be deplored. The individual is top-heavy and unbalanced, and cannot see things in their general relations.

A somewhat unsuspected effect of civilisation is the awakening of the dormant self-consciousness of *the race.* When white men first appeared in South Africa, the natives seem to have had no consciousness that they formed a class opposed to the white men. One tribe regarded the next tribe as its eternal enemy. The natives were intensely conscious of the tribal bonds, but it never occurred to them that they had a bond of "colour." The effect of civilisation and education has been to draw their attention to this racial conflict; and the way many unwise philanthropists have talked to the natives about the antithesis of black and white has had a most potent effect in awakening a sense of racial, as opposed to a tribal, solidarity.

In olden days, before the advent of civilisation, the various tribes were kept apart by distance and by wars; but civilisation has abolished both these barriers. With the impossibility of exercising the fighting habit, the natives have grown less hostile to each other. The sheer, wanton hatred of tribe for tribe grew by the wars it fed on. Distance no longer keeps the natives apart, for we have covered South Africa with a network of railways and have supplied focus-points where tribe meets tribe. The effect of this has been to break down some of the tribal hostility, for the white man makes natives of different tribes live amicably side by side: thus at Johannesburg a Zulu comes to find that a Pondo is not such a "baboon" as he thought; a Swazie discovers that a Basuto can be quite a decent fellow; a Shangaan is surprised to note that a Bechuana is quite a gentleman. In addition to this, semi-civilised Kafirs of all tribes meet in Mission schools and Mission churches with a new and common bond, and set to work to hatch a common grievance. Since nothing draws people together like a common grievance, large centres, such as Johannesburg and Durban, become hot-beds of Ethiopian discontent, and the pernicious seed of race-hatred, like thistle-down in a wind, is carried away to the remotest kraal in the country. The very massing of tens of thousands of natives in one district teaches the Kafirs their power. Civilisation also gives the natives a Press of their own, which not only spreads discontent but also hastens on the dawn of national self-consciousness. It may be argued that all this is for the ultimate good of the country. Possibly it is; possibly it is not. But whatever may be the ultimate result, the immediate one is fraught with danger; for civilisation supplies the machinery for wrecking itself, and colonists do well to be anxious.

This dawn of racial self-consciousness leads naturally

to a desire for new kinds of self-government, for the Kafirs are told by injudicious white men that they are being ill-treated. When the half-educated Kafir is told that the white man is keeping some of his "rights" from him, he is apt, not unnaturally, to grow suspicious; and the spirit of discontent that is thus awakened is not wholly a divine thing. Hitherto the Zulu, let us say, has never heard of the franchise, and does not even know what it is. Either at Johannesburg, or through some political agitator, he hears that certain natives in the Cape Colony have votes while he has none. He naturally feels that he has a grievance, and readily lends himself as a tool to any nimble-witted Ethiopian who has an axe to grind.

On the top of all this there arises a desire for something more than self-government. I refer to the wish that is not unmanifested in the nursery or dame-school for a person not only to manage his own affairs but also to control those of others. There is not much use in hiding the fact that the chief reason why the civilised natives want the franchise is that they know that they could then not so much manage their own affairs as dominate, or get rid of, the hated white man. It is idle to suppose that anything short of this will ever permanently satisfy the natives who have broken loose from their Clan-System. Every boon the white man gives such people is accepted and promptly used to undermine the position of the giver.

The effect of civilisation is thus seen to be unfortunate. Individualism at first spoils the native; breaks up the clan; sets the black man against the white; binds certain black men together in new ways; leads to discontent and crude self-assertion; introduces poverty where it was unknown before; sets one class of Kafir against another class; and, finally, is used against those who introduce it. The problem becomes acute just in proportion to the number of whites living in close proximity to the natives. It is therefore most acute in Natal, where Englishmen, Kafirs and Indians are huddled up together in almost inconceivable confusion; and it is comparatively slight in many other districts, such as Cape Colony, where the whites press upon the natives, but to a very slight extent.

It is not pleasant to think what the result will be when the country is filled with educated Kafirs—educated on the system now in vogue. What will happen when there are hundreds of thousands of perfectly useless, poverty-stricken, ill-educated Kafirs, who will be fit for nothing, but who will wander round the country seeking employment, unwilling or unfit to engage in manual work? Puffed up with a vain idea that they can find a living by their comparatively feeble brain-work, they will find all posts available for them occupied by Europeans or by better educated Kafirs. At present South Africa may be able to absorb, either for purposes of education or trade, all the natives Mission schools turn out; but there is certain to be a slump one of these days, and the economic consequences of such a state of affairs will be a menace to the country.

Does it not call for almost superhuman wisdom in steering the bark of civilisation in South Africa between Scylla and Charybdis? And do we not well to halt at times so that we may examine the situation and take stock of our methods, lest by chance we be steering towards sunken reefs? It is time the missionary stopped chafing under the criticism of the colonists and set to work seriously to find out and alter the defects in an educational system that has grown up in a haphazard fashion.

## II. The Case for Education

If we ask the missionary what he has to say to these charges, he will reply that there is much exaggeration in the indictment. He will possibly say that the colonist judges a Kafir's value by the readiness with which he will serve the ends of the white men. No one cares to have his servants too well educated or too enlightened. Some missionary will accept the challenge, and will go round certain towns and ask the various employers of labour whether they are satisfied with certain boys who attended a certain school. The results of one such inquiry are before me in a pamphlet published by Mr. Le Roy of the American Zulu Mission. This missionary has been connected for years with the Amanzimtoti educational institution. The Americans are nothing if not practical and resourceful; they ought to be able to show good results—and they can. He says that "sixty of our graduates are now engaged as teachers in the schools of South Africa. One of these, Rev. John Dube, by his own enterprise has organised, and is carrying on successfully, a Christian Industrial School, and is also the editor and publisher of a leading native paper." It was unfortunate for the argument that this man was picked out by name, for he has subsequently written the most virulent long letter in his own paper, stirring up race hatred. The colonist will with justice, as I think, take hold of this point. But let us imagine that Dube is an unfortunate exception. Mr. Le Roy arranged to get the employers' opinion of all the boys who had been at his educational establishment and who were working in Durban. The employers of forty-seven were interviewed, and they were asked whether the boys were good workers, whether they were truthful, respectful and trustworthy, and whether they compared favourably with raw Kafirs. In the case of forty-four out of the forty-seven, the verdict given by the employers was one of *unqualified approval*. There were forty-four boys who had been in the Institute who were found to be working at Johannesburg. Their employers were consulted in a similar way. And thirty-eight out of the forty-four boys were reported as being quite satisfactory. The verdicts (on both sides) are expressed in vigorous and colloquial language, and I quote a few samples: "All rattling good boys; never any trouble; hard workers"; "The best boy I have"; "Good boys, but exceptions. Mission natives worthless"; "A fine fellow. No complaint"; "Was here a year but knew too much"; "No fault to find whatever; but does not learning English usually spoil the native?"; "Good boy. Wouldn't have raw Kafirs"; "No good. All Kafirs no good, no exceptions. This one a bad egg, always a bad egg. We had him a *long* time"; "A credit to missionaries. Wish there were more like him"; "Good boy; very respectful"; "Good fellow; civil, always ready for work. No fault to find"; "Absolutely the best boy I've had"; "Very good boy, well educated, no complaint"; "Two boys, both good, the best we have. Most trouble with boys comes through the way they are treated"; "First-rate boy"; &c. &c.

The men who give the boys such characters—and the

bulk of the criticisms are just like these, which I have picked out indiscriminately—are all business men in Durban or Johannesburg, the heads of large commercial houses or mine officials. It is impossible to form any quantitive conclusions on but the hundred cases available, even though these boys represented the entire number of old students that could be traced at these two centres. But these verdicts are sufficient to show that the missionary can, under some conditions, show unexpectedly good results. Quite a number of the employers emphasise the fact that the boys in question were "exceptional" boys, and that all other educated boys are worthless. But it looks a little strange that when common talk is tested by actual facts there should be found to be so many exceptions. Clearly no great conclusion can be drawn from these figures, for many facts are not taken into consideration. We naturally ask what can be said about the rest of the natives educated at the Institute. Those fittest for work would survive in employment in commercial houses; and so no idea can be drawn from these figures as to the total result of education. It is a fair question to ask whether all educational institutions could show a similar record. And moreover it would be possible to urge the fact that the bulk of natives are not being educated in institutions where several hours a day are devoted to manual work, as is the case at Amanzimtoti. And yet again it is strange that the missionary did not seek to dissociate religion from education in his analysis. It is very difficult, no doubt, to define a Christian: yet a missionary can feel the difference between a Christian and an educated "heathen" more easily than he can formulate it. When these facts are borne in mind it becomes evident that it is very difficult to say how far the results were due to education, and how far to religious principle. But even when that is pointed out, the evidence in favour of combined religious and educational instruction appears very strong, and shows that *the missionary can make out a very good case for Mission schools precisely in the direction where his cause is thought to be unsatisfactory and weak.* If all these Kafirs were Christian boys, they show that a Christian native can carry a good deal of educational sail without becoming top-heavy.

The missionary will next point to the Report of the Native Commissioners, who adopt an optimistic tone when speaking of education. Their report shows that there is a considerable section of people who think that education is highly beneficial to the native. This argument looks very strong indeed, for here are sensible, level-headed men, who have had every opportunity of hearing both sides of the case, and they pronounce strongly in favour of educating the native. The Colonist, however, might well maintain that this evidence is not final.

There are advancing waves even on an ebbing tide, and there are retreating waves on a flowing one. To discount all the accidental elements, and to gauge the actual advance, is by no means an easy task. In South Africa there is a general feeling that the Commissioners said the best that could possibly be urged on behalf of education. They did not err on the side of being pessimistic : perhaps they were, if anything, a little too sanguine. It must also be remembered that the Commissioners were not trained ethnologists who examined everything for themselves, and who discarded all "evidence" that had no scientific value Much of their evidence was drawn from mere hearsay and from interested parties who were deeply committed to the existing *régime*. And it does not appear that the Commission sought to dissociate the effects of *education* from the effects of *religion*. This I am seeking to do, and I would speak much more hopefully of the *Christian* than of the merely *educated* native. Not a few of those who gave "evidence" were exposed to the danger of putting down to the account of education what should have been put down to the account of religion: yet that did not prevent them from entering the same sums later on under the columns of the religious account as well. By this spurious "double entry" they have probably somewhat swelled the total account. The giver of evidence is also, when asked to give an account of his assets, perilously in danger of thinking more of his successes than of his failures.

Again, students at such schools as Lovedale or Amanzimtoti are apt to be taken as typical of the class produced by education, for a Commission can visit such large institutions and pays especial attention to the opinion of the managers of such schools, but cannot visit the small schools far away from civilisation. Yet it is in such schools that the great bulk of the scholars is to be found. I have on two occasions spent a week at Lovedale, and so I hope I am not forgetting it and a few other excellent institutions when I fix my attention mainly on the small Mission schools never visited by Commissions. In those schools the education is carried on for the most part by native teachers, who teach the children their alphabet and to recite unintelligible words parrot-fashion. The vast bulk of educated natives never rises beyond that condition, though a few Kafirs become highly educated. Those who are satisfied with the present educational *régime* are, of course, satisfied with turning out native teachers suited to carry on such a type of education, and naturally approve of the result. I admit that every now and then a fine specimen of Kafir is produced, but I think this is perhaps more in spite of, than because of, the methods in vogue. Indeed it is very often the case that religion rather than education is accountable for these remarkable cases. It is possible to point to such men as Tiyo Soga, and to say he is a proof of what is being done with Kafirs. I quite agree with Mr. Theal when he describes Soga as "An earnest, enlightened, zealous, self-denying Christian missionary, such a man as any nation in the world might be proud of"; and yet we must remember that this man, on the breaking out of the War of the Axe, was sent to Scotland for his education; that he married a Scotch wife; and that he was placed in an environment—religious and social—that was exceptional. He may be an earnest of what the educated Kafir may *ultimately* become, but he cannot be adduced as a proof of the value of *existing educational* methods in South Africa, or as an example of the *general product* of our Mission schools.

But the missionary has many other arguments to bring forward. He might say that people have expected far too much from educated Kafirs, and that they are quite unreasonable in the way they condemn a native for not being the equal of the white man. The Englishman is known all the world over for his intolerance of all that is unfamiliar. The missionary might point out that it is the nature of human knowledge to lead to experiment in things that are evil as well as in things that are good. In the language of religious allegory, he might say that eating of the Tree of Life ever leads to the knowledge of both good and evil. He might quote Rousseau's remark that modesty is born only with the knowledge of evil: and what is true of modesty is also true of some of the finest qualities in human nature. It is too late in the day to put down all the evil to the credit of some defect in the educating process, for much of it is due to contact with Western individualism, to the nature of things, and to the natural and inherent imperfection of the material on which the missionary has to work. The symptom complained of may be admitted, but the suggested cause may be denied. The missionary might go on to point out that much of the evil complained of is not due to formal education, but to intercourse of the Kafir with the civilised white man himself.

Again, what do the critics expect? Do they seriously imagine that they will ever find perfection amongst the Kafirs? That would be a strange place to look for it, seeing it cannot be found even amongst white colonists. We must all admit that increase of capacity must necessarily mean increase of power to do either good or evil; and the whole problem is whether the individualistic *régime*, with its corollary of the fostering of the faculties, can be justified on existing conditions. There is no reason for expecting the Kafirs to be free from the educational measles and all the other childish complaints experienced all the world over by educational immaturity. The so-called "educated" Kafirs are in no adequate sense educated.

We are just beginning to educate them: that is all. No doubt those natives who with much difficulty have advanced in their studies about so far as an English boy of twelve years of age imagine themselves to be prodigies of learning. So they are when compared with the kraal Kafirs; so they are not when compared with the most ignorant white man. We call them "educated" in a complimentary sense and out of courtesy; for there are but few natives that really deserve to be called educated. When a small boy, who has just put on his first pair of trousers, pulls himself up to his full height, and says, "See, I'm a big man now, with trousers!" we humour him and say in baby-language, "Yes, you are indeed a man now." Even so, we smile and tell the "educated" Kafirs that they are men of education and culture. Why should it be thought that Kafirs should spring, Minerva-like, fully educated out of the head of some educational Zeus? The preliminary stages of a process can never be taken as indicative of the end aimed at. No process is ever justified by its beginning, and it is absurd to expect the preliminary stages of the education of the Kafirs to be taken as a criterion of the whole process. It is ever from the end of a process that we learn its value, for it can never be justified by its early stages. It therefore follows that we cannot fairly judge of the whole problem of educating the natives by the few specimens to be met with away from Mission circles. The critics are often not even sufficiently fair to take the trouble to go and visit the chief educational centres such as Lovedale and Amanzimtoti, but judge the process from any chance half-baked Kafir they meet in towns. The missionary might go on to point out that what we have to do with in this workaday world is practical politics. The Kafir is going to be educated because his heart is getting increasingly bent on it. He will not stop and ask us for our opinion on the subject. Contact with civilisation in the mine, on the farm, and in domestic service opens his mind, and he wants to know how he, too, can do the cunning things the white man does. It is useless to imagine that a forward race can exploit a backward one for financial purposes and yet deny it other civilised advantages. A forward race is bound to educate the backward one it comes in contact with, just because the forward race imagines that its own progress is largely due to its own education. To say that the Kafir must not be educated is as idle as to say he must not breathe, or that he must not be exploited by civilised nations.

Though the missionary might make out a very good case from his own point of view, yet I think he would do the cause of education a grievous injury if he refused to admit that there was much truth in the indictment of his work. There is a *cause* for the undoubted phenomenon of colonial hostility to Kafir education. If the missionary were to raise the question of method, and if he were to admit that there is room for improvement in this direction, he would take a step that would prove the most progressive he has ever taken. At present he is apt to put down colonial hostility to mere prejudice, and thereby loses all the stimulus he might receive from level-headed criticism. By admitting some failure, the missionary would short-circuit much current opposition. The moment he asked his critics for advice as to how the system of education could be improved, he would discover to them the fact that many of them had no constructive policy to suggest. But very few people would care publicly and seriously to suggest that the natives should be left alone. The man who advocated such a policy would at once call public attention to his own lack of education, and would write himself down as uncultured. Not a little of the popular hostility of the colonists towards educating the Kafir is due to the fact that some of the men who are loudest in their objections are suspiciously weak in education themselves: their education was stopped at a preliminary stage, and they are scarcely the best people in the world to raise the whole question of the value of education. Men are cowards and take colour, like chameleons, from their surroundings. So one objector makes a dozen others. The cure for some hostility to education is more education of the enemy and more independence of thought. I have noticed that very few highly educated people in South Africa condemn the work of missions, though they frequently see the weak points in the missionary's methods. The Press in South Africa is becoming more and more inclined to side with education of the natives, though it would —very wisely, in my opinion—urge that there should be much more industrial work and much less book-learning undertaken.

The missionary, by refraining from showing resentment under hostile criticism, and by offering the other cheek— to drop metaphor, by asking for advice how to improve matters—would put his critics in a quandary. The moment any one tries to suggest alterations in educational methods, he either gives advice which does much to strengthen the case for education by improving its quality, and by showing that it can be conducted with good effect, or he is forced to admit that he has no constructive policy to suggest, and that very little change can be made, since most of the evils he has complained of are due, not so much to education as to the inherent quality of the human nature of the people educated. Thus without resorting to a *tu quoque,* and without pointing out that it is partly the disturbing presence of the white man that makes the education of the Kafirs so difficult, the missionary would educate the European objector, and would, perchance, teach himself that his own methods in the past had been faulty and defective. Perhaps that is the most important lesson the missionary could learn; and he is not the missionary's best friend who allows his sentiment to cover over the grave errors made in educational methods to-day.

By adopting the line of defence pointed out above, the missionary would cease to throw the glamour and irradiation of his sentiment over the subject in dispute, and would at once lift the argument out of the heated atmosphere in which it is usually discussed; and he would be prevented from making that most pitiful of all errors—the mistake of imagining his educational methods to be incapable of improvement.

### III. The Causes of our Success and Failure

It has been said that to muddle is to labour with effects without paying regard to causes. If that is so, then we must admit that we have muddled considerably in South Africa; for we have not even taken the trouble to make quite sure about the effects we complain of. Until we are quite certain as to symptoms, we are not likely to make a wise diagnosis or discover causes.

It is symptomatic of nothing but childhood and immaturity to contend that all educated Kafirs are extremely good or extremely bad. It is natural for children to see the salient features of things, and to fail in observing the half-tones, for they see things largely in masses and in outline, and adopt refreshingly simple systems of classification. To them, men are good or bad—never middling. But those who are busy educating the Kafirs cannot be classified into good teachers or bad teachers, for most of them are very indifferent teachers, just as most of the educated Kafirs are very indifferently educated Kafirs. Colonists are far too exacting in their demands about education: they are like many an old Kafir I have seen who has come along to learn to read, and who, after half an hour, has left the missionary saying indignantly that it is all nonsense: books don't talk to him as they do to white men.

It is essential to recognise two things in connection with the education of the Kafir. The first is that a wise education can do as much as or more than any other single factor to elevate the man. The second thing is that educational work must, from the nature of the case, be largely carried on by missionaries. When one million white people have to see to the education of their own children under peculiar difficulties, it is idle to expect them to be able to take entire control also of the education of the children of many millions of black people. It is not practicable, as yet, to dispense with Mission schools. We must recognise the fact that missionaries freely give to the country an immense amount of energy, and are in actual possession of the field. It may be possible to insist on a larger amount of governmental oversight in education, but at present this can only be obtained by increasing educational grants to existing schools. Since there is a limit to what the white man is willing to pay for the education of the Kafirs, there must be a limitation of his control of that education, unless it be decided that the problem is so important that emergency legislation is called for.

There has been a tendency in modern times for Governments to control many human activities which in past ages were freely open to people devoid of the necessary qualifications. Public opinion demands certified efficiency in its doctors, lawyers, hospital nurses, chemists, as well as in other trades and professions. In England we do not care to have inefficient people in positions of trust, but demand certain certificates of capacity or of adequate training in those who administer to our bodily or mental needs. But here we are dealing with that most difficult of all problems, the government and progress of a backward race, and we allow the most inefficient teachers, whose only qualification for the difficult work is their own kind hearts, to form the character of the rising generation and to complicate immensely our difficulties. We might as well try to cure cancer by kindness as to educate savages by it. The quality of the education we give to the Kafirs, probably more than anything else, decides the entire future of the natives: and yet, while there are many excellent and efficient Mission schools, we also allow the most inefficient people to mis-educate the Kafirs. I know not a few missionaries who deliberately choose to go without a

Government grant so that they may perpetuate the system of education they imagine to be best for the natives. I do not ask, has a State the right to prevent this sort of thing, but has a State the right to *allow* unqualified people to intensify national problems in this gratuitous fashion? The future of the Kafirs is, in some cases, being decided by people with the narrowest outlook.

On the other hand, we allow, in some cases, utterly unsuitable traders to complicate the problem in a different direction. Many traders, like many missionaries, are good, average people: but there are undesirable traders as there are unwise and unsuitable missionaries. If we are going to rule parentally—and surely there can be but little doubt that this is our duty—we should do so firmly, and have the courage of our convictions. An aboriginal race emerging from barbarism is an exceptional thing—as even John Stuart Mill admitted in his famous work on "Liberty"—and it is also a very dangerous thing: if ever special circumstances called for special treatment, they would seem to do so in the case of the natives, for the destiny of the country is at stake. The Kafirs say that pots are made while the clay is in good condition: if we delay much longer, we shall one day awake only to find that some of the irresponsible people who are moved by blind moral impulse have given ungainly and dangerous form to the pots. When once the clay is baked, it is useless to mourn over the shape of the pot.

We must now consider a few details in connection with the education of the natives, for destructive criticism is much easier to supply than constructive advice.

(1) The Governments should start a number of their own institutions for training teachers. At present it is proposed that such training institutes should be worked through existing missionary agencies. This is, of course, better than nothing, but it will inevitably lead to the retention of some undesirable elements. It is, perhaps, impossible to overrate the value of religious instruction in the case of the Kafirs, and it would be a grave mistake for the Government to alienate the sympathy of the missionaries, who at present have the educating of the Kafirs in their hands. But the missionaries would listen to reason. If the Government started a training institute for both white and black teachers, and gave increased grants of money to schools that employed such certificated teachers, it would begin to control native education.

It would be well for State schools to be started in suitable centres so that the Government might experiment as to the efficiency of various educational methods. If it were once demonstrated to the colonists that education could be devised so as immensely to improve the Kafir as a labourer, there would be an end to the common talk against native education.

(2) We should give the natives a very simple and yet very varied kind of education. The stimuli we have applied have been too complex and too violent. We should apply a greater variety of very simple stimuli, never over-pressing one form. Instead of pinning our faith to books, we should call to our aid every conceivable form of training that has been found useful in the education of the feeble-minded in Europe and in America. We should reduce book-education to a minimum. We might almost

as well return to the methods of the old schoolmen and set the natives discussing how many angels can stand comfortably on the point of a needle, as teach them Latin or force them to repeat pages of unintelligible English jargon parrot-fashion. For many a day our work would be cut out for us if we would but begin to train intelligently the muscle-nerve mechanisms by simple kindergarten work, and by the most elementary exercises. If we could but see that the object of education is to draw out and develop the existing faculties, and not to cram into the child's head an indigestible mass of ready-made learning, we might do the Kafirs some good. We should make full use of the immense educative value of play. Thus we should make the school hour a delight instead of a burden; and the children, whose parents refused to allow them to go to school, would become envious of those who had a better fortune.

The subject of child-study has been sadly neglected in South Africa. When wishing to publish a book on "Savage Childhood" I was astonished to find that there was no book in English treating of the subject of the Kafir child. This is an amazing fact, and it shows how little we have studied *causes*. We are never tired of saying that the child is father of the man; we say we are anxious to create good men, and yet we have not studied the children! If this does not reveal a policy of muddle, it would be interesting to know what could indicate such a policy. To educate wisely we need to study *origins* and *ends*. Until we know exactly what sort of product we wish to turn out, we are not likely to turn it out: until we know the capacity and the tricks of the clay, we shall not be very likely to make the vessels we desire. Now, missionaries and colonists differ as to what it would be good to turn out: no wonder they differ as to their verdicts of what is actually turned out.

So long as we look at the children, we see no reason why many of them should not become very intelligent and active. They are brimful of life and of energy, being fully as lively as white children. They are smart and intelligent within certain limits and in certain directions; and when wisely taught, they keep pace with white children for many years. But just when we hope to produce a good result, the mental development seems to become arrested, and the children return at puberty to the kraal and disappoint all our hopes. There are exceptions, but there is little doubt as to the general rule. Now, what is the cause of this arrest of the development of the higher powers? After puberty the body continues for years to develop splendidly, but the mind, the imagination, the logical processes, the higher regions of intelligence, all seem to suffer from a blight. Is it not possible that if we discovered the cause of this arrest of development, and if we discovered the reason why some Kafirs do *not* deteriorate after puberty, we might be able to overcome the difficulty?

The savage child lives under conditions that lead to a great development of the lower faculties. As a result, he can make a clever bird-trap at an earlier age than can a white child. He can throw sticks at birds, and hit them while flying in a way very few white children can. He can follow a spoor, and can come to sound logical conclusions from insignificant trifles, such as the attitude of a leaf, a blade of grass, or a piece of stick, in a way that would seem magical to a white child. The Kafir child lives entirely in a region of sense-perceptions and is trained to a high degree in certain kinds of observation. Within a very narrow compass it can perceive sensations and argue from them to definite and limited conclusions. All its nervous energy is diverted through the channel of its animal needs. The black child can detect a buck in the veld more readily than can a white child, not because it has better eyes, but because it has trained its sight in this direction. But in the kraals children are discouraged from asking questions; and parents throw cold water on any inquiring mind. In other words, the child has not been trained *in reflection*. The faculty of sense-perception is highly trained, while other faculties are neglected. The memory is wonderfully strong and keen, and impressions are retained very tenaciously. This is a great asset to the teacher, but also a great snare. I entirely agree with the following foot-note found in a translation of Rousseau's "Emile":

"With respect to reason and judgment, and what may be called the higher life of the mind, the memory is a subsidiary and subordinate faculty, but a faculty without which these higher activities cannot be maintained. The very possibility of education is dependent on memory. We must not only remember what we have understood, but we must remember in order that we may understand; the memory must hold not only the finished products of thought, but also the crude materials for thinking."

But if there is a faculty in the Kafir child that does not need developing it is the memory. No sooner, however, does the child go to school than the teacher, who does not think out his method, catches hold of this faculty, and saves himself endless trouble by working it for all it is worth. Lessons are learned by rote, though the child often has not the remotest idea what it is repeating. It would repeat lessons in Hindustani or Chinese equally well, without knowing the meaning of a word of either language. Thus the teacher develops the apex, or the most developed faculty of the child : the result is very showy and seems to reflect great credit on the teacher. Sometimes the pupil exposes the sham, when showing off, by not quite knowing where to begin or end in his lesson; but that is thought a trifle to be laughed at. Instead of teaching the child to *reflect*, the teacher has trained it to *remember*. The lesson has therefore not only had no educative value, but it has done the child harm, for it confirms a bad habit and deepens the channel of the child's plastic thought in a vicious manner.

"The apparent facility with which children learn is the cause of their ruin. We do not see that this very facility is the proof that they are learning nothing. Their smooth and polished brain reflects like a mirror the objects that are presented to it; but nothing remains, nothing penetrates it. The child retains the words, but ideas are reflected." In these words Rousseau has pointed out a fact often forgotten in South Africa. He has also (in the following passage), with fine insight, drawn attention to the way teachers are misled by the seeming dulness of some of their most promising pupils. "Nothing is more difficult than to distinguish, in infancy, real stupidity from that apparent and deceptive stupidity which is the indication of strong characters." The whole book ("Emile") from which these extracts are taken should be studied by every school teacher in South Africa.

Another fault is that the teacher keeps the child far too long at one thing: he repeats and drones away until the child gets dazed. The immature mind gets tired, then listless, then weary, and finally exhausted. The teacher, intending to be thorough, literally inhibits all development. The pupil gets accustomed to the sound and forgets, if he ever knew, the sense. A habit is formed; and when a lesson is repeated by sheer habit, it has ceased to have any educative value. The mind gets clogged, and it becomes more difficult than ever for the child to reflect and think. The child comes to mix up names and things in a general jumble, and confuses sound with sense. It is, in other words, thrown back on sense-perceptions, and even has these confused for him.

Now this is what Mr. William Harris, the American educationist, has called "A training in idiocy." "For," asks Mr. Harris, "what is an idiot but one who sees all things in their superficial relations—confuses things with names, and causes with effects?" The logical reflective and imaginative faculties have become, in too many cases, crushed or atrophied through the ignorant actions of the very person whose duty it was to develop them.

We come to a further cause of trouble. In England one does not need to point out that too much occupation with the emotions and sentiments inhibits intelligence. We have only to listen to sentimental questions asked in the House of Commons to see that undisciplined and over-developed emotion is not to be found in people of high intelligence. We never find a well-balanced statesman asking some trivial and sensational question: it is always the little men who do that. When a Kafir reaches the age of puberty,* emotions of the most turbulent nature awake within him, and there is great danger that his intelligence should be crowded out in the struggle for nutrition. The boy's nerve-energy is all drained off away from the brain-centres whose function is reflection. The master has not developed the boy's power of reflection—or his imagination—sufficiently to resist the degenerative changes that set in. The boy leaves school, too often, at this critical age, and is so undeveloped in brain that future progress amid the kraal-life is impossible. His mind dwells ever on sex, for he listens to talk of but little else in the kraal. He becomes engrossed with his emotions, and thus his higher mental activity is inhibited. He settles down into an ordinary sort of Kafir, having just sufficient veneer of education to make him really objectionable. No wonder the colonist can see little good in him.

Now if we contrast with this dismal picture I have drawn —and I have seen it so often that I am sure I am not exaggerating—the method by which the native is educated at the most enlightened training institutes, we find a great difference. In proportion as the defects pointed out above

With regard to the onset of puberty, Rousseau has offered the following most suggestive hint:

"The instructions of nature are tardy and slow, while those of men are almost always premature. In the first case, the senses arouse the imagination; and in the second, the imagination arouses the senses and gives them a precocious activity which cannot fail to enervate and enfeeble, first the individual, and then, in the course of time, the species itself. A more general and a more trustworthy observation than that of the effect of climate is that puberty and sexual power always come earlier among educated and refined people than among ignorant and barbarous people."—"Emile."

are avoided, so far is the education truly educative in tendency. And in so far as the boys can be kept at school after puberty so as to give the higher faculties a chance to ripen, and in so far as they can be kept away until their character is sufficiently developed not to be ruined by the conversation of the kraal, and in so far as they are taught to work at trades or at industrial employment so that their minds may be healthily occupied—so far are they able to continue to rise in the scale after puberty; their faculties have had an all-round development and are able to withstand the mentally blighting dawn of strong emotion at the period of puberty. If at that critical stage the growth of the boy's faculties becomes arrested, all his nervous energy flows along the line of least resistance, and those who know the Kafir know what that direction is. That is why, I think, the natives who are taken to Europe for their education rise higher than those who stay at home: they are brought into an environment vastly different from that which they would live in even at the best industrial school in South Africa. Unfortunately, a voyage to England is very apt to give the Kafir a swollen head, and to make him unsuited to South African life. It is therefore not well to send a few natives home, for such a voyage raises aspirations that cannot be satisfied in South Africa. It also separates the native too much from his fellows; and the pampering he receives at home by well-meaning but injudicious friends proves a cruel kindness in the long run. Every here and there a Kafir passes through the ordeal safely, but far more are marred than improved by residence in Europe. It is not fair to the Kafir to subject him to the process. To send Kafirs to England for their education is not a practical solution of the difficulty: the natives must be educated in their own country.

So important is this subject of arrest of faculty at puberty that it must be referred to again in a later chapter (*see* pp. 236–241).

A common complaint brought against educated Kafirs by people who are truly interested in them is that they show so little originality. They all conform to type, and merely imitate white men. The cause of this is worth hunting for.

One of the most fundamental things about mental activity is its spontaneity. We see this in the play of children. The spontaneity of play has great value in developing the sense of personality. In the kraal, custom throws its spell over the children at an early age, and spontaneity is thus checked, with the consequence that the latent sense of personality is nipped in the bud. The child goes to school and finds he must also conform to type. Here too, any spontaneity or originality is stamped out of the pupil by the teacher who conducts a large class. All the children are set droning away at their lessons. If much more kindergarten exercise was indulged in, the child would get more scope for spontaneity, together with a certain amount of discipline. Curiosity and imitation are two principles that can be of infinite use in education, for curiosity is very strong in savages, and leads to attention and concentration of the mind. If work were made more interesting to the children, and if kindergarten exercises were used as a sort of break between the kraal-life and the school-life, the curiosity and pleasure of the child would greatly help the teacher. Tumultuous excitement is bad from an educational point of view, as it dissipates attention;

but great educationists have ever sought to win over the curiosity of their pupils. Socrates would produce a pain in his hearers while at the same time he let them see that he intended slowly to remove it and to turn it into a pleasure. He thus riveted the attention of his wriggling victims, much to their profit as well as the enjoyment of future ages.

By remembering that an idea has motor-force, we can see how we may use the imitative faculty for our ends. Instead of nagging at the children and telling them what *not* to do (as so many native teachers do), we should show them the right action, and would find that the children imitated the action half unconsciously. But the white teacher should decide as to what is to be imitated. Unfortunately, the Kafir wants to lay down the law as to what he shall be taught. In some institutions there is a rule that all natives shall put in a certain number of hours' work every day at industrial pursuits : but too often the Kafir dislikes the regulation, and offers to pay something extra to be let off the manual work. Some missionaries, most weakly, permit the Kafirs to decide this question, and feebly say that if they insisted on the manual labour, the Kafirs would go to other institutions where their whims would be given way to. Thus it comes about that the taught dictate to the teachers and largely decide what is to be learned. The desire to learn is sometimes very great, and Kafirs often are willing to pay more for the education of their children than are white people. But if missionaries cannot combine to save the Kafir from himself, then they must be prepared for poor results, for if the Kafirs can decide the type of education they are to receive, the results will be lamentable. We must allow room for spontaneity, but must not mistake mere whim for that excellent quality. The Kafir wants to imitate the last educated native he saw, and if possible to surpass him in glitter. He loves book-education best: it is this that he hankers after. Unfortunately it is the missionary who has set the fashion, for he is so anxious that the native should be able to read the Bible. As a result, the fashion is stereotyped in custom, and the Kafir is bent on reading books, even though he does not understand what they are all about. But book-education does not open the mind of the native in a healthy way, for there is an immense amount of work to be done, as all scientific educationists know, before the mind can profit by such education. The natives should be treated as if they were mentally deficient, for that is what they actually are. They should be trained by experts in the art of curing feeble-mindedness and arrested mental development. They cannot be truly compared with European children, for they have been trained differently from the cradle. When we have to train a feeble-minded child, we have an immense amount of work to do before we can set the child to book-work. The nervous system wants training and discipline, the nerve-centres need co-ordinating, and the entire nature requires strengthening so as to supply a solid base on which to build the future edifice. In the case of those feeble-minded people, the Kafirs, all this is largely neglected; the pace is forced; and book-education leaves the higher powers of the mind vacant, and the hands idle.

Yet when missionaries train the natives in industrial pursuits, the colonists—especially "labour" colonists—too often cry out and say that the white man's work will be taken from him: they say it will lead to competition, and that the native will cut out the white labourer. In one breath such a colonist says the native is lazy, is no good and cannot rise in the scale: in the next he says the native will rise far too high and will be too active. What does he mean? Does he know himself what he means? As the Trade Unions develop in South Africa they will more and more knock their heads against this knotty problem, for to boycott the Kafir will be impossible. To prevent the colonist from grumbling about the way the Kafirs threaten to cut out the white working man, some teachers are apt to withhold industrial training and to give the native a book-education. But all in vain: the colonist refuses to rejoice or lament no matter whether the missionary pipes or mourns. As a result of this lopsided education the political agitator obtains ready to his hand just the material he wants. He finds it easy to instil into the mind that is empty, swept and garnished the pernicious seed of discontent.

(3) We should advance slowly. Time is nothing to savages: it has no value in their eyes, for they are scarcely conscious of its flow. While people are in a primitive stage of culture they should be given ample time for the lessons to soak into their minds. Hurried education does but confuse simple-minded folk. There are many people, even in England, who would not be benefited by advanced education. George Gissing, basing his remarks on fact, makes Henry Rycroft say of his excellent old servant: "I find her one of the few women I have known who merit the term excellent. She can read and write—that is all. More instruction would, I am sure, have harmed her, for

it would have confused her natural motives without supplying any clear ray of mental guidance." If there are thousands of excellent people in England at that stage, must there not be hundreds of thousands of Kafirs in the same position? But with a lack of discrimination, some teachers insist on giving the Kafirs a wholly unsuitable education that simply passes over their heads. Nay, it is worse than that: the education these natives receive is just sufficient to lead them to question their old categorical imperative of clan-restraint, while it does not give them any clear ray of guidance to take the place of the old familiar rules of conduct. It will be ages before higher education will supply the Kafir with any guidance in the perplexities that a hasty education raises. If we give the Kafirs a very simple and elementary education, we shall not spoil them by making them unfit to remain good, sensible members of Kafir society; but the hastily and half-educated mother will neglect her home and will want to ape the white woman; while the hastily educated men will be fit for nothing. It is our impatient insistence in cramming unsuitable knowledge into the thick skulls of the Kafirs that guarantees a maximum of risk to us and a minimum of good to the natives. If, instead of seeking to hurry a few Kafirs through centuries of growth within the space of a few years, we were to recognise the limits of their capacity, and were to give a larger number of Kafirs a more simple training, we should at least minimise our risks. There are to-day thousands of simple-minded Kafirs who are good, honest folk, and who serve their day and generation according to their lights and capacities: but we are ruining them by forcing them into our wretchedly unsuitable European mould, and one day we shall turn them out as useless, crippled members of society. A very little simple education would improve them, but more education would at the present stage undermine their very virtues.

(4) The training should be largely industrial. While book-education seems in too many cases to close the mind, or to open it in a distorted fashion, industrial work has an excellent effect. I have sometimes given a native a piece of wood and a few tools, and have allowed him to experiment with them. It is striking to notice how contact with such physical things opens the mind. The Kafirs who work in iron (I refer to the tribal blacksmiths) are by far the most intelligent of the natives. Their work has educative value, for it makes them think. If a native is set to learn a trade, it is impossible for him to make such apparent profit out of his memory as he can do when reading books. We have made too much flashy profit out of the memory of the natives, and have in consequence crippled their intelligence. The Kafirs who are educated chiefly by books do not seem to lose their crudity in the

* Speaking of the failure of civilisation in Russia, Rousseau says: "The Russians will never be civilised, because they have been civilised too early. Peter had an imaginative genius; he had not the true genius that creates and produces anything from nothing. Some of his measures were beneficial, but the majority were ill-timed. He saw that his people were barbarous, but he did not see that they were unripe for civilisation; he wished to civilise them, when it was necessary only to discipline them. He wished to produce at once Germans or Englishmen, when he should have begun by making Russians; he prevented his subjects from ever becoming what they might have been, by persuading them that they were what they were not. It is in this way that a French tutor trains his pupil to shine for a moment in childhood, and then to be for ever a nonentity."—"The Social Contract," Tozer's trans., p. 139.

way natives do when they are taught by industrial methods. The good memory of the Kafirs is an educational snare—a sort of "booby-trap" for the unwary teacher. The native scholar may get full marks in an examination though he has but the remotest idea of the meaning of what he repeats by rote. His education has not led to the development of his logical, imaginative or intellectual faculties. But the fellow cannot play tricks on nature in the same way as he can on the too lenient and often unobservant teacher. It is a striking fact that every one in South Africa has a good word for the Trappists, who, above all others, make use of industrial education.

There are many trades at which the natives can do passably well. They make fairly good compositors in the printer's trade, and take to the work well, for they have infinite patience; they can be made into moderately good gardeners if suitably trained; they can be trained as blacksmiths, carpenters, masons, painters. The women can be taught washing, ironing, sewing and other suitable occupations. But in all these departments of labour they need white supervision, a fact which seems to point to the conclusion that more and more the white man will be a highly paid controller and director of labour rather than a moderately well-paid labourer. It would not be wise, therefore, from this point of view, to flood the country with unskilled white labourers. That policy will be but the laying up of gigantic evil for the days to come. As soon as we frankly recognise the fact that the Kafirs are going to rise in the scale of civilisation, and yet are not going to become imitation white men, we shall be able to adopt a sensible and far-seeing policy, and shall be saved from the need of listening to home journals that, without having adequate knowledge of all the conditions of the country, press on South Africa theoretical and impossible solutions of their difficulties.

(5) I should like to see every school holding an ignorance class once every week. One of the gravest defects of the present type of education given to the natives is the way it leads to conceit as to mental capacity. As soon as a native can read and write, he swaggers in a most aggravating manner. Who has not seen one of these fellows (who has, perhaps, been to a night school at Johannesburg or Durban) as he takes up his position where he can attract public attention? The fellow, anxious to show all the wealth of his wit in a moment, takes his book out of his pocket, and, with prodigious show, points with his clumsy finger to some word which he spells out aloud: he tries to read a few words, every now and then looking up from his book to see how many white people are remarking what a clever fellow he is. Or he stands gazing at a shop window, and reads out aloud any words he can find printed on show-cards. He blocks the way while some white person wishes to pass on the narrow pavement; and, instead of thinking himself an intolerable nuisance, he shows by his peacock vanity that he imagines himself to be a paragon of knowledge. If these people were taught regularly how infinitely insignificant is their little stock of learning, it might save them from making themselves so peculiarly and unnecessarily offensive to white men.

In the ignorance class, the simplest things might be taught to the Kafirs. They might have pointed out to them how they were ignorant of even the superficial wonders to be found in the very weeds in their kraal. The simplest lesson in botany might be given, not to teach the natives that science, but to show them how infinite was their ignorance of the commonest things. And aspects of nature might be chosen in which the natives thought they saw caprice : if the simplest of natural processes were explained to them, they might come to see that Nature was orderly, and that the belief in magic was based on defective observation. Hitherto the type of education given to the Kafir has proved most ineffective for the removing of the belief in magic.

At these ignorance classes we need only teach the Kafirs the sort of thing an English child of ten years of age knows. In fact it would be a good plan to tell the "educated" natives that they were to be taught some of the things, now hidden from them, that were known to small children in Europe. Such ignorance classes would prepare the people for more positive education later on ; for the newer knowledge would then no longer be some wholly incongruous mixture taken from a book, the understanding of which demands an immense amount of previous knowledge, and which is at present unrelated to the rest of their information. I know some highly intelligent "educated" natives who have been open-mouthed with wonder when I explained to them some elementary fact that a small English child of ten would not need to be told. If instead of seeking to educate the apex of the mental nature, we set to work to enlighten the mind where its ignorance is densest and most dangerous, we should be doing the Kafirs a good turn, though we might not have any showy results to point to. By ignorance classes we might break down the pernicious idea that the native is the equal of the white man.

In these ignorance classes the children might be taught the outlines of their own history, and might thus come to see how very backward and primitive they are. Their mental poverty might be emphasised by telling the children one of their own primitive nursery tales, and by contrasting it with a more imaginative European fairy story. This might stimulate the imagination.

(6) Latent aptitudes and capacity should be developed. Who that has seen the children making small clay models of oxen, horses, sheep and other animals, can doubt but that much educational advantage could be taken of such a natural aptitude? The faculty of imitation is very strong in the children, and this could be used along the line of the plastic arts. Wood-carving affords an excellent training method; Kafirs take to it keenly. It is not that the *results* would have any value: it is the *process* and training that would be so important and advantageous. The school should foster all the hobbies that, from the nature of the case, cannot thrive in the kraal. Existing industries, such as basket-making and pottery manufacture, could easily be improved, but where does one find a missionary who thinks this work worth the while?

(7) We should teach the people the value of thrift. At present an immense amount of grain is absolutely wasted in a few weeks after harvesting, for enormous beer-drinks are held with prodigal waste. No wonder the people find "famine beginning to gnaw" before the next season's crop is ripe. If we could but make the Kafirs realise the value of a good crop, we might do much to foster improvements

in methods of agriculture. We can generally appeal to Kafirs through the stomach, though missionaries are apt to regard that unruly member as beneath their notice.

Improvidence is one of the minor vices of even the highly educated natives: as a result they are for ever running into debt: they have to borrow money as best they can when in acute difficulty, and not unnaturally find that exorbitant rates of interest are demanded because the security is uncertain. This last factor in the problem is beyond their comprehension, for the educated natives are now turning round—Dube has done so—and demand that the Government should fix the limits as to the rate of interest. The Kafirs have the solving of the problem in their own hands, but they seem unable to overcome their own improvidence. Did they but treat *the cause*, and did the missionary (some missionaries are doing so) but help them to do so, the trouble would soon vanish. But educated Kafirs are apt to demand that the Government should tinker at effects, while they themselves leave the causes unchanged. There is thrift and thrift, and the grace can become a curse; but since the whole past training of the Kafir prevents him from becoming niggardly, it would be well to develop his nature so as to make the man more provident.

It is, perhaps, useless to go further into details, for what I am contending for is the adoption of rational principles that might be worked out in detail with infinite variety according to local need. I have tried to show that we are bewildering the native, not by our naughtiness—that bugbear of the sentimentalist—but by the very complexity of the benevolent civilising process. We expose savages to the highly complex stimuli of individualism, labour demands, economic pressure, violent legal changes, trade, clothing, industries, a lofty spiritual religion: and to all these we add a wholly unsuitable system of book-learning, which in itself affords a complexity of stimuli of a varied nature: and then we are surprised when colonists tell us that the native is being spoiled. We are in danger of causing spasm by the very complexity of the stimuli. If we could but grasp the fact that there is no virtue in everything that goes by the name of "education," but that the value is to be determined by *the suitability of the means to reach the desired end*, we should be saved on the one hand from unreasoning dislike of education, and on the other from the idolatry of books.

Most of us cherish the splendid faith that the freedom of the Press is, on the whole, a good thing. Faith in the future of the educational process in the case of the natives is an equally heroic one. Those who are at present educating the Kafir seem to take it for granted that such education will ever remain in their own hands; and that they will for ever and a day be able to decide what books the natives shall, and what books they shall not, read. But one of the very first effects of education is to make the natives anxious to manage their own affairs: they will soon demand the right of directing their own education, and after that the deluge.

As soon as Kafirs begin to publish their own literature, and to organise their own educational societies, they will adopt many most pernicious books. Missionaries may have it all their own way now, and may flood the country with the "Pilgrim's Progress" and the "Peep of Day."

But do they fondly imagine it will be ever thus? Father Waggett has told us how a Kafir chief puzzled his missionary by a reference to Darwin's books. When the educative process has advanced a little more, it will pay the destructive societies in Europe and America to flood the country with cheap, agnostic, atheistical and anarchist literature. The missionaries are but preparing the people to arrive at a state in which they will be able to appreciate the most clap-trap arguments against Christianity. When Kafirs begin to discuss the Higher Criticism, the missionary will be most embarrassed. To the natural race-hatred of the raw native will be added the race-envy of the educated Kafir. The Ethiopians have shown us something of the sort of thing we may expect; but this movement is mild compared to other movements that must perforce spring up—especially if we are too indifferent to prevent the natives from going to America for special inoculation with a virulent virus of race-hatred. Only the stupid, easy-going, liberty-loving spirit of the Briton would suffer this American peril.

Since it is the odd and the bizarre that especially appeal to the half-educated native, the effect of unsuitable literature will probably be ruinous; it will be much more dangerous than in the case of Indian races, which have more sense of balance and of proportion, to say nothing of delicacy of thought and feeling. Clever natives will catch at the idlest, and most irresponsible, and unpatriotic of questions asked in the House of Commons by some sentimentalist, and will spread the silly questions into every South African kraal.

Another danger looms ahead. We hear much about

the "inconsequent" Kafir, which really is based on little more than the inconsequence of the white person who writes on a subject that he or she has not studied carefully. But even if the Kafir be so inherently inconsequent as is made out, our education must modify that trait, for it is largely the result of ignorance, difference as to data, point of view and lack of training. Our education must of necessity be directed to the development of the imaginative powers—so pregnant with good and evil—of the Kafirs; for if it deals chiefly with what Carlyle called the arithmetical understanding, it will prove sterile; it will be found to be essential to plough deep into the imagination of the people. When missionaries find this out, education will produce strange effects. Unless we have disciplined the man's nature, we shall develop the imagination of the Kafir for one purpose, and he will, probably, use the quickened capacity for quite another. At present the Kafirs have not the imaginative grasp necessary to think-out the necessity for a carefully designed plan for a long campaign. They have not yet the imaginative power required to appreciate the disproportion between black and white men. The raw Kafirs think in a vague way that the white man can do anything by his strong medicine and powerful magic. But even a little education dispels this idea, and the slightly educated Kafir thinks himself quite as capable as the developed white man. A half-educated Kafir would gaily offer to run the British Navy—or Empire, if necessary. We have therefore the immediate danger that the half-educated Kafir may rise in rebellion, in the vain idea that the white man can easily be driven into the sea. The immediate result would be a massacre of the whites; but this would be followed up by a decimation of the native races, who are not yet ready finally to expel the white man. But in the long run, as the imagination becomes developed, a graver danger will arise. War against the whites would then be thought out seriously, and plans would be laid more carefully. The result would be much more serious. It is some such ultimate risk we must run if we educate the Kafirs. Our greatest blunder would be to live in a fool's paradise and to ignore the dangers connected with our policy. The risks must be taken; but, equally, they must not be ignored.

It has been suggested by the friends of education that it would be better for us to have to bargain with educated rather than with uneducated natives; that the educated natives would listen to our proposals more readily; that we should get better terms out of them; that we could bring them to their senses more quickly. The argument seems to betray a lack of insight into Kafir character. It is probable that we should do much better for ourselves if we were bargaining with the raw Kafirs, for they are more moderate in their demands, more balanced in their judgments, and more open to appeals to common sense than are the educated Kafirs.

In so far as the educated Kafir has proved unsuitable, it is partly our fault, and partly the fault of the man's nature and antecedents. We cannot hope to make a silk purse out of our sow's ear, and we had better give up the attempt. When the Kafir receives a sensible education, he shows a most unexpected capacity for responding to our stimulus. If taught to work, he will show himself industrious, as the confessions of Durban and Johannesburg merchants given above show. If he is given too much book-learning by a stupid teacher, he will be utterly ruined by his faulty education. The reason that so many white men denounce native education lies largely in the fact that they do not see the best results produced, for the missionaries keep their best Kafirs for their own purposes. But even if we adopt the wisest methods of education, we shal but build up for ourselves an edifice that may at any time fall about our ears. We shall produce a class of reliable Kafir workers who will, undoubtedly, replace some of the inefficient, lazy, drunken Trade Union white men who shirk a good day's work; and shall thus foster race-antagonism of a very pronounced type; for it will be the least intelligent and least self-disciplined white men who will cry out. A faulty education will lead to endless trouble, and the more rapid the process of education the greater the risks we run. Looking far ahead it is difficult to see how we can stay the tide of education, or avoid the ultimate clash that must ensue when educated Kafirs will form so large a body that they will threaten to drive the white man, either by peaceable or warlike means, out of the country. It will be our democratic ideals, our individualism, and our good intentions that will be our undoing. We start by making the Kafirs the victims of our benevolence, and shall probably end up by being ourselves the victims of this policy.

## CHAPTER V

### CAN THE ETHIOPIAN CHANGE HIS SKIN? A BIOLOGICAL ARGUMENT

THE final issue of the conflict arising from the clash of Western Individualism with Kafir Socialism obviously depends in a large measure on the capacity of the natives to rise in the scale of civilisation—in metaphorical language, on the ability of the Ethiopian to change his skin. Our native policy will, naturally, be affected by our ideas on this subject; for if we are convinced that the Kafirs are doomed either to extinction or to permanent degradation, we shall adopt one type of policy: if we think they will increase in numbers, and also in intelligence and culture, we shall adopt another. The question is therefore intensely practical; and a mistake in presuppositions will be fatal.

Of all answer-begging questions, the words at the head of this chapter would be difficult to surpass. To ask the question is a picturesque method of stifling all discussion by an appeal to the gallery. Like jesting Pilate, the man who asks the question stays not for an answer.

The words ask three very different questions: *First*, Can the Ethiopian become a European? *Secondly*, Can the *individual Ethiopian* rise immensely higher than the average of his race succeeds in doing to-day? *Thirdly*, Can *the race* evolve to something vastly different from what it is at present? We shall have to take these three questions in order. But before we do so, we need to ask a preliminary question, Will the Backward race survive in contact with the Forward one? This question is most important, for many races have died out when brought into contact with European civilisation; and unless it seems probable that the Kafirs will survive, it is not much use to discuss the question of their capacity to change and develop.

In problems of racial contact there are but four possibilities. These have been summed up by Mr. Bryce in his "Romanes Lecture" as follows: "When two races differing in strength, that is to say, either in numbers or in physical capacity, or in material development, or in military resources, come into political or social contact, some one of four possible results follows. Either the weaker race dies out before the stronger; or it is absorbed into the stronger, the latter remaining practically unaffected; or the two become commingled into something different from what either was before; or, finally, the two continue to dwell together unmixed, each preserving a character of its own."* Let us glance at each of these four possible results and see which will most probably hold in the case of the Kafirs. Let us consider first the possibility of the weaker race becoming absorbed into the stronger.

This can only take place by intermarriage. In the case of Kafirs and Europeans any such commingling of stocks appears to lead, not to a loss of Kafir character, but to a third type of thing, that *tertium quid* the half-caste. Opinion is divided as to whether in such hybrids characters blend or tend to segregate: but even if it should be found

* *Loc. cit.* pp. 10, 11.

that they *do* segregate, it would be practically impossible to prevent the constant appearance of fresh hybrids. We do not enter on the stage of prophecy when we say that the Kafirs will not be absorbed into the European population and lose their distinctive elements. We have experiment in the past, and not mere unsupported speculation as to the future, on which to base our conclusion.

The second theoretical possibility is that both the races may lose their distinctive elements, and may blend, and so become fused into a conglomerate type intermediate between the original stocks. Mendelism may, or may not, have much to say as to the physical aspect of a problem of this nature; but when we note that there is an element of sentiment in the question, and when we further remember that this element of sentiment has for centuries kept the races from intermarriage, we are bound to conclude that, with the increased friction that now obtains owing to the clash of racial interests, there is no practical possibility that the problem will be solved by the elimination of the European and the Kafir in the formation of an all-embracing half-caste population.

We are therefore left with but two possible endings of the problem. Either one of the two races will be exterminated by disease or war, or else both will survive and live side by side with differing aims and ideals. To believe that the two races should permanently live on side by side seems at first sight a splendid faith too difficult to hold. We therefore postpone it for the present, and ask what chance there is of the Kafir's dying out in the blighting presence of civilisation.

As we look round the world we see aboriginal races

dying out in the presence of civilisation; we note how the ship that carries the missionary and the Bible into the South Seas also carries the germs of diseases that decimate the natives. We see the Hottentots and the Bushmen vanishing before the advance of the Kafirs or of civilisation, and we want to know whether the Kafirs will follow the example of all such races.

Disease, Drink and Clothing form Civilisation's trinity of evil, in so far as the physical well-being of most savage races is concerned. European diseases kill far more savages than European rifles. There is no lack of evidence on this point. For example, R. L. Stevenson writes: "The tribe of Hapaa is said to have numbered some four hundred when small-pox came and reduced them by one-fourth. Six months later a woman developed tubercular consumption; the disease spread like wild-fire about the valley, and in less than a year two survivors, a man and a woman, fled from the newly created solitude. . . . Early in the year of my visit . . . a first case of phthisis appeared in a household of seventeen persons, and by the end of August, when the tale was told me, one soul survived, a boy who had been absent at his schooling."

We see in this case what frightful havoc an imported disease causes in races that have never known it before. Dr. Archdall Reid, from whose "Principles of Heredity" I have taken this extract, says: "The Caribs of the West Indies are almost extinct. The Red Indians are going fast, as are the aborigines of cold and temperate South America. The Tasmanians have gone. The Australians and the Maoris are but a dwindling remnant. As surely as the trader with his clothes or the missionary with his church and schoolroom appears, the work of extermination begins on the Polynesian Islands. Throughout the whole vast extent of the New World the only pure aborigines who seem destined to persist are those who live remote in mountains or in the depths of fever-haunted forests, where the white man is unable to build the towns and cities with which he has studded the cooler and more 'healthy' regions of North and South."

It matters but little what the newly imported disease is, so long as it is lethal. In 1876 some forty thousand of a population of one hundred and fifty thousand in Fiji were killed off by measles. The trouble, which with us is but a moderately mild children's disease, becomes a devastating plague in countries where it is introduced for the first time. Small-pox and whooping-cough can tell the same tale. Wherever a lethal disease makes its appearance for the first time in a virgin soil, the loss of life is enormous.

While there may be much that is still obscure in connection with the varying capacity of different races to resist disease, a few main principles seem to be fairly well established. It is impossible in this place to go fully into the scientific aspect of the matter ; those who wish to do so may, as a preliminary, study Dr. Reid's book on "Heredity," and especially his chapters on Evolution against Disease, The Origins of Zimotic Disease, and Bacteria as Empire Builders. With regard to the special problem of the Kafirs, it may be briefly summarised that when a new disease is imported into a region where it has hitherto been unknown, a certain number of the people succumbs

* *Op. cit.* p. 151.

at once to the disease, while a certain number is able to resist it. Those least fit to persist under the changed conditions of environment die off, and fail to reproduce their stock: those who resist the disease best have the most offspring; and thus, in course of time, through the action of natural selection, the race becomes able to resist the malady. In England every person is exposed to infection from tubercular trouble,* and yet, owing to our past familiarity with the disease, we are moderately capable of resisting it, or have such resisting power that we are able to recover from slight attacks. An enormous number of people have some slight tubercular lesions. Professor Sir Clifford Allbutt recently stated in an address: "I am guilty of no extravagance when I suggest that one-third of you who hear me, wittingly or unwittingly, are, or have been, infected with tubercle." At the other end of the scale come the races of the New World, which, as we have seen, suffer the most fearful havoc when phthisis first appears in their midst. Negroes have not had so much experience of the disease as have Europeans, but they have had much more experience of it than have the races of the New World. Consequently they come between the English and the inhabitants of the New World in their capacity to resist the disease. Says Dr. Reid: "No colony of Africans has ever succeeded in Europe or Asia, where the mortality from tuberculosis grows so great that the immigrants soon become extinct. Nevertheless, even in West African forests negroes have undergone some evolution

* In the case of *pulmonary* tubercular trouble, 39·9 in every 10,000 persons died of this disease in 1838; 27·7 in every 10,000 in 1855; 11·5 per 10,000 in 1906. The diminishing rate is significant.

against tuberculosis. It was not enough to enable them to persist in densely peopled parts of Europe and Asia, but it was enough to enable them to persist under the conditions they found in the islands and on the mainland of America. In America, tuberculosis, as compared to its prevalence in Southern Europe and Asia, has as yet spread but little. The slaves were taken to the warmer parts of the country and employed mainly in agriculture. They had a special start, and were placed under conditions that grew worse only very slowly as the density of the population slowly increased. As a result they underwent evolution, and are now able to persist even in towns and cities of the United States, though, as their high mortality shows, with difficulty." *

Phthisis has been taken as an example, but many other diseases, such as small-pox or measles, might just as well have been chosen. As Dr. Reid says: "In 1841 Catlin wrote of the United States: 'Thirty millions of white men are now scuffling for the goods and luxuries of life over the bones of twelve millions of red men, six millions of whom have fallen victims to small-pox.' " †

And almost any other race might have been chosen to illustrate the principle. Thus: "In New Zealand phthisis has made frightful ravages among the natives, and has been one of the chief causes of the gradual extinction of that race." ‡

* *Op. cit.* p. 184. † *Op. cit.* p. 182.

‡ Hirsch, quoted by Dr. Reid, *op. cit.* p. 147. It is, perhaps, not fair to Dr. Reid to quote from his pages on this subject without at the same time giving the following passage, which lies at the base of his whole argument:

"There is not an iota of evidence that any race whatever has undergone degeneration through the action of any disease, nor that the acquire-

Whether or not the Kafirs, who have had a moderate acquaintance with phthisis, will die off from the disease, seems, therefore, to depend on the local condition of the environment; where that is favourable, and where the daily occupation takes the Kafirs into the open air, the natives can persist: where the surrounding population is too great, or where the conditions of work are unfavourable, and where the natives are deprived of sunlight and of fresh air, the chance is that they will suffer extremely. Dr. Reid quotes from Bartolacci's work on Ceylon as follows: "It is a remarkable fact that of 9000 Kafirs (negroes from the East Coast of Africa) who had been imported at various times by the Dutch Government into Ceylon, and had been drafted into regiments, scarcely a trace of their descendants remains; and they would certainly not be recognised at all among the present popula-

ment of immunity during any number of generations has resulted in an evolution of inborn immunity. On the contrary, every race that has been exposed to a lethal disease is resistant to that particular disease precisely in proportion to its past experience of it. When the disease is one against which immunity *cannot* be acquired, the race has undergone an evolution of *inborn* immunity; thus Europeans who have suffered severely from tuberculosis for thousands of years resist infection by it, or when infected recover from it more easily than African negroes who have suffered less, and much more easily than American Indians, who until lately had no experience of the disease. When the disease is one against which immunity *can* be acquired, the race has undergone an evolution of the *power of acquiring* immunity, never of inborn immunity; thus English children, whose race has long been afflicted by measles and whooping-cough, contract those maladies as easily as Polynesians to whom they were familiarised only during last century. But whereas English children, as a rule, recover readily, Polynesians perish in great numbers. When the disease is non-lethal no effect on the race can be observed. Thus Polynesians are infected as easily and recover as easily, but not more easily, than Englishmen, from chicken-pox."—*Op. cit.* p. 135.

tion of the island. In the years 1813 and 1810 the British Government imported three or four thousand negroes from Mozambique into Ceylon to form into regiments; of these, in December 1820, there were left just 440, including male descendants." And in a second reference to this quotation, Dr. Reid adds: "All the rest had perished mainly from tuberculosis." *

Now, the mining industry at Johannesburg supplies the worst possible conditions for the Kafirs with regard to their resistance to tuberculosis. The men who, owing to contact with Europeans, are exposed to infection, work underground; they come up perspiring profusely, and then sit in cotton blankets in the wind so as to cool down. As a result they are peculiarly susceptible to pulmonary complaints and to infection from phthisis, which is also complicated by "miner's phthisis," brought on by the irritating dust derived from rock-drilling. The Kafirs, who are ignorant of sanitation, expectorate freely, and thus become a source of increased danger to themselves and to the white population on the Rand. The natives suffering from the disease go home to their kraals and spread it everywhere. It is possible that the bacteria become especially virulent when they find a suitable medium in which to propagate themselves. The resident medical attendant at an Open-air Home in Natal assured me a short time ago that he noticed that Europeans who contracted the disease in South Africa nearly always succumbed to it, for in such cases it seemed to be especially virulent; while those who visited South Africa with tuberculosis contracted in England seemed to do remarkably well. If for a

* *Op. cit.* pp. 141, 149.

moment we may consider the problem of imported labour at Johannesburg from a non-party point of view, we must heartily wish we could find some substitute for Kafir labour on the Rand. We must not forget, moreover, that even if we manage to reduce the enormous death-rate of Kafir labourers *at the mines*, it does not follow that all is going well. We may still be sending back to the kraals thousands of Kafirs suffering from tuberculosis.

By seeking to introduce a great number of cheap white labourers to work alongside the native miners, we should probably do much to spread tuberculosis all over the country; and since the disease when contracted in South Africa seems to be so fatal, we should be doing a grievous wrong to the colonists. But in this matter, as in so many others of vital importance, we are in need of fuller and more reliable statistics. Nothing has been said about the very obvious danger of our introducing Bovine Tuberculosis by the cattle we import to improve the stock in Kafir cattle-kraals. Yet we must never shut our eyes to the danger.

Tuberculosis does not appear to have affected the birth-rate of the Kafirs to any great extent, nor have the natives become alive to the insidious dangers to their health that they meet at the mines. When they leave the mine infected with tubercle, and return to their open-air life in the kraal, they may recover, though with difficulty. But they must infect others during their convalescence. When the consumptive natives remain on at Johannesburg as house-boys, the case is even worse, for the crowding of a number of such servants in small and ill-ventilated rooms—and how ill-ventilated they are is beyond telling *—must make them a source of infection to the European population. The moment the Kafirs awake to the fact that Johannesburg is a death-trap—and the native editors will make a point of using this fact to show how wicked the white man is—there will be an end to native recruiting.

We are now ready to answer the question as to whether we can expect the Kafirs living in their own country to be swept off by our imported diseases. We find that they have been for so long in contact with us that they have developed a certain stock that is moderately well—but only moderately well—able to resist our imported diseases. Small-pox still causes considerable loss of life, but the natives on the whole are sensible enough to see the value of vaccination, though they naturally dislike submitting to any small operation at the hands of a white doctor. If some native editor were but worked upon by some anti-vaccination faddist, the result might be deplorable; for it would be easy to appeal to every particle of superstition and fear of the white man so as to get the natives to refuse to submit to vaccination.

The natives showed that they were peculiarly susceptible to plague,† when the country was threatened some time ago, and it might seem that some such disease might decimate the Kafirs. But the white man will do so much

* It is quite a common thing for such house-boys to paste strips of brown paper round the windows so as to keep out all draughts. Three boys may occupy the room; but as often as not they have three or four friends sleeping with them. To make the room warmer, the natives put mats or old coats up against the door, and so stop all ventilation. There is need for strict municipal regulations on this point.

† Possibly this was due simply to unhygienic environment.

to prevent such diseases as plague, or cholera, or sleeping-sickness from taking hold of the country that we may reasonably hope no such diseases will ever get the chance of decimating the natives. The one real danger lies in the possible spread of tuberculosis through the crowding of natives at the Rand.

To bring home once more to the reader the seriousness of the question, I will give another quotation from Dr. Reid: "The British conquest of North America and Australia resembles the Saxon conquests of Great Britain. The natives have been exterminated within the area of settlement. It is in sharp contrast to their conquests in Asia and Africa. Both in the Old World and in the New the subjugation of the natives was accompanied by many wars and much bloodshed, and probably the conflicts in the former were more prolonged and destructive than those in the latter. But in no part of the Old World have the British exterminated the natives. They do not supplant them, they merely govern them. Southern Asia and East and West Africa are defended by malaria. The British cannot colonise them,* and the natives have undergone such evolution against tuberculosis that they are capable, under favourable conditions, like the American slaves, of resisting the hard conditions imposed on them by modern civilisation. In South Africa, where there is little malaria, Europeans share the land with the natives, but the latter are likely to remain an overwhelming majority. If history teaches any lesson with clearness it is this, that conquest to be permanent must be accompanied with

* We may, however, possibly destroy the *seed* of this disease even if it takes too long to improve the *soil* of the white races.

extermination; otherwise in the fulness of time the natives expel or absorb the conquerors."

The second of the evil trinity that accompanies civilisation is dress; and while it is accountable for a vast amount of illness in the case of the Kafirs, it does not seem appreciably to diminish the native population. The trade in cheap cotton blankets is a most lucrative one, especially to the English manufacturer: but it is responsible for not a little Kafir mortality. In this, as in other matters, the natives will soon learn to take better care of themselves, and much of the evil that results from the importation of European clothing will be overcome.

There remains then but to discuss the question as to whether the natives may not be exterminated by drink. It is certain that, if we were to withdraw the restrictions about liquor, an immense number of natives would drink themselves to death in a comparatively short period. Kafirs have practically no self-control in this matter. When at a beer-drink it takes a prodigious quantity of the native small beer to make the men drunk. The natives do not become quarrelsome on the first twelve hours' debauch, though they drink gallons of beer. It is on the second or third day of continuous drinking (with alternate periods of perspiring in the sun) that beer-drinking leads to serious intoxication. When the natives get raw spirits, they therefore drink the most disastrous quantities, and become so much the slaves of the drink habit that resistance is out of the question. I have frequently been in traders' stores up-country when natives have come in, and, not being able

*Op. cit.* pp. 185, 186.

to buy brandy, have bought large quantities of eau-de-cologne, which they swallowed by the bottleful on the spot. The removal of the restrictions as to the sale of liquor would lead not only to innumerable deaths, but also to a falling off of the birth-rate.

A moderate amount of well-diluted alcohol seems to suit the natives very well. Possibly they would be better off without it ; but it is utopian to ask them to discontinue its use. They are accustomed to it from of old, and their native beer seems to be wholesome and to have some slight antiscorbutic properties. It is both food and drink, for it is something like a thin gruel. But the introduction of European spirits leads to hopeless consequences. The restriction of the sale of liquor to the natives is therefore our very sheet-anchor, and we must not listen to educated natives like Dube, who demand the removal of liquor restrictions. On no consideration whatever must existing restrictions be tampered with unless we want to kill off the native races. If our liquor restrictions were removed, the natives might exterminate themselves rapidly, and so terminate the Native Problem. But it is impossible to regard such an ending as in any true sense a " solution " of the difficulty. It would be a national crime for us to allow such a disaster : and I would here repeat the warning given in an earlier chapter, namely, that a wide extension of the franchise must one day lead to a lessening, or removal, of liquor restrictions.

Those who will study Dr. Reid's book on " Heredity " will find an illuminating chapter on narcotics and drink. Some of his conclusions are strongly opposed by men as well informed as Dr. Reid, but there is, to say the least, very much evidence that points to the fact that the races living round the Mediterranean have eliminated by natural selection those strains in their stock that are peculiarly susceptible to drink. Travelling up the East Coast, I was talking to the Austrian doctor on board, and he told me that the sailors employed by the Austrian Lloyd Company were selected from races along the coasts of the Adriatic, and that none of them ever drank to excess. When asked by British travellers to "have a drink," they invariably replied that they did not care to drink between meals. Their ancestors had, through heavy drinking, apparently weeded out all the strains in their stock that were peculiarly susceptible to the charms of alcohol. This method may be the only final solution of the drink problem, but we can scarcely submit the Kafirs to the process. In England the process of weeding out of our bad stock is going on now, but in South Africa it has not fairly commenced amongst the Kafirs. The initial stages of such drastic natural selection mean the decimation of a people, and a race has to be under favourable conditions if it is to recuperate itself and propagate healthy stock. We cannot hope that the Kafir will become able to drink with impunity for at least a dozen generations, and therefore we may conclude that there can be no relaxation of the liquor laws in our days or in the days of our grandchildren.

When we combine together the progress of science, the moral consciousness of the forward race, and the Kafir's past acquaintance with, and consequent capacity for resisting, disease, we must but conclude that the natives are not likely to die out from the attacks of imported diseases. The birth-rate does not seem to be appreciably affected by the contagious diseases brought in by the white men. We conclude therefore that the Native Problem will *not* be solved by the dying out of the natives ; if the Kafirs are to vanish, it must be through military extermination. There is left but one possible ending of the problem, and that is, that the whites and blacks have got to live on together in South Africa as best they may, without any intermingling of stocks. If the two races do not live together amicably, either the whites will have to exterminate the natives by war, or the blacks will, by sheer increase of numbers, squeeze out the Europeans. It is therefore well worth discussing the capacity of the Kafirs for improvement.

We are ready now to pass on to a consideration of the three questions contained in the ambiguous words, Can the Ethiopian change his skin ? We proceed to discuss these questions in order.

(1) *Can the Ethiopian become a European ?*—When we seek to put all race-prejudice aside and examine the capacity of the Kafir to absorb and assimilate Western civilisation in such a way that he shall practically cease to exhibit the peculiarities of the negro, and shall become Western in thought and feeling, I think we must admit, from cases before our very faces to-day, that he can apparently sometimes do this to a much greater extent than is thought by most people to be possible. But yet there seems to remain something—is it in the texture of the man's mind ?—that prevents him, even in the best cases, from becoming altogether Western. It is doubtful whether he can quite adopt the European standpoint in anything,

for he seems to lack that indefinable something which, after all, makes so much difference even in the best instances. There is lacking a subtle quality, illusive and difficult to define, that somehow or other makes us say,

> The little more, and how much it is:
> The little less, and what worlds away.

And it is difficult to believe that this illusive $x$ could be gained—I doubt whether it could ever be gained—without a greatly preponderating loss of some essentially good Kafir qualities. I am talking of to-day's practical politics, and do not pause at present to ask whether this difficulty might not be overcome in, say, ten more centuries of help from the white man. At present the individual Kafir may occasionally rise very high, and yet he does not cease to be a Kafir. Progress is a social product, and it may be that in the absence of the "evolution of his environment" no educated Kafir has yet enjoyed the stimulating atmosphere, formed by a sufficient number of his equally educated and congenial fellows, which might enable him to rise to greater heights. And I do not think that it would be a good thing to place a few Kafirs in a hothouse so that they might outstrip the rest of their race in their mental growth.

The average colonist feels that "Exeter Hall" ambitions and methods lead but to a coating of Western veneer over the savage nature. He asks what can be the good of such an accretion of an unabsorbable civilisation which leaves the savage still a savage at heart. Even in the preliminary stages, this philanthropic elevating of the Kafir tends to make the most immature native think he is equal to the white man. While a few exceptional Kafirs have advanced surprisingly high, the *average* educated Kafir has, of course, not in the slightest degree changed his nature: he has only added to it some highly unsuitable and discordant elements of a very superficial character. He has put on something over his skin—usually dirty clothes—rather than made a change beneath it. But though we recognise that this has been the result of our philanthropy in the great majority of cases, we need not jump to the conclusion that the few exceptional natives who have been wisely handled, and who have enjoyed most favourable environment, have not advanced as far beyond the average Kafir as they are yet behind the average white man. And, once more, it does not follow because we believe the Kafir to be capable of advancing very far toward Western ideals that therefore it is wise for us to help a few natives to do so at once. It may be better to help on a larger number to a lesser degree. What may be good for the individual, viewed in the abstract, and in isolation from his race-duties, may be bad for him when this immensely important aspect of the matter is considered. But because one does not wish to see a few Kafirs educated far beyond the bulk of their fellows, one need not deny that they are capable of such development. And it is important to recognise what I believe may safely be called a fact, namely, that the Kafir cannot as yet advance much if left to himself without European guidance. When free from that guidance he will ape the white man in mere externals; and this can be stated definitely, not by appealing to analogy, and by showing that it is what has actually occurred in Hayti where Black rules White, but, because the Kafir in South Africa has actually done so when left to himself. The Ethiopian movement shows how utterly superficial, pernicious, and bizarre is the civilisation of the natives who break loose from European guidance.

I, for one, am not inclined to blame the colonist for being sceptical as to the Kafir's capacity to develop. Very much has been done by friends of the Kafirs to break down colonial belief in the capacity of the Kafir. The renowned Dr. Philip was a very pugnacious man, and he fought the colonists most rigorously—not to say cruelly—about the Kafir. In Mr. Theal's words, he "laid down a theory that the coloured races were in all respects, except education, mentally equal to the European colonists, and that they were wrongfully and cruelly oppressed by the white people and the Government. With this as a professed motive for exertion, he stood forth as their champion." * Later on in life he found out how disastrous had been his advocacy—even from the standpoint of Kafir interests. "After he had enjoyed almost unlimited political influence, and had seen the schemes which he devised result in bloodshed and confusion, he became a comparatively gentle old man, and abandoned politics." † He was but an example of the man who willed the good, and yet who thereby wrought the bad. Apart from the immediate suffering his mistaken philanthropy brought to the Kafirs, he did very much, by his intemperate advocacy of the natives, to wreck colonial belief in the capacity of the Kafirs to advance at all. That the average colonist should, in the

* "History of South Africa," vol. 1795–1834, pp. 345, 346.

† *Op. cit.* p. 345.

face of the extreme advocacy of Kafir equality to the whites, run to the opposite extreme, and say that the Kafir is scarcely capable of any improvement at all, is very natural and very human, even if it is not fully accurate.

In answer to our first question, I should be tempted to reply that there is good evidence for saying that while the individual Kafir can, nay, does now and then in exceptional cases under suitable white guidance, reach a surprisingly close approximation to the European, yet at present he always falls short, and moreover falls short in some strange way that makes it quite impossible for the most kindly critic to regard him as the equal of the white man. In this sense the Ethiopian, probably, can never change his skin.

(2) *Can the individual Kafir rise immensely higher than the average of his race?*—It is certainly a pity that our race-prejudice should sometimes hide from us the fact that it is immensely to our interest that the Ethiopian should change his skin. Unless he can do so, it will be a very bad look-out for the white man in South Africa: if the native is to remain, for example, as ruthless as he was during the Border Wars, if he is to foster for ever the hatred of the white man that he now undoubtedly cherishes, if he is to continue to become top-heavy and unbalanced when educated, then the fate of South Africa is sealed, for it is only a matter of time before the whites will either be massacred or squeezed out of the country. But if the Ethiopian can change his skin there is hope.

It is most interesting to read what an American negro

has to say on the latent capacity of the black races to rise in the scale of civilisation. Du Bois, at least so I have been told by an old friend of his, is more white than black, and yet glories far more in his negro than in his European inheritance. Perhaps it is not fair to take him as a specimen of the height to which the average Kafir may hope to attain. Yet it is instructive to read what he has written as to the capacity of the negro to rise.

"The silently growing assumption of this age is that the probation of races is past, and that the backward races of to-day are of proven inefficiency, and are not worth saving. Such an assumption is the arrogance of peoples irreverent towards Time, and ignorant of the deeds of men. A thousand years ago such an assumption, easily possible, would have made it difficult for the Teuton to prove his right to life. Two thousand years ago such a dogmatism, readily welcome, would have scouted the idea of blonde races ever leading civilisation. So woefully unorganised is sociological knowledge that the meaning of progress and the meaning of 'swift' and 'slow' in human doing and the limits of human perfectibility are veiled, unanswerable sphinxes on the shore of science." * Yet we are sometimes told by colonists in South Africa that the individual Kafir comes of a bad stock, and "inherits" no civilised traits or "characters," and therefore cannot make up for his hopeless handicap. It will be interesting to seek to trace where the truth lies in this matter.

Those who have studied recent developments of biology do not need to be told that an organism has great, and

* W. E. Du Bois, "The Souls of Black Folk," p. 262.

often unsuspected, capacity for responding to suitable stimuli. Nature is fuller of resources than our imagination, or the lack of it, would sometimes lead us to believe; and we are coming to perceive that the individual can respond to stimuli far more than we had thought. There are three factors to be considered in all questions of possible progress in the animal kingdom: these are heredity, capacity for variation, and the power of the environment to modify the organism: but for the present let us confine ourselves to the subject of heredity, for we shall approach the two other subjects at a later stage of our argument.

Popular thought on the subject of heredity has been so misled by the exuberant, though inexact, fancy of novelists that people are slow to listen to and grasp the facts that have been observed by trained biologists. It is popularly thought that we "inherit" our culture and civilisation through parents who pass on to their children the "modifications" they have acquired during life. The word "inherit" is used in the vaguest way by popular writers, and would cover the inheritance of a quick temper as well as that of money or lands: but in biological circles the word has a very definite connotation which must be explained. The "characters" of an organism are divided into two distinct categories. On the one hand we find *inborn* characters which are passed on from generation to generation by the germ-plasm, and on the other hand the modifications or *acquired* characters that are the result of individual use or of the environment. These acquired characters are the result of the play of the environment, or of personal habits, on the stock of previously inborn characters. All inborn characters take their origin from the germ, while all—or nearly all—acquired characters seem to be acquired by the individual by his own direct action, and are but modifications of inborn characters. It is becoming more and more clear that—at least in animals—acquired characters—or "use-acquirements" or "modifications" as they are often called—cannot at the present stage of evolution be passed on by heredity. The term "heredity" is therefore used to connote the passing on of characters by the germ-cells. Civilisation and culture are use-acquirements and not inborn characters: therefore, on our hypothesis, they cannot be passed on by germinal means, and so are not hereditary. "Man," says Dr. Reid, "has not evolved into a civilised being; he has merely developed into one. The change in him consists solely or principally in a change of mental acquirements, not in a germinal change. He transmits his civilised habits by tradition and not by inheritance." This would seem to be the reason why a high state of civilisation was difficult, if not impossible, to attain until man had invented some method of writing that would render tradition more permanent. Had culture been passed on by heredity, the progress of mankind should have been enormously rapid. The fact that, previous to the invention of writing, human progress was so slow would seem to be corroborative evidence of the hypothesis that acquired habits are not hereditary.

Mr. Lock, in his most interesting work, "Variation, Heredity and Evolution," says: "The principles of heredity teach us that education and training, however beneficial they may be to the individuals, have no material effect upon the stock itself. If they have any effect at all, this is undoubtedly unimportant in comparison with the effect which would be produced by the selection of individuals which exhibit desirable qualities." *

Man has for countless ages made that complex compound of use-acquirements that we call speech: yet he has not passed on to his offspring the power of speaking without exertion, training, and exercise on the part of every fresh individual. Every child has to make these use-acquirements for himself so that he may modify or train the inborn characters that he derives from his parents: he inherits the inborn capacities but not the use-acquirements of thousands of ancestors. When once this basal fact is grasped, the whole problem of heredity is taken out of the atmosphere of fog in which popular writers have immersed it.

We start then with the idea that the personal gains acquired during life by the individual are not passed on to the offspring because, presumably, they do not affect the germ-cells. Let us take the case of a child born of exceptionally musical parents. The little boy does not inherit the benefit of his father's years of practice at five-finger exercises, but has to begin at the very start, and must learn to play his scales. The father's diligence or sloth in this matter affect but himself—not his offspring. The child has to train his nerve-muscle mechanisms just

* P. 258. In somewhat more technical terms, Professor A. J. Thomson has pointed out that "modifications" (acquired characters) "are exogenous, somatogenic changes, as contrasted with endogenous, blastogenic changes" (or variations). They are the direct result of peculiarities in "nurture" as contrasted with inborn changes in the inherited "nature."—"Sociological Papers," 1906, p. 164.

as his father had to before him. What he can inherit is the delicate structure (the inborn character) that is capable of profiting by exercise. The use-acquirements (or neglect) of the parents are not stored up and passed on to the child, but die with the individual. But the delicacy of nervous constitution—which lies at the root of ability, or of the capacity to acquire special skill—is a germinal character: it was received by heredity, and is capable of being passed on by heredity.

All this holds good with regard to culture, which is the matter in hand in the case of the Kafirs. The literary man inherits a nature that makes him peculiarly susceptible to the charms of literature: he spends his life over books and his mind consequently becomes highly cultured. He only passes on to his child the peculiar nervous structure which is at the base of his susceptibility for profiting by reading good literature, that "runs in the family." He does not pass on to his child the knowledge he has acquired by the use of his brain. The son has to learn his alphabet just as any other child, for he does not "come into" his father's accumulated knowledge as he may "come into" his father's money. The child may inherit such a delicate and sensitive constitution that he is enabled to learn his alphabet much faster than other children. He inherits the ability or the nervous constitution that is at the base of his capacity for acquiring culture rapidly: he does not inherit the culture itself. Use-acquirements are gains, solely, or almost solely, to the individual. "At the present day the consensus of opinion among experts is undoubtedly to the effect that acquired characters are not inherited at all, except in so far as better nutrition may lead to more vigorous offspring. And it seems clear that such an effect as the latter cannot go on accumulating for more than a few generations." *

At first sight all this may seem to offer but a depressing and pessimistic view of life, for an appalling amount of individual effort thus seems to be ephemeral. Is this, we ask, the fate of all the "struggling sighs of sacrifice"? But a little further reflection will show us that there is a very bright side to this hypothesis. *First*, no man is hopelessly doomed to cultural poverty because his ancestors have been slack. No Kafir can be pronounced incapable of rising simply because his father did not rise. We cannot say the stock is bad until successive generations have had a fair chance, for mental capacity can lie dormant for ages and yet ultimately awake to life. *Secondly*, the hypothesis indicates to us how to set to work. Philanthropists in the past have thought they could quickly improve *the stock* by educating the individual: they were therefore apt to work at a high tension for a short period, and then to leave their *protégés* to stand or fall by themselves. The moment they saw a slight improvement in the individual, they mistakenly thought they had permanently improved the stock. But germinal changes are very slowly brought about; and we now see that if we would directly improve the stock, we must pay attention to artificial selection rather than to education. To this subject we shall return presently. *Thirdly*, we now know that, when we look away from the stock to the individual, we can, by maintaining through successive generations a sort of *external* heritage of culture—

* R. H. Lock, "Recent Progress in the Study of Variation, Heredity and Evolution," p. 115.

a very laborious process that must never be relaxed—uplift each successive generation; for men everywhere possess much more capacity for making acquirements, when placed under suitable conditions, than they can ever hope to make use of in their lifetime. But we see that this culture does not affect the germ-plasm, and so it is essential that we should not relax our stimulus. We cannot make human nature perfect, and then leave it to take care of itself, for each successive generation must see to its own culture. Civilisations have waxed and waned because cultural atmospheres are easily destroyed. And past civilisations have left no impress on the germ-cells, for it is not in the power of culture to effect such changes. Yet the individual, if rightly handled, is capable of almost endless advance because he possesses enormous, and somewhat unlooked-for, capacity for responding to suitable stimuli. Science joins hands with poetry at this point, and Browning's "Rabbi Ben Ezra" will occur to all:

> All instincts immature,
> All purposes unsure
> That weighed not as his work, yet swelled the man's account.
>
> * * * * *
>
> All I could never be,
> All men ignored in me,
> This was I worth to God, whose wheel the pitcher shaped.

If a child should be permanently deprived of the use of both its hands, it will often learn to use its toes to a marvellous extent, and can even be taught to thread a needle, or to hold its paint-brush with its toes.* It will not pass on such use-acquirements (or its mutilations) to its offspring,

* Some twenty years ago the writer saw the well-known artist at Antwerp—or was it Brussels?—who had lost both his arms and used to paint with a brush held between his toes.

who will not be able to thread needles with their toes because their parent did so for many years. If they wish to perform such marvels they will have to exercise their own toes. If culture were based on a germinal change, and if it could only be passed on by heredity, progress would be very unequal, and the world would become a very patchy place. A few lucky strains that happened to be nature's favourites, or that happened to get a start in the race, would soon become by such accumulations nature's millionaires, while the bulk of people would be doomed to cultural poverty.

Instead of saying that the individual Kafir cannot rise above the level of his race, we must admit that if he can respond to stimuli—and if suitable stimuli can be applied—there is every hope that the individual thus stimulated may rise surprisingly high above the present low level of his fellows. And all the Kafirs may be raised enormously, though to different degrees, if all are suitably stimulated. The capacity for responding to stimuli varies with the personal equation; and one Kafir, like one white man, can rise higher than another. Each man has to work up his own cultural fortune, and we can never say that the individual Kafir cannot rise until we have exhausted every kind of stimulus that might help him to do so. In this matter we must be empiricists, and indeed pragmatists, seeking to make real and actual what we now suspect to be but a latent possibility. The individual Kafir is not doomed to remain a savage *because* his ancestors were savages. The only thing that could condemn him to remain a savage would be his own individual incapacity to respond to a stimulus. It is idle, therefore, to say that the individual Ethiopian cannot change his skin until we have tried all possible methods for enabling him to do so and have failed in our attempts. And I submit that we *have* tried the experiment in the past, though in the most bungling and unintelligent fashion; and yet amidst the many failures we have, as a matter of fact, produced educated Kafirs who seem centuries ahead of the bulk of the people. The average colonist avoids educated Kafirs, and has of course never met such men; he therefore does not know the facts of the case.

It is now our business to discover why we often failed, why we sometimes succeeded, and how we may test the effects of the stimuli we apply in the future to the natives. If those of us who are interested in the Kafir could but be induced to moderate the pace, and could be persuaded to seek to find out in what direction we are going and ought to go, it would be a good thing. We are like people riding on horses (hobby-horses) we know not whither. We keep calling to one another to "keep moving"; and when some one halts and says, "But whither are we going?" the others shout out, "Never mind that: just keep moving and all will come right." We have been going on so unintelligently that the illustration that seems suitable is that of a little child who has been given a number of toys, on hitting a certain part of one of which a bell sounds: the child, ignorant of the causes of the sound, aimlessly hits everything within reach so as to produce a repetition of the noise: every now and then it happens accidentally and half-unintentionally to hit the right thing, and points to its occasional good luck as a sign of its cleverness and success. We have stimulated hundreds of thousands of

Kafirs with our tangled mixture of stimuli arising from civilisation, education and religion : we simply daze and bewilder most of them, but every now and then by some lucky accident a Kafir responds to the confused mass of stimuli and shoots out far ahead of his fellows. We do not know why he did so : one of us thinks it was the stimulus of religion, another that it was the stimulus of education or political propaganda, a third that it was the stimulus of civilisation that produced the result. But we know so little as to how the result was produced that we cannot go on producing similar cases at will. It is this fact that the Kafirs have shown every now and then that they are capable of reacting to our stimuli that is both our hope and our despair : it is our hope for the Kafir, because the result happens too often to be looked on as a case of a "sport"; it is our despair as to our own lack of wisdom, because the result happens too seldom to give us any reason for thinking that our methods are rational, intelligent, and suited to the mass of the Kafirs. There is evidently some factor in our methods that is radically faulty. To discover it would possibly be the work of ages in the case of isolated men working at the problem ; whereas an Ethnological Bureau that organised research might possibly hit upon the source of all our trouble in a very short time. When the Kafirs can throw up not a few striking characters, they must surely have some latent capacity lurking somewhere in their nature. And it is a question whether the occasional geniuses that have been thrown up have not appeared rather in spite of our mistaken methods than as a result of them. A Kafir renaissance is not altogether a utopian hope. The few bright cases of Kafirs who rise show that the nerve-tissue of the Kafir is not wholly degenerate or incapable of high development. But the Kafir certainly does not respond to our educational methods as we had hoped. It is easy to put all the blame to the Kafir—possibly some causes of failure lie in the nature of the man—and none to the unsuitable nature of the stimulus; but it is not very sensible.

There certainly seems to be a sort of general simmering of latent faculty amongst the members of most of the Kafir tribes. It is not merely the fact that there is one Kafir who can understand, let us say, the *Nineteenth Century*, but that there are perhaps fifty who can do so, that gives us hope. At the same time the fact that out of the tens of thousands of educated Kafirs there are not thousands who could do this is a pregnant fact, which throws light on the inadequacy of our methods of elevating the natives. It would seem as if the Kafirs required some peculiar correlation of stimulus and environment before they could profit by our benevolent efforts.

I have referred above to but one aspect of progress. I might take any other point, such as military or musical capacity. Those who have listened to the monotonous jingles of the Kafirs in the kraals, and who have felt how elementary is the sense of melody as distinguished from the delight in rhythm, and who have further heard a Kafir like John Knox Bokwe of Lovedale play his own musical compositions on the piano, must admit that the Kafir is capable of rising in this matter. Bokwe's compositions—it is a doubtful com liment—are quite up to the level of our modern drawing-room songs. As I listened to Bokwe, it was difficult to believe at first that a black man actually composed the tunes he was playing. My race-prejudice certainly received a well-merited rebuff by the experience.

If we take the subject of oratory, we find the Kafir of the kraal quite up to the level of the European, and indeed often very much beyond him. Yet how little is being done to use this special aptitude for cultural purposes. It is being exploited by Ethiopian agitators for political and hostile ends, but we are doing practically nothing to make use of it for good ends. I was once at a native debate at a Mission station in Basutoland where the French missionaries showed their great, and usual, good sense by fostering this faculty. The educative effect of the debate, which was on the question as to whether man gets more pleasure through the eye or the ear, was obvious. The function of public speech in the education of the Greeks is a favourite theme of philosophical historians : yet the use of oratory for educating the Kafirs is confined to but a very few Mission stations.

The Greeks are a most interesting example as to the unexpected capacity that can lie dormant in human nature, ready to be awakened by a suitable stimulus. They were to start with but a race of barbarians devoid of any special intellectual promise. Suddenly they threw up a number of intellectual and artistic giants, only to revert in a few generations to a condition of mediocrity. There can be little doubt that this amazing efflorescence was not due to a germinal change, but to the direct influence of the finest educational system the world has ever seen. Another example is found in the case of the Maoris : under a suitable training they emerged in a generation or two from a state of cannibalism to a high condition of civilisation. It is superfluous to point to the Japanese, for everybody is talking about their sudden awakening through a suitable education and political policy. The Kafirs have *not* risen to a high state of culture; but it is difficult to see how they, or any race, could have done so with the faulty kind of education to which they have been subjected. The negative fact of the Kafirs' failure to rise is in no sense a proof that they are incapable of rising: the fact that some Kafirs have been elevated to a very high state of culture seems to indicate that the fault has been not in the germ but in the environment.

It is also necessary for us to remember that progress is a social product, and that we cannot expect amongst the Kafirs Beethovens, Newtons, or Shakespeares, who did but give expression to the simmering ideas and emotions of their age, until we lift up the low average of the Kafirs *as a whole*, so that it may be somewhat comparable to the state of European society when it threw up such men. These men were but the mountain peaks arising out of national mountain ranges or table-lands. They did not rise in isolation out of the ocean. Until we lift up the general level of the Kafirs, we cannot expect to find some of them towering above the ordinary European, for all they can do is to tower above their submerged fellow Kafirs. And a mountain peak arising out of a submerged bed of ocean may seem a mountain peak to creatures living on that bed, though it is not conspicuous to people living far above that level. We think of Caliban upon Setebos, or of the young witch in "Pauline," and remember how her blue eyes drew down a god, who said even in his perishing, "I am still a god—to thee": and we begin to see that, though the Kafir genius may be no genius to us, he may be one to his fellows.

I conclude, therefore, that in this second sense of the words the Ethiopian can change his skin. He may not be able to become a European, but he can become a Super-Kafir.

(3) *Can the Kafirs as a race be elevated? And if so, how?* —Before discussing some interesting theoretical aspects of this question, let us ask what history has to teach us about the natives' racial capacity. We know that since the sixteenth century the Kafirs have not progressed in civilisation to any marked degree. If anything the native races of South Africa have sunk in the scale. Even if we take into consideration the effect of our civilising efforts, the result must appear very unpromising. We have already pointed out in a previous chapter that our contact with the backward race has led, not to a marked increase of any original capacity, but rather to the inhibition, or stifling, of what little enterprise the natives once possessed. Civilised ideas are not absorbed by the mass of the Kafirs: they are held as accretions to be put off or on as if they were external things, such as clothing. The conspicuous failure of the natives to develop anything in the nature of architecture, art, poetry, writing, music, religion or philosophy has been pointed out, and must be emphasised once more to prevent the reader from imagining that the present writer is under any illusion as to the *seemingly* inherent defects of the Kafir's nature. It certainly looks at first sight as if the natives were on the down-grade, for we can almost see the degenerative process at work before our very eyes. The Kafirs still live in the same rude type

of hut that their ancestors lived in centuries ago, and have lost much of the arts and crafts in which they once excelled. If ever there was a people that *seemed* inherently opposed to progress and indissolubly wedded to conservative modes of life, it is the natives of South Africa. Certainly a very strong case can be made out for the belief that the Kafirs *as a race* are incapable of rising in the scale. There is no need to labour this aspect of the matter.

There are, however, very weighty considerations to be stated on the other side; and since it is these that are generally neglected, I propose to give fuller consideration to them. Nothing so strikes the traveller who starts at the Kei River and journeys up to Lake Nyassa as the progressive increase of intelligence in the natives he meets on his overland journey. Very few white men have made such a journey, and consequently the fact is not well known. In Pondoland one finds the very lowest rung of the ladder. The Pondos are very low in the scale with respect to intelligence and culture. Crossing into Natal one finds the natives much more intelligent and energetic. When close to Delagoa Bay the natives are found to be considerably smarter than the Zulus, though not so fine in physique. The natives in Gazaland are yet more intelligent than the natives around Delagoa Bay. On the Zambesi the Sena-speaking natives are immeasurably above the Pondos, and much superior in intelligence when compared with the natives of Gazaland. Again, proceeding north we find that in the Shire Highlands the natives are yet more bright and quick at entering into the new ideas of the white man. My own personal observations stop at Blantyre; but those who have lived on the shores of Lakes Nyassa and Tanganyika have assured me that the farther north one goes the more intelligent do the natives become. It is a matter of general knowledge that the Uganda natives are very far advanced in a civilisation of their own,* and have shown by their social and civil administration how superior they are to the natives living far down south.

So much for a brief sketch of the strange rise in mental capacity that is to be found in the natives as one travels north from the Umtata River.

There can be little doubt but that the Kafirs have come down from the north at some remote period: in this the natives and ethnologists are agreed. But how shall we account for the very striking fact of this graduated lessening of intelligence and of culture to be observed in the tribes as one travels south? There must be a cause for this effect. We have little but conjecture to help us here. It looks as if, brain being a stronger force than muscle, the more intelligent tribes expelled the less intelligent ones, who, however, were their superiors in physique. Did some degenerative mental process set in amongst certain of the tribes so that they became incapable of resisting the more intelligent ones? Was it a germinal change due to the effect of the faulty, or of too close (or not sufficiently close), inter-breeding? We know the Kafir is not pure negro, but that he has a mingling of other strains in his stock. Did the excessive multiplication and isolation of tribes lead to unwise narrowing of the area from which new and energising strains might have been secured? Did the marriage customs adopted lead to the breeding-

* A missionary assured me that the Uganda natives have completely solved the drink problem.

out of intellect and the breeding-in of physique? Or did the mere fact of migration necessitate the breaking up of the cultural environment and the consequent loss of stimulus in the case of individuals? Did incessant wars make the culture of the arts of peace impossible, until—in the absence of written records—the races forgot their past achievements? If this be the case, then, since the change is one of *nurture* rather than of *nature*, there is every hope that by supplying a suitable stimulus we should elevate the Kafirs. These and many similar questions that rise to our lips cannot be answered, largely because we have not seriously tried to accumulate the facts or evidence that would lead us to the answer. Carefully conducted research in connection with the customs, traditions, folk-lore and history of the natives might possibly supply us with most valuable information that would enable us to trace the faults made by the Kafirs in the past, and, by avoiding them, to improve their stock.

Before we can decide the question as to whether or not a backward race can rise, we need to understand how such a rise could be brought about. We can then discuss the question as to whether we can fulfil the necessary conditions in the case before us. In other words, we need to study the horse before we study the cart.

A race can be elevated in two ways: *first*, by attending to the culture of *the individuals* composing the existing generation, and by repeating that process in every succeeding generation; and *secondly*, by working a permanent improvement in *the stock* (germ-plasm) through the agency of Artificial Selection. Let us take these two points in order.

(A) *Improvement of the Individual.*—This is a social and educational problem. Man, as we have seen, passes on his culture, not by heredity, but by tradition: he makes a cultural atmosphere which influences all those who come within its reach. This may be a very rapid process, for the gains accumulate; but it is a laborious process, because it has to be maintained by incessant and strenuous effort, since it produces no germinal change which is passed on by heredity. Professor Thomson has suggested that this process "may be so effective that its results come almost to the same thing as if acquired characters were transmitted. They are re-impressed on the bodies and minds of successive generations, though never ingrained in the germ-plasm." . . . "The useful fact to emphasise is that man, though slowly or slightly *variable*, is rapidly and exceedingly *modifiable*, and that social organisation provides a means—an external heritage—whereby the results of modifications may be practicably transmissible, though not organically entailed." † However, the drawback to this method of elevating a race consists in the necessity of the maintenance of the social and educative process. Many a civilisation has waxed and waned because nations have first of all built up a suitable cultural environment, and then have had that environment broken up by war or by some other accident. They neglected eugenics, and so the gains were but ephemeral. The very fact that past civilisations have absolutely vanished, leaving behind them no impress on the germ or stock, is an eloquent fact. But the advantage of elevating a race by the culture of its individuals is that a backward race need not be left alone to

* "Sociological Papers," 1906, p. 165. † *Ibid.* p. 163.

fight its way unaided, because a forward race can supply it with a cultural environment and so give it a splendid start.

In educating native children it is essential to ensure that the gain they receive through education shall not be lost and turned into an evil thing owing to the premature break-up of the elevating environment under which they have been placed. Too often we prematurely send back the educated native child to live in the kraal, which does not provide an environment that will foster and perpetuate the new life received. We have produced no effect that is able to withstand the blighting influences of kraal-life: too often we leave the Kafir just at the one supremely important period of his life, namely, the stage that follows the arrival of puberty. Thus our initial success is followed by a subsequent deep demoralisation and degeneration which often leaves the individual in a far worse condition than that in which we found him.

I believe this is the secret of our past failure. In those cases in which we have been able to save the boy or girl from the blighting influence of the incessant talk about sex which forms the atmosphere of the kraal, we have been wonderfully successful in raising the individual. Where we have sent the sharp and intelligent little boy back to the kraal at puberty, he has lost, and often more than lost, all we have given him. His sharpened intelligence may even be an extra snare to him, as his quickened imagination dwells in an atmosphere of incessant talk about sensual things. Tiyo Soga, who stands out as one of the most pre-eminent of educated Kafirs, was, as we have seen, taken to Scotland when a lad, and was shielded from kraal-influences until long after puberty. He continued to develop in mental vigour long after that period, and did not dwindle in capacity as do nearly nine-tenths of the Kafirs. But we cannot send all Kafirs to Scotland for their education, nor would it be a good thing to do so if we could. At the present state of affairs it is not good to get a few Kafirs far ahead of their fellows, for all sorts of side-effects are produced, and these tend to alter the total of the account. If we want the race to advance *as a race*, then we must clearly educate them at their homes and not in Europe or America.

It is generally recognised in scientific circles that the development in the individual is a sort of "recapitulation" of the development of the species. It has been said wittily that every individual has to climb his genealogical tree. To put it in more technical language, the ontogenetic development follows the line of phylogenetic development. Professor Mark Baldwin has published an interesting volume on the subject, under the title of "The Mental Development in the Child and the Race," and he points out some suggestive gaps in the "recapitulation" of the individual. Now, Mr. Andrew Lang has advanced certain reasons for supposing that Zulu myth and religion indicate that the race has fallen from a higher state of culture, and that the Zulus are therefore a decadent or degenerating race. The problem thus opened to us is of vital importance in a treatment of the Native Problem, and a careful study of the children of the Kafirs might throw a flood of light on the probable past history of the natives, and might either support or negative Mr. Lang's most important suggestion. The short study I have written on "Savage Childhood" certainly seems, when coupled with Mr. Lang's hypothesis, and with the doctrine of "recapitulation," and also with the progressive lessening of mental capacity shown in the tribes as they journeyed southwards, to throw some light on the matter. Since the Kafir is at his best, intellectually, emotionally and morally at the age of the onset of puberty; and since he begins, as a rule, to deteriorate in all these directions after the development of his sexual nature has become established—it seems probable that in past generations the race of the Kafirs had reached a much higher stage of development than the individual Kafir does to-day. The child, urged from within by the forces that tend to the "recapitulation" of phylogenetic development, shoots beyond the level he finally attains as his normal experience. The tendency to recapitulate the past experience of his race forces him to a temporary efflorescence of faculty which he cannot now permanently sustain amid the unsuitable environment which surrounds him.* He therefore sinks back after puberty to a lower stage than he had reached at that crisis. This apparent over-shooting of the mark in the individual, when coupled with the fact of the increasing degeneracy of the tribes as they came down south, seems therefore to lend support to Mr. Lang's idea that Kafir religion and culture are decadent, and that the Kafirs once attained a far higher development. And it further seems to indicate the probability that it is the faulty environment, and not a germ-plasm change, that is accountable for the low state of the average Kafir. If it could be proved that this speculation

* I have noticed that sexual customs seem to become grosser the further south the tribe has migrated. This would possibly account for much of the unsuitability of the environment referred to.

were sound, it would be of immense importance to us in our future legislation, for we could seek to trace in the child the line of a past development, and, if we were to discover this, we might adopt it as the path along which to travel in our attempts to regain the comparative Paradise Lost. The Kafir being, on this hypothesis, a fallen creature might be capable of redemption. But at present all this line of things is so neglected by our administrators, who seem content to legislate in spite of their ignorance, that it is but thin speculation. It is to our shame that it is nothing more than speculation, for knowledge is within our reach if we would seriously set to work to study the subject.

I have suggested in a previous chapter that this strange arrest of capacity at puberty may be due to the bad environment the adolescent finds in the kraal. The everlasting talk and thought about matters of sex draws off the imagination from more healthy topics. The formation and retention of culture depend largely on the maintenance of a suitable atmosphere or environment. Most Europeans believe that puberty sets in two or three years earlier in the case of the Kafir than it does in the case of a white child: but I think this is a mistake. Delayed puberty or prolonged childhood are of great value to a race, and the dulness of the Kafir can hardly be accounted for along that line, if my observations as to the age at which puberty sets in amongst the natives be correct. To change the environment of the adolescent, and to make the kraal a more wholesome place for the growing lads and maidens to live in, is a difficult problem; but if some of the attention that is now paid to less important things were diverted to this channel it would be well. We might at least set to work to produce *evolution of the environment* if we are too prudish to set to work to institute evolution of the germ-plasm by eugenics. That we should sit with folded hands and watch generation after generation of smart little Kafir children developing into dull men and women is a most grievous shame; it is a discredit to our national intelligence and a loss to the Empire.

It is difficult to over-estimate the practical importance of knowing for certain whether the arrest of mental faculty at puberty is due to defective environment or to some radical defect perpetuated through the germ-plasm: for if it be the latter, then it is hopeless to seek to cure the trouble by altering the environment; for the trouble, in that case, could only be overcome by selecting those individuals who showed that they could develop mentally after puberty; we should thus give them every advantage in propagating their special stock, while we made it difficult for the bad stock to multiply. We should thus by Artificial Selection breed-out the bad stock and breed-in the good. But if, on the other hand, investigation showed clearly that the difficulty was wholly created by the bad environment of the kraal-life, then we should pay but little thought to Artificial Selection, and should direct all our attention to the question of environment. It is really of but little use to go on blundering without studying *the causes* of the trouble: for while we may accidentally stumble on a solution, we are much more likely to waste time, energy and money, only to harm the very people we wish to improve. In this matter accurate investigation is an absolute essential.

Only when we know what can, and what cannot, be done

by environment, shall we see the problem clearly enough to develop a wise policy of education. We cannot hope for this great pubertal difficulty to be overcome by a germinal change, if the difficulty is, as I believe (perhaps wrongly), wholly a result of bad environment at that stage of life. To recognise this fact—if it be such—immensely simplifies our problem. If what I have written above about "recapitulation" and the great efflorescence of the higher faculties up to the time of puberty and their subsequent degeneration be correct, then the individual and the race are capable of a much greater elevation than is generally thought possible. If the Kafir could only be kept as bright and intelligent and withal as quick at assimilating good influences as he is before puberty, it would be a splendid thing for the race. Wherever that portentous period is reached and passed in safety there is immense hope for the individual's subsequent continuous and further progress. The more I study the subject and look ahead, the more do I feel that this is after all the crux of the educational—and possibly of the *native*—problem. If we can overcome the pubertal difficulty, we shall be able to mould the Kafir into a most excellent member of the Empire. If we want to deal with the *environment* of the Kafirs at all, then this is the period at which we should do so. And if that period is the most critical one in the case of school-boys in Europe, where the masters can call to their aid every good influence of religion and moral tone, how much more critical must it be in the case of the Kafirs, where a missionary has to control his pupils with all the evil influence of the kraal, and all the evil influence of the boy's companions, and all the immeasurably stronger sexual nature of a Kafir ranged against him. It is a subject that must be dealt with if we would see our hopes for the Kafirs fulfilled. But we must hasten on.

(B) *Improvement of the Stock.*—We have seen that the educational environment and social atmosphere are of immense importance to us when we seek to raise the level of the existing members of the race. But we have also seen that we do not affect *the stock* by such processes. We now ask whether it is possible to help matters by producing advantageous and permanent germinal changes in the race. It is easy to see how we can get at the individual so as to improve him: but how can we get at the stock or stirp so as to improve that? We can do so by attending to eugenics—either direct or indirect. The direct method works through the intelligent selection of suitable parents: the indirect method works through a number of seemingly trifling causes that together indirectly and yet profoundly affect the stock. Let us consider these latter first.

(*a*) *The Indirect Method.*—Like the Frenchman who was surprised to find that he had been talking prose all his life without knowing it, we awake with astonishment to the fact that we have been unconsciously and unintelligently experimenting in indirect eugenics for countless ages. It is merely proposed that we should do intelligently, and for the highest motives, what we have been doing bunglingly for less worthy ones. Our social customs exert an immense influence on the qualities lovers seek and prize in one another. People are complaining that our existing generation is sadly weedy as to the legs. Why, we are asked, do we find a falling off in shapely calves? Instead of looking somewhere in the skies for the answer, it would pay us to look at our social customs. Novelists may be poor teachers of science, but they are good recorders of passing social custom, for they hold the mirror up to society and are rewarded with great popularity if their mirror catches the superficial aspect of things. If we would know what values ruled in the matrimonial market in early Victorian days, we need but read our Dickens or our Thackeray and we shall see, for example, how the piano was used by every scheming mother to give additional matrimonial value to her daughter. The dress of past centuries gave a distinct matrimonial advantage to the men who had shapely legs. Novelists, such as Fielding, Richardson and Thackeray, make a great amount of literary capital out of allusions to the subject. But we hide the legs and so prevent a fine limb from exerting its attraction. Nowadays we worship money, and physical excellences are but secondary concerns. As a result, the man with atrocious legs, but with a good income, stands a better chance of being accepted as a lover than the man who has merely magnificently shaped calves. Our ancestors put a premium on shapely legs: we have taken off that premium, and have so put a stop to the secondary sexual attraction of fine legs. The unfit in this respect stand as good a chance as the fit: and we consequently breed-in poor legs and breed-out fine ones. Doctors complain to-day about the prevalence of varicose veins. What Greek or Roman—or what Kafir—with varicose veins stood a chance of winning the finest wife, or indeed any wife at all? When the leg was exposed, all deformities were visible, and a defect of a striking nature placed a man at a great disadvantage in comparison with those who were possessed of beauty of form. Our social customs have changed all that, and people with varicose veins stand as good a chance of perpetuating their stock as the man with sound veins does of propagating his. We are apparently breeding-in varicose veins owing to our social customs in connection with dress. There may be other factors also at work; but the idea was suggested to me by a medical man who is a student of genetics.

The bandaging of Chinese feet is a striking object-lesson to us as to how *not* to do things. The Chinese admire small feet, and yet they have set to work in the most wrong-headed manner imaginable to produce them. For countless ages the Chinese have been bandaging the feet of the children, in spite of the endless pain the process has entailed. They have tinkered at symptoms and have ignored causes. Perhaps they thought that acquired mutilations would become hereditary. Had they worked according to knowledge, they would have adopted the very opposite process, and would have exposed, rather than have bandaged, the feet. Had they done this, they would have allowed the secondary sexual attraction of small feet to work, and those fortunate women with the smallest feet would have become the favourite wives, while women with large, ungainly feet would have had but a poor chance. As a result of exposing the feet the Chinese would have bred-in small feet and would have bred-out large ones: thus they would have gained their end without submitting millions of human beings to utterly unnecessary and excruciating pain. The acquired mutilation of the feet cannot be passed on by heredity; but sexual selection can give handicap to the coveted smallness of foot. The extent to which they could have reduced the size of the foot would, of course, have depended on the amount of capacity for variation possessed by the foot—probably a strictly limited quantity.

Why do we so rarely find any kind of deformity, or physical defect such as hare-lip or cleft-palate, amongst the Kafirs ? Partly because they adopt the most drastic of all *direct* eugenic methods, and kill off deformed children so that they may not propagate their deformities ; partly because a Kafir with any defect stands a poor chance in life—and especially in matrimony. But it would seem that the chief reason why personal blemishes, such as varicose veins, do not occur, consists in the social custom in virtue of which the body is left undraped. A Kafir woman scorns to marry a man with any defect of a conspicuous nature, and the man is unable to hide the defect. The Kafirs thus adopt unconsciously a powerful *indirect* method of eugenics. By taking this fact into consideration we might do much to maintain Kafir physique, which is now threatened by our stopping of inter-tribal wars (through which natural selection once worked), by inventing a suitable and rational dress for the civilised natives. Our European clothing is bad for them from many points of view. We should thus counteract one of the evil consequences of civilisation. Again, why should we not seek to affect Kafir custom so that mental superiority should also be recognised as a valuable trait in a man or woman ?

In England we are all, by virtue of our social judgments, working every day of our life at indirect eugenics; for every person who rightly values physique and mental and moral qualities is giving such things extra marriageable value. Those who set the fashion in exalting beauty of face above all other qualities are doing their part to preserve beauty in our descendants. Chivalry in olden days did much to preserve stock that possessed beauty, grace, courage, bravery and manliness; and the result is visible to-day. Had chivalry but placed a greater premium on brains as well, it would have been the means of untold good. We *are* working at eugenics every day of our life, and the only question is as to whether we shall do this sensibly and with knowledge or stupidly and by blind impulse. In an inaugural address delivered at the London School of Economics, Professor Westermarck is reported (the *Times*, December 18, 1907) to have said that legislators and lawyers might well profit by the comparative study of social institutions—how laws should adapt themselves to the social environment, and how they had a tendency to survive the conditions under which they were devised. It was something to know how laws might be improved, even if we had to learn something from savages. It had been said that the suggested law to prevent undesirable persons from contracting marriage was impracticable. Yet many savage tribes had tried the experiment and had succeeded.

The importance of marriage customs can scarcely be over-estimated. By such means we can indirectly affect the stock. "Isolation" is the term generally applied to the narrowing of the radius of inter-crossing. Professor Thomson has said that: "It tends to the segregation of species into sub-species, it makes it easier for new variations to establish themselves, it promotes prepotency or what the breeders call 'transmitting power,' it fixes character.

. . . There seems much to be said for Reibmayr's thesis that the establishment of a successful race or stock requires the alternation of periods of in-breeding (endogamy) in which characters are fixed, and periods of out-breeding (exogeny) in which by the introduction of fresh blood new variations are promoted. Perhaps the Jews may serve to illustrate the influence of isolation in promoting stability of type and prepotency; perhaps the Americans may serve to illustrate the variability which a mixture of different stocks tends to bring about. In historical inquiry into the difficult problem of the origin of distinct races, it seems legitimate to think of periods of 'mutations'—of discontinuous sporting—which led to numerous offshoots from the main stock, of the migration of these variants into new environments where in relative isolation they became prepotent and stable." *

Professor Thomson has also given the following example of the way some great change in the species may be brought about, especially if it be favoured by in-breeding or some form of isolation: "It seems certain that a definite breed of cattle may arise in a single farm-yard, may be in-bred until it obtains dominant prepotency, and may after a while persist in its integrity in spite of occasional intercrossing. If this be so, we can better understand how a particular human strain—such as the 'Celtic type'—may be so prepotent that it persists as an important social factor in spite of much mingling of stocks. On the other hand, a genius is a transilient variation who usually does not come to stay, except as an immortal spirit embodied in literature or art." †

* "Sociological Papers," 1906, p. 184. † *Ibid.* p. 163.

But not only do we work at indirect eugenics by social custom : we also experiment by means of legislation. When we pass legislative measures that handicap the inefficient in morals, in brains, in energy or in physique, we work at pernicious and inverted "eugenics"—a sort of *kakogenics*—for we foster and aid the multiplication of the worst elements in our stock. When we seek to remove the symptoms of poverty or crime without paying regard to the causes, we too often do but shield and screen the inefficient and the vicious so that they may propagate their inefficient and vicious stock at the nation's expense. We remove the evil symptom that distresses our sentiment, but, not seeking for causes, we feed the disease and ensure the continuance and increase of the evil by our ill-chosen methods. The present Liberal Government seems to be intent on this *kakogenics*, for by its ill-considered legislative measures, freighted with socialistic tendencies, it is screening the unfit and the vicious from the consequences of their unfitness, improvidence and laziness. They propose granting old-age pensions rather than seeking to prevent old-age poverty. By unwise State interference in the feeding of children, and by discriminative legislation in favour of the least desirable of our population, we shall but aggravate the diseases we deplore. We so relieve the distressing symptoms of poverty that we manufacture a larger number of paupers, and perpetuate the disease to cause us fresh and increased distress in the future. We are treating symptoms and leaving the causes untouched. It is becoming increasingly easy for the improvident and the vicious to burden the State with the bad stock they propagate so quickly. It is important to remember that the biologically fit may be the sociologically undesirable. A worthless and vicious member of the pauper community—a man who is extremely fertile and biologically fit—can marry at eighteen and cast the burden and care of his children on to other shoulders; yet many of our professional classes—men who are sociologically desirable—cannot marry till thirty, and even then cannot afford to have as large families as can the improvident, the unintelligent and the feckless; for they have too much self-respect to cast the responsibility of providing for their children on to others. When we remember further that it is possible that highly individuated and sociologically desirable stock is less fertile than the more animal and biologically fit stock, it appears that our best stock is being doubly handicapped; first of all by nature, and secondly by the bungling of our politicians. There is therefore placed a double premium on parental neglect and improvidence, and a double penalty on self-respect, providence and brains. Why should we not remit taxation in the case of some of our struggling men of ability? They are, comparatively speaking, poorer than the "poor," for their self-respect makes them aim at maintaining a higher and costlier and worthier type of civilised life. Of course starving children must be fed; but equally they must not so be fed as to increase the number of hungry children. By wise legislation no one's sense of delicacy would be offended, for who would realise that we were working at eugenics? Every Member of Parliament is to-day working at indirect eugenics, though he might possibly be astonished and not a little scandalised if he were told that fact. The only question, then, is, Shall we plan our legislative measures on the basis of sound knowledge, and with definite ends in view, or shall we muddle along unintelligently as in the past? Possibly we hide behind our prudishness and say that sentiment should not be ignored. We forget that it is the best stock that already has the best sentiment: but in their case our artificial statecraft hinders them from giving effect to their sentiment, while it favours the low sentiment of the undesirable. There are thousands of excellent people who have the needed sentiment, but who lack the needed financial means for marriage.

We see then that we can improve the stock indirectly by attending to such things as social custom and legislation. Moreover, we can use these forces in one of two ways: we can adopt such methods to prevent the multiplication of our worst stock on the one hand, or else to improve the quality—and quantity—of our best stock on the other. It would seem as if we should do both these things at one and the same time, working simultaneously at each end of the scale. We now pass on to see how we can improve the stock by more direct methods.

(*b*) *Direct Eugenics.*—With regard to improving the stock by direct eugenics, a few years ago we could have done little more than feel our way by rule of thumb or by guesswork; but owing to the advances made recently by biologists, owing also to the studies (amongst many others) of Mr. Francis Galton, Professor Karl Pearson and Dr. Archdall Reid, and to the recent re-discovery of Mendelism —we at last see the main bearings of the problem. Genetics, from being a mass of rules of thumb, is becoming a science. It is perhaps hopeless to seek to explain the present position of the subject adequately in a few pages, for in a popular statement nine-tenths of the technical terms generally used must be left out: but all the same, some rough attempt must be made to indicate the chief problems concerned, and also the lie of the land. The consideration of the deepest well-being of posterity is surely a department of human thought in which our highest patriotic, social, moral, and religious duties unite, and it is worth while taking a little trouble to bring our knowledge up to date. A nation can, within certain limits, decide the destiny of the unborn generation. To say, "After us the deluge," is to show a callous spirit that few of us would care to exhibit, for it would expose our bad citizenship, our selfishness, and our irreligion. But our practical indifference to the interests of posterity is only too palpable, and betrays us at every point.

If we do not possess sufficiently accurate knowledge to enable us to make, with certainty, as many experiments in direct eugenics as we could wish, we at least know the lines of the necessary investigation and experiment. We can get clear knowledge if we take the trouble to do so—and that is a great point gained.

We are most of us more or less familiar with the epoch-making work of Darwin, and know that individuals of a single species vary; and that nature, by means of natura selection, has weeded out the unsuitable variations and preserved those that are beneficial. The biologically fit survive and perpetuate their stock, while the unfit are handicapped. Certain variations had survival-value or selection-value, and in the struggle for existence individua which possessed them were at an advantage compared with organisms that were less fit, or whose variations had no such value. Biologists are not yet agreed as to whether the variations that have been selected were those that differed but slightly or those that differed largely from the mean. The former slight variations are sometimes technically called fluctuations, while the latter are called mutations, discontinuous variations or sports. Some Mendelists are inclined to think that species were largely formed owing to the selection of these mutations or discontinuous variations: while many selectionists maintain that such mutations are practically never selected by nature for they seem to be accompanied by an instability of the equilibrium of the organism. We can, however, retain such mutations (in plants) by artificially cultivating and shielding the plant, which shows these great variations, from the struggle for existence. When such plants are placed under natural conditions, the modifications we have artificially fostered tend to vanish.

When we come to the case of man, we find it very difficult to determine whether improvement in the stock should be expected through the summation and accumulation of slight fluctuations from the mean, or whether we should seek for the greater variations. According to Mendelism, "characters" in an organism tend to segregate and to get sifted out from one another. But many biologists think that "characters" in man tend to blend and not to segregate. The difference of opinion exists solely because we have not yet collected sufficient evidence (or made experiments) to test the truth of these opposed hypotheses. We are all familiar with the patent fact that when white races mate with black ones, the hybrid shows a blending of colour. If Mendelian principles obtain in the case of man as they do in the case of plants, and if the colouration of skin, the form of hair, and the distinctive features are Mendelian "characters" that segregate, it should be possible, by suitable interbreeding, to take a mass of half-castes, and in the course of a few generations to sift out from them the two original stocks from which they sprang—thus eliminating the half-caste. The interest of this question is very great, and the dispute that is now going on amongst the two different schools of biologists could easily be settled by observation and experiment.

It would be hopeless to point out in this chapter the principles that Mendelians are seeking to establish, for it would take pages to explain the meaning of allelomorphs, gametes, heterozygotes, and all the other technical terms necessary to a discussion of the subject. But it is possible to give an example of the sort of practical problem in horticulture that can now be solved by using Mendelian principles of intercrossing. Mr. Lock, in his work on "Heredity," supplies for our consideration several examples, from which I extract the following facts.

There are very many kinds of wheat that can be grown in England, and yet none of them fetch so high a price as several varieties of grain grown in America. On seeking to grow American varieties in England, most of them are found rapidly to lose their good qualities, though one of them continues to give a good grain. Unfortunately this variety yields in England too small a crop per acre to make it worth while cultivating. A Mendelian worker attacked the problem, and by cross-breeding an American and an English variety was able to produce a wheat that showed all the good qualities of the American grain as well as the desirable qualities of the home-grown varieties. "The problem has therefore been completely solved, and there can be little doubt," says Mr. Lock, "that when these new types are brought into general cultivation the profit obtaining from the growing of a wheat in this country will be increased by several shillings to the acre of crop grown." *

This solution of the problem was not obtained by mere rule of thumb, but was the result of a definite following of what are called Mendelian principles. But a still more striking achievement has been effected. Many millions of pounds are lost annually by the attack of rust, which ruins the wheat crop. Certain varieties of grain are practically immune to this rust, though they are wanting in other very desirable qualities. It seemed too good to hope that a variety might be obtained by cross-breeding that would be rust-free and yet possessed of the desirable qualities. Experiments were carried out on the Cambridge experimental farm, and Mendelian principles were again adopted. A variety that was practically rust-free was crossed with another variety that was excellent in all points except that it invariably suffered from rust. By crossing these varieties, and by selecting, according to Mendelian principles, certain of the young plants, and by cultivating these alone, it was possible to produce a stock that bred true, and that was both rust-free and possessed of all the other desirable qualities. Acting according to principle, and not by rule of thumb, this feat was performed in only three generations.

It might be thought—indeed it has been suggested—that what holds good in the case of plants should hold

* "Variation, Heredity and Evolution," pp. 218, 219.

good in the case of man. It by no means follows that they do hold good in this case. If these principles were found to hold in the case of man, we might be able to produce the most extraordinary developments in human nature. But as yet we do not know for certain whether any valuable human "characters" blend or whether they segregate according to Mendelian principles.* At present the dust of battle is raging; and we must wait until those who are now, along with observers such as Mr. Mudge, investigating the question of the intercrossing of races have completed their observations. It would be of great interest to collect evidence and pedigrees of half-caste families in South Africa, as well as to test the effect of intercrossing between South African tribes, such as, say, the Fingos and the Basutos, each of which is noted for a somewhat different type of intellect and physique.†

With regard to the question as to the latent capacity for variation possessed by the Kafirs, we can at present neither affirm nor deny that they have bred-out or exhausted their capacity for variation. There is much evidence to lead biologists to think that variation was once much more ample and abundant (and evolution more rapid) than it is to-day. Nature has been at work for ages, and by natural selection has weeded out useless variations and has stereotyped the useful ones. Thus she has standardised her patterns, as it were, and is now working in such a way that variation is of much less selection-value or survival-value than formerly. The

* It would seem as if *disadvantageous* variations, such as hare-lip, cleft-palate, &c., behaved as Mendelian characters.

† There are several types of colouration in the case of the Kafirs—a fact that might be borne in mind by investigators.

useless patterns have become discarded, and perhaps with these ill-adapted patterns has gone the concomitant capacity for variation. Fixity of type seems to have been nature's goal, and so it has come about that forms are now more stable than they were ages since. We have not experimented or observed facts sufficiently to say whether the human race has, or has not, nearly reached the end of its tether in the matter of variation; nor do we yet know how long such capacity can lie latent without becoming lost. Old races are certainly vanishing rapidly, and only the fortunate ones that are wisely handled can hope to survive. Civilisation has been as severe as natural selection, or has possibly been one of the tools natural selection has employed to weed out the unfit races.

Discussing the question as to whether man's evolution has ceased or not, Dr. Reid points out the two sides to the matter. On the one hand it is possible to argue that man is regressing, as most of the occasions for selection have ceased to exist. Some of the races in the stone age seem to have surpassed us in size of body as the ancient Greeks seem to have surpassed us in intelligence. But on the other hand there are reasons for thinking we have progressed, since, for example, modern Norwegians are able to introduce but one hand into the two-handed sword-hilts of their ancestors, while the intellectual achievements of the Greeks seem to have been due more to the excellence of their mental training—to their environment—than to the greatness of their mental powers. The Greek youth was taught *how* to think while we teach our youth *what* to think: in other words, the Greeks *educated* their youth while we stifle their opening minds. Dr. Reid says: "Other writers maintain that man is undergoing, not regression, but a great and rapid evolution. They point, as proof, to his recent wonderful advance in civilisation. But here the word evolution is not used in its biological sense. The existence of the steam-engine and the electric telegraph do not imply any intrinsic change in mind or body. They belong, not to human evolution, but to what has been termed 'evolution in human environment.' The truth appears to be that the gradual cessation of the old causes of elimination has caused, or is causing, human evolution on ancient lines to cease; but as yet the time has not been sufficient to permit appreciable regression. Just as hands and feet ceased to evolve hundreds of thousands of years ago, just as heart and lungs ceased to evolve at a period still more remote, so the evolution in size, strength and intelligence has probably reached its term. In all these particulars the race is so well adapted to the environment that the amount of elimination which now obtains merely sustains, but does not add to, the antecedent evolution. But if, in the future, as modern socialistic tendencies seem to indicate, the labourer receives, not according to the result achieved, but according to the labour expended, if the weak in muscle and brain survive and have offspring equally with the strong, very slow regression will follow no doubt; unless, indeed, in an era more enlightened than our own, Artificial Selection takes up the task which Natural Selection has laid down, and, by a careful selection of parents, raises mankind to a pinnacle of strength and intelligence as yet undreamed of." *

All this has several profound relations to our Kafir

" Principles of Heredity," pp. 107, 108.

problem, but only one point need be touched on here. When discussing the Clan-System it was pointed out how it was suited to a general low level of mediocrity. However, there were tribal wars to ensure that there should be no deterioration of muscle and of the lower animal faculties, such as cunning. These tribal fights prevented the physique from degenerating; and our stopping of inter-tribal wars will almost certainly lead to a falling off of physical stamina in the Kafirs. But the Clan-System did nothing to stimulate the intellect, and Dr. Reid's words, "If the weak in brain survive and have offspring equally with the strong very slow regression will follow," might have been written with a view to argue from the Kafirs. It may be argued that unless we can so modify the Clan-System as to allow excellence of brain to have survival-value, the system must prevent the highest possible elevation of the natives. And, indeed, the regression of the Kafirs, if it has taken place in the distant past, as has been suggested above, may have commenced with the institution of the present form of the Clan-System and its marriage customs: in that case the social, if not the socialistic, elements wrapt up with that system may, after all, be the cause of the Kafir's present low mental condition: for the natives would have been handicapped, first of all by too much exogamous breeding (which appears to tend to the production of a moderately low average of the stock), and then also by their socialistic organisation, which seems to tend to mediocrity.

There is another aspect of the whole problem. We know that a species undergoes evolution only under somewhat adverse conditions, and that it suffers regression in the absence of struggle and consequent natural selection.

Superabundance of food-supply is a gain to the individual, but it may prove a loss to the species; for selection under such conditions may not be sufficiently stringent to weed out the individuals that are unfit. Disease is a loss to the individual, and yet, owing to its drastic selective action, it may be (if not excessive) a gain to the species by weeding out the unfit. What is required is a balancing of these two forces. It must also be remembered, once more, that the biologically fit are not necessarily the sociologically desirable. Unless there is a certain amount of shielding from undue struggle, the arts and amenities of life have no scope for development. We need first of all a broad basis of stock that is biologically fit, so as to give physical strength to the nation; and having got that, we need to favour those individuals who are sociologically desirable. In the case of direct eugenics, as in that of indirect eugenics, we can work at either end of the scale, preventing the formation of bad stock, or encouraging the formation of good stock—or we can combine both these methods.

We have been experimenting in direct eugenics for ages, and even those who are scandalised by the very word have been working at eugenics, though it may have been in an unintelligent fashion. Every time a self-respecting man carefully considers the physical, mental, and moral characters of the woman who is to be the mother of his children, he is working at direct eugenics; and so is the woman who bears these factors in mind when she receives an offer of marriage. When the Vicar of Wakefield "began to think seriously and chose his wife, as she did her wedding-gown, not for a fine glossy surface, but for such qualities as would wear well," he was also working at direct eugenics. When doctors persuade people not to marry epileptics or degenerates, they are working at the same science. It is therefore absurd for people to cry out when it is proposed that what is done feebly and often in a bungling fashion should be done by combining accurate knowledge with sound scientific sense so as to ensure the greatest possible amount of good for posterity. There is much truth in the words of Mr. Bernard Shaw when he says in his *Man and Superman*, "Being cowards, we defeat natural selection under cover of philanthropy: being sluggards, we neglect artificial selection under cover of delicacy and morality." These words apply with peculiar force to our philanthropic efforts amongst the Kafirs. We have deluged them with philanthropy, but have done nothing to shield them from the inevitable and evil side-issues of our propaganda. We even talk of destroying the one custom that would make it unusually easy to try experiments in direct eugenics in the kraals. The custom I refer to is that of *lobola*, in virtue of which a man gives a number of cattle to the father of the girl he marries. The great bulk of the Kafirs do not marry "for love," as we use that phrase. The average young Kafir, like a primitive Vicar of Wakefield, looks round the kraals for a good, fat, strong, hard-working, restrained-tongue wench. He wants a woman who will bear him healthy children, cook his dinner, hoe his fields, carry his water, and attend to all domestic matters without plaguing him with her tongue. So long as he can find a few of these qualities combined in any woman, he is moderately satisfied, and, like a man, pays up his ten head of cattle to the girl's father. In nine cases out of ten, the girl goes unquestioningly to the man who has bargained for her. Every now and then men choose wives out of special love, and every now and then a girl refuses to go to the man she does not like. But the bulk of the people, who seem to think that marriage was made for man and not man for marriage, find the custom very convenient and satisfactory. The educated natives dislike the custom, for, amongst other reasons, they want to get their wives—as they want to get so many other things—without paying anything.

It must be obvious that mankind can never expect to have a better opportunity for studying problems in direct eugenics. This *lobola* custom * would enable us to start investigations, for through it we could "arrange" suitable marriages, even as we "arrange" the most unsuitable money-marriages in English society. There is practically no delicacy—except our own—to stand in the way, for the investigations could be carried on without the natives knowing what the strange white man was up to. The state of our knowledge would hardly justify us in applying immediately much heroic social surgery: for a considerable time to come we should have to confine ourselves chiefly to accurate observations of the effect of past marriages; and we could begin with very simple problems, for the Kafirs would not present such complex tangles of numerous emotional and intellectual factors as would be the case in Europe. We should thus get a most valuable set of simple observations to guide us in the more complicated problems that must face us in the future. It would seem that the nation that has the pluck to start experiments in direct eugenics will have a good chance of ruling the world: and

* I have described this custom at some length in "The Essential Kafir."

it is not improbable that the Japanese will soon apply, in this matter as in so many others, Western Science to Eastern problems.

By experimenting with the Kafirs, we should not offend their sense of propriety, for they have very little or none in this matter. Indeed we should do something to redeem the custom of *lobola* from some of its abuses, while at the same time we should improve their stock from a physical point of view. We seem scarcely justified in breaking up native customs unless we are also willing to help the people to adopt safeguards against some of the evils that follow as a result of our action. If we were to cleanse the custom of *lobola* we might stop, or lessen, some of the degenerating defects of our interference in Kafir affairs. By uprooting the *lobola* custom, we should but offend Kafir sentiment, destroy the black woman's one safeguard from ill-treatment, and throw away our opportunity of improving the stock of the people. We might at least take an initial step to improve that stock if we wished, but we are, as Mr. Shaw says, too cowardly or too sluggish to set to work at the problem before us. Our sentiment prevents us from taking the one precaution that would ward off some of the evil effects caused by our sentiment and moral impulses.

The Kafirs happen to present us with a magnificent field for such experimental work, for they are broken up into a number of tribes, each of which has preserved for countless years certain types that seem to breed true. They also practise polygamy, which would enable us to make the most valuable comparative studies which are obviously impossible in Europe. In other words, the Kafirs, by means of their tribal organisation and marriage customs, have been for ages preparing the ground for experiments in eugenics. We have thus a most fruitful field for experiment and study.

We have now examined the horse—in other words, we see more or less clearly the conditions that must be fulfilled if the Kafirs are to rise. If we wish to know whether the Kafirs as a race can rise, we have only got to ask ourselves the questions: *first*, whether we have tried to fulfil the conditions, and *secondly*, whether we intend to try them. I think it is obvious that we have never made the least attempt to fulfil the conditions, and consequently cannot be justified in maintaining that the Kafirs as a race cannot rise. There would seem to be every reason for thinking that they are capable of vast improvement: but it must be confessed that when we think of the present condition of South African politics and Home opinion, it is extremely doubtful whether we shall adopt suitable methods. There is, however, one thing we certainly might do: we might collect accurate evidence and data, as well as reliable pedigrees of half-castes and full-blooded Kafirs, so as to pass on to a generation that we hope will be more intelligent than the present one, reliable data on a subject they will be certain to study.

It will perhaps make the drift of my biological argument clearer if I sum up thus. It would seem that in the case of the Kafirs, the race will not fuse with the whites and will not die out through the importation of European disease, but will live on and multiply side by side with the Europeans. Further, it appears as if the individual Kafir, owing to some idiosyncrasy of his stock, can never become the equal of the white man, though he has a great and undeveloped capacity for progress. If left to himself, the Kafir will not be able to rise very high; for our civilisation supplies an unsuitable environment, the evil of which he cannot resist unless he is guided by the white man. Nevertheless, if he is wisely educated by experts in education, he may develop in intelligence, in moral sentiment, in industry, in will-power, in religion, in art, and in most of the amenities of civilised life far more than is generally thought possible. Thousands of individuals may be raised possibly as high above the level of the average Kafir of to-day as we are above the worshippers of Woden. But this would take time as well as very careful—and yet firm and bold—handling of the Kafir. Left to the tender mercies of amateur educationists, the natives would probably end in something worse than what we contemptuously call savagery.

With regard to the education of the Kafirs, we have a magnificent object-lesson in Brooker Washington's Institute at Tuskegge, where the attention is turned away from politics and is chiefly centred on the formation of character; and where the negroes are taught trades, industry, practical agriculture, honesty, thrift and self-reliance, being given only as much book-education as will strengthen and cement together the various items of the curriculum. The *esprit de corps* at that Institute has a most potent influence; for the students feel that they have a reputation to live up to, and they find that they must work hard so as to support themselves. Here, and not at the polls, lies the work of the educated Kafir. If Ethiopianism could be purged of its politics, and if it could be turned to the forming of solid character—a work that does not glitter half so much—it might be a truly valuable force in the uplifting of each successive generation of the race, even though such work will not produce a direct and permanent effect in the stock.

With regard to the *race* (in distinction from the *individual*), we can by the adoption of wise social and political remedies, indirectly affect the stock. But if we wish to produce still more germinal change, we shall have to work at direct eugenics, breeding-out the sociologically undesirable and breeding-in the qualities we value. By combining education, which affects the individual, with social custom and political legislation and direct eugenics, which affect the stock, we should elevate the Kafirs all round, and do our simple duty: and it is difficult to say whether the Kafirs or we ourselves would benefit the more.

## CHAPTER VI

### THE FIRST STEP TOWARDS THE SOLUTION OF THE NATIVE PROBLEM

THERE are a dozen important things we should do if we would solve the Native Problem: but since this book is only an *introduction* to the study of the subject, and since its main object is to call a halt and to provoke inquiry, it is not necessary to discuss at length the solution of the problem. Indeed, it is to be doubted whether at the present stage much good can result from the propounding of "solutions," for we have not yet taken the most obvious preliminary step. The Kafirs say that the Eye crosses the full river: but the Body does not; and until we have taken the first step, it is scarcely worth while to let our imagination go roaming while we discuss details of the later parts of our journey. Beyond all reasonable doubt the first thing that should be done—and it is an endless cause for wonder that it was not done a century ago—is to start an Ethnological Bureau which should discover for us the basal facts of the problem.

I should be sorry if it were thought that in these pages I have been scoffing at sentiment. The Native Problem will no more be solved without sentiment than it will be solved by it. I hold firmly that a strong, healthy sentiment, based on sound knowledge, is the only thing that will give us the energy and motive-power to do our duty:

it is a soft effeminate sentiment, based on hysterical fancies and imaginings, and uncontrolled by intelligence, that I regard as our greatest enemy. Let us have facts first and sentiment afterwards.

The days of the devising of imaginative cures for diseases have passed away. We are now aware that if we seek, not a palliative, but a cure, we must do something more than treat symptoms, the study of which is of value mainly for diagnostic purposes. Our medical text-books consist largely of a description of the nature, causes, consequences, and diagnosis of disease; and we are slowly beginning to realise that we must follow a similar line of action with regard to the diseases of the body politic. When we give syrup of opium to quiet a restless child; when we give sixpence to a beggar who appeals to our pity; or when we, through the State, feed hungry children without considering the causes that have led to their hunger; we do but treat symptoms, and as often as not aggravate and propagate the diseases of poverty and parental indifference or neglect. The danger of manufacturing paupers by applying palliatives to lessen the distressing symptoms of poverty is now fairly well recognised by the average intelligent person; though popular theories whose fallacies have been exposed to all the world are apt to seek the privileged shelter of the House of Commons, just as faiths and philosophies go to Oxford when they die. But outside the House of Commons and Party Politics no one believes that we can cure national evils by sentiment, or doubts the necessity of making an organised study of the causes of trouble whether the subject be cancer, or crime, or poverty, or the falling off in the birth-rate, or physical deterioration. The days in which some Paracelsus sought to cherish his selfish ambition in solitary study so that he might astound the world have well-nigh vanished; for we now recognise that progress in knowledge is a social product. We therefore start societies and committees to devise experiment, and to gather and collate evidence. A hundred brains all work in unison, and each profits by the experience of each; the greater the problem, the vaster the issues of our policy, the more intricate the problem, the more necessary does it appear to us to co-ordinate the investigations of many workers in the field. Only thus can we hope to find a remedy. Yet, though we are in a great measure responsible for the happiness and destiny of millions of our backward fellow countrymen in South Africa, we have done little, as a body of white rulers, to study native thought, aspiration, and custom. Instead of investigating facts, we have been occupied with opinions, and have looked at the natives through the eyes of Home sentiment or dividends. "At the present stage," writes Dr. Haddon, the head and moving spirit of the Cambridge Ethnological School, "knowledge will not be advanced much by looking at laggard peoples through the spectacles of old-world civilisation." Yet this is precisely what our rulers persist in doing. Sir Harry Johnston, writing in *Nature* (May 19, 1904), said: "It is a national humiliation to us to reflect that as a Government we have been connected with South Africa for more than a century, that is to say, two-thirds as long as our Imperial connection with India has lasted, and yet that by Government endeavour or private research so little of value has been published in the English language of the native human races of Africa south of the Zambesi." The writer went on to point out the main works published, but it is a meagre list, valuable as are some of the books. Sir Harry Johnston has done so much in his tenure of office in Central Africa to advance the study of the native races we have to govern that his remarks carry all the weight of a practical administrator. But who will listen to them? The verdict of the scholar living remote from the hubbub of Colonial administration is to the same effect. Dr. Frazer, the well-known author of "The Golden Bough," has done much to explain the ideas underlying primitive thought; he recently wrote in the *Daily Mail*,* when reviewing an ethnological book: "It is a pity that our Government, in its dealing with native races, has no Bureau of Ethnology or advisory board of anthropologists to consult. If it had, it might have been saved from many blunders which have cost the nation dear in blood and treasure."

Mr. Andrew Lang told us some years ago, when discussing in the *Morning Post* Dr. Haddon's plea for an Ethnological Bureau for Greater Britain, that the British had not sufficient imagination to see that it would be worth while to pay for such a thing; for in England we do not value abstract knowledge very highly. But he went on to point out that: "In Africa it really would be money in our pockets to understand the native law and custom, which is elaborate and complex, and can scarcely be disregarded with impunity. When questions of dowry and property are mixed up with witchcraft, an administrator must understand the native point of view."

It is not suggested that sentiment should be banished

* November 24, 1906.

from our view of the native race, for only the most petrified and desiccated ethnologist of the study would have workers in the field act as if Kafirs were so many apes or monkeys, or would wish us to forget that the people examined are throbbing with rich human blood. The sentiments, customs, emotions, and ideas of the backward race are precisely the subjects the ethnologist in the field would study. We want common sense and knowledge to be "touched with emotion," but only touched: it would be most pernicious to swamp facts in an ocean of sentiment, whether financial, political or "Exeter Hall." Nothing so blinds the eyes as race-prejudice, religious enthusiasm, and self-interest; where they come in as disturbing factors we need an impartial tribunal, composed of men specially trained to sift knowledge, to determine and interpret the facts. It is no cause for wonder that the Johannesburg financier imagines that the Native Problem is in essence a question of the economic development of the native labour-supply; that the politician conceives it to be a question of the suffrage; that the missionary regards it as chiefly a problem in religion; that the teacher thinks it is a question of education; that the doctor insists that it is mainly a problem of race-survival and disease. Where shall we find a man so filled with the grace of detachment as to form a dispassionate and impartial judgment of values in a question where his interests or sentiments are deeply engaged? An ethnologist may not be perfect, but, owing to training and freedom from personal interests, he is at least more likely than most people to keep his balance in this matter. He is sympathetically disposed towards the race he studies—else he could never get the information he seeks—and yet is alert and interested in the broad aspect of all social problems.

I am aware that in tacitly assuming that the white man in South Africa knows almost nothing, as he should know, of the native races, I am running counter to the usual colonial talk. This has been summed up by Mr. Lionel Philips in his "Transvaal Problems." "English statesmen," he writes, "should bear in mind that the colonists have an intimate personal acquaintance with the native" * (p. 139). He also gives a good example of how politicians talk when he adds: "The Native Affairs Commission has gone fully into the tribal system, &c." (p. 140). I should be the last to wish to underrate the most excellent and valuable report of the Commission, but cannot help noticing that the Commissioners gave but a few pages of very large type to the subject. It would have been difficult for them to have said more in the space at their disposal; but for the public to be told that the Commissioners "went fully" into the subject shows how lightly politicians value such matters. An Ethnological Bureau might find a hundred times as many pages all too little for a full examination of this most important subject. The Commissioners did but touch the fringe of the subject, and they would be the first to admit the fact. To devise a policy on the insufficient knowledge we have of native thought and character is to court failure: to think we know all about the natives is to ensure it.

* If Mr. Philips only intended to convey the impression that South African ignorance of Kafir thought and custom, when contrasted with European ignorance on the subject, appeared to be deep knowledge, then I agree with him.

It is true that we have from time to time appointed Native Commissions to investigate Kafir customs, and we may well be thankful for the invaluable help these reports have been to us. That fact alone is sufficient to substantiate my plea; for if one or two Commissions have done so much good, what would be the effect of an Ethnological Bureau? But it must be borne in mind that such Commissions have rarely been composed of men who have had a scientific training, or who have been taught to sift ethnological information, though they may have been astute magistrates or lawyers. The legal training and habit of mind that make a man an adroit barrister, capable of worrying a witness until the worse case appears the better, are poles asunder from the scientific training and temper that enable a man to ascertain the positive facts in an ethnological puzzle. Therefore we may reasonably expect great results from the founding of a Bureau.

The Bureau that I suggest would popularise accurate knowledge as to native custom and thought, and would, little by little, undermine hide-bound prejudices and popular fallacies without the public being aware of the fact that its opinion was being affected. Knowledge, instead of opinion, would become the basis of our legislation; and as a result we should not continue to knock our heads against hard facts. Until we are better informed than we are at present, we may well hold our hand from making drastic changes in our methods, and from devising a uinform policy for all the different South African States, for we have no guarantee that we should not but shift our building from one patch of sand to another. There can, however, be no conceivable danger in the immediate starting of the Ethnological Bureau.

The following brief outline may show some of the advantages that we might reasonably hope to gain from such a Bureau: but we must remember that the mere creation of an establishment, though it may supply us with information, will not solve the problem. We must not expect, savage-like, that a Bureau or anything else will act by magical influence and save us all the trouble and responsibility of clear thinking, sensible feeling, and strong willing. In pointing out some of the results that we may expect, there is a danger of imitating advertisers of patent medicines who say that their remedies will cure "all the ills that flesh is heir to": yet some of the advantages of an organised study of the natives may be enumerated.

(1) At present one of our greatest dangers consists in the way politicians are seeking to solve the Native Problem by fancy policies evolved from their own inner consciousness. It is not so much the actual needs of the natives that prompts these schemes as the exigencies of white politics. There is not much likelihood that any of such proposals will really solve the problem; for the most important person of all is the one person least considered. By studying native custom and thought it may be possible for us to trace symptoms until we arrive at causes, and so get to the roots of the problem. There are few more difficult things than this, for natives do not readily supply to men of an alien race information as to their inner thoughts and aspirations. An illustration may be given. An ethnologist recently spent a few months studying a certain race of primitive people. A missionary, who had been

working amongst these people for more years than the ethnologist had been working months, on seeing the results of the ethnologist's work, said he felt ashamed and worthless; here was a man who, without knowing the language, had discovered more about the customs of the people in a few months than he had during a whole lifetime devoted to this special object. The one knew what to look for and had been trained how to look for it, while the other had bungled along, groping in the darkness and deceived by the people amongst whom he was living.

(2) Starting with the study of Kafir children, we should study the inborn capacities of the race as well as the environment of the child; and should probably discover amongst many other equally important things why it is that there is so often an arrest of progress at puberty. We should study the "recapitulation" shown by the child, and might thus get clues to many things that puzzle us in the adult.

(3) We should watch the effect of educational methods, and note whether they were defective or effective. Though it may be impossible to-day, yet later on the Government will have to take a greater control of native education. The Bureau would study educational methods in Europe and America—especially such excellent methods as those used by Brooker Washington at Tuskegee—and test their efficacy in the case of the Kafirs. They would also spread information amongst missionaries as to recent educational methods.

(4) The Bureau would undertake anthropometric measurements of the various races of South Africa, and would apprise us of any incipient changes in physique, or in other characters, as a result of changed environment.

By adopting a uniform system of measurement, the results arrived at in the different tribes would be strictly comparable, and would be of immense value even in the study of many European problems. It is difficult to estimate the value of a series of such measurements of the adolescent Kafir when compared with similar measurements that are now being taken at such public schools as Eton. A series of measurements of Kafir infants would also be of great value.

It is clear to us that we are suffering under great disabilities simply on account of the indifference of a past generation to anthropological and ethnological investigation: the least we can do is to see to it that we do not similarly handicap our children, who will be faced with a larger native population. If we have the least regard for posterity we should set to work at once.

(5) The Bureau would not only increase our stock of scientific knowledge, which would be of infinite value in future ages; it would also study problems of immediate importance, such as the latent talent of the Kafirs for industrial pursuits. Directly or indirectly it would foster, and experiment in, native capacity for working in iron, and it might revive this almost lost art that the trader and missionary have unintentionally combined to kill. It may show what natives can do in this direction if I mention that on the Zambesi a friend of mine pointed out to me a native who had welded into his self-made iron hammer a steel facing made from old broken files. My friend had been the chief engineer of one of the mines at Johannesburg, and was extremely handy with his fingers, being able to make everything he required, from his clothing to his house; yet he said that he would not like,

with the poor apparatus the native used, to attempt the same feat.

In a somewhat similar way it would be possible to foster the many existing native manufactures, such as mat-making, basket-work, pottery manufacture, dyeing, cotton-spinning, gold- and silver-smithing, weaving, &c., many of which arts are only practised in a few isolated districts I have seen all these arts carried to a considerable degree of excellence in different tribes. It would seem probable that what natives in one district can do, natives in other districts could be taught; but at present there is no machinery for developing the native industries from a common centre that is in touch with the scattered tribes. When one has seen natives plaiting grass baskets that will hold water without leaking, one cannot but feel that a great deal more might be made of the dormant industrial faculties of the people.

(6) It may be said that theoretically speaking the improvement of agriculture and pastoral pursuits is the business of the Agricultural Departments of the various Governments: but if the Kafirs have got to wait until this theory is adequately turned into practice, they will have to wait a very long time. Such Government Departments seem, not alone in South Africa, to be overburdened and to get into ruts. If an Ethnological Bureau began to experiment with the capacity of the Kafirs to improve their stock or their methods of agriculture, they would not only directly stimulate the Kafirs, but would probably rouse the emulation of some sleeping Department, and so lead indirectly to a surprising amount of energy. The existence of a progressive tribe in one colony far out-

stripping another in a different colony, at present leads to no stimulus for improvement; but the Bureau could use one tribe to inculcate a healthy jealousy in another and more backward tribe: by arranging for a deputation of the principal men of the backward tribe to inspect the results obtained by another tribe, it would be possible to stimulate all parties to do the best they could. Two or three native head-men from Pondoland could with but little expense be taken to Rhodesia, for example, to see the methods used on a farm or on a cattle-ranch: and the experience thus gained might mean the beginning of Pondo progress. Tree-planting throughout the denuded native territories might also be fostered by a Bureau that was in far closer contact with the natives than is a Department of Woods and Forests, which has done but little, compared to what it might do, to help the raw Kafirs to take an intelligent interest in the subject. Apart altogether from the asset of the actual timber, the indirect effect would be felt everywhere, creating even in the most unexpected quarters a new interest in the Kafirs. It would also have a reflex effect on the native community; and the mere fact that the mind of the Kafirs was kept occupied would tend to make the people less restless, while it would lead to their healthy social and economic development in a way no amount of book-learning ever could.

(7) The Bureau might have a special department for dealing with problems of commerce and trade, and would thus serve as a sort of centre for the co-ordinating of information concerning the native labour-supply, the possibility of opening fresh markets, the introduction of new lines of goods, &c. It could study the subject of the creation of

fresh wants, which seems to be one of the central thoughts of civilisation.

(8) The Bureau would form an expert body to be consulted by people in the various States of South Africa. It would prove helpful to most classes of society: magistrates, traders, mine-managers, missionaries, and, above all, natives would find it of great value. It could keep an eye on the Native Press, watch Kafir aspirations and ideals, study changes in thought produced by Missions, labour demands, commerce and economics, and generally act as a sort of buffer between the native races and the white men. Kafirs, who for obvious reasons are shy of the magistrates, would soon come to open their minds about their difficulties and their needs to men who understood them, but who had no executive power, and who, above all, wished to keep up kindly relations so as the better to gain the information they sought. Ethnologists would take broader views of racial customs than could financiers, missionaries, magistrates or politicians with their more departmental interests; and natives would soon come to appreciate this fact.

(9) The Bureau, by enlightening Home opinion about the Kafir, would form the best possible bulwark against uninformed and unintelligent interference from home. Time was when the world considered that a slave was a person (*a*) who was forced to leave his country against his will; (*b*) who was not paid for his labour; (*c*) and who was not allowed to return to his home. We all knew where we were in those days. Now a Political Party can win an election and can affect the affairs of a Colony at the other end of the world by so curious a procedure as maintaining that a person (*a*) who leaves his country of

his own free will; (*b*) who is well paid for his labour; (*c*) and who voluntarily undertakes to return home, at his employer's expense, when his contract is finished, is a slave. When that sort of thing can happen, the affairs of the Colonies are in an unfortunate and perilous condition. We may any day be faced by a popular party cry about the Kafirs, almost as ridiculous as this contention about the Chinese. An Ethnological Bureau would be a great asset if such a thing were to happen.

(10) Finally, the Bureau could have an official and corresponding member * in England who would be able authoritatively to correct at a moment's notice the egregious blunders and misstatements made about the Kafirs in the Home Press. Let a fact that was mentioned above be referred to again as an example The other day a writer in the halfpenny Press appealed to the democratic sentiments of the people at home by stating that the Kafirs were a "pure democracy." A possible effect of such a misstatement—which may have been the result of mere ignorance—is not difficult to divine. A reader, wishing to find ammunition for his warfare against his own kith and kin in the Colonies, would put that paper down and cry out: "Now just look here! Do you see how the brutal colonist is tyrannically smashing up the democratic customs of these poor defenceless, voiceless, voteless Kafirs? Is it not time the Home Government interfered and stood up for this 'pure democracy' which is defenceless before its tyrants? Let us memorialise our Liberal Premier, and in the sacred name of democracy put a stop to this outrage on humanity."

* No Agent-General could possibly be expected to fill this function.

Now what are the facts of the case? There probably never was a people on the face of the earth less friendly to the whole spirit of individualism and democracy than the Kafirs: it is *the colonist* who is inoculating him with democratic ideals, and who is calling out for the abolition of those tyrants, the chiefs. Not only would the corresponding member of an Ethnological Bureau immediately correct such a error, but also the knowledge of the fact that there was a man fully informed as to native custom and thought, ever on the alert to expose them to ridicule, would make such irresponsible writers more cautious as to what they published. If the Bureau could do nothing else than keep the Home Press a little more straight in such matters, it would pay for its unkeep several times over.

Sir Richard Temple, when speaking about the relation of ethnology to our success and failure in governing India, remarked: "Tact is instinctive anthropological knowledge." Unfortunately it is not every one who possesses such *instinctive* knowledge: but there is not a single person who could not, if he took the trouble to avail himself of the information collected by an Ethnological Bureau, gain *acquired* anthropological knowledge. Moreover, even in the case of those fortunate people who have the instinctive knowledge, the addition of definite information would prove of immense value.

Professor Westermarck, in the address referred to in the previous chapter, is reported to have said: "Another class of persons to whom the study of social anthropology would be most useful would be colonial officials and others having to deal with alien races. It was amazing that no knowledge of the customs of non-European peoples was required of the persons who were sent to rule over them. No error could be greater than to suppose that such officials acquired the necessary knowledge in the course of their duty. Ignorance had been the main cause of the trouble that had occurred in European contact with native races."

A good deal more might be suggested as to the possible results to be obtained from the institution of the Bureau. I agree with Mr. Andrew Lang in thinking that there really would be money in it: but the chief value would seem to consist in the probability that the starting of such an institution would be the dawn of a new day for both natives and white men in South Africa.

The Americans are not generally supposed to be blind to their own interests when driving a bargain, yet, though they have but a very small number of aborigines in their country, they spend a good many thousand pounds annually in support of the Ethnological Department of their Smithsonian Institute. Moreover, their millionaires support independent ethnological work in a princely fashion, as may be seen in the case of the Curtis Ethnological Survey of the Red Indians, which is largely financed by Mr. Pierpont Morgan. The magnitude of the undertaking is shown by the fact that the full series of volumes enshrining the results of this undertaking is to cost about £600 per copy. If the South African Governments cannot see the value of an Ethnological Bureau, may we not look to some South African millionaire to take a hint from America?

It is strange how easy it is to forget *the native* when considering the Native Problem. The politician is so slightly acquainted with the Kafir of the kraal, and lives so remote from him in an utterly different environment, that he naturally thinks more of the political problem than of the pawns or counters in the game. The philanthropist is so close to his own work, and is so intensely conscious of the evil symptoms of his patient, and also of the conflict between his own love of "light" and the Kafir's love of "darkness," that he, too often, finds little time or inclination for studying the object on which he is experimenting. He is apt to regard Kafir customs as so degrading that he hesitates to taint his own mind by studying the subject. As Mr. Havelock Ellis has said, when speaking of the late appearance of anthropology and psychology amongst the sciences: "Men studied the stars, but their own souls and bodies seemed to them too sacred or too shameful for study." So few people seem to study the problem from the point of view of the Kafir that the thoughts and ideals of this most interested party get forgotten. The actual kraal-Kafir is therefore voiceless in the discussion—for no one can pretend that the educated native tries in the very slightest to express the opinion of the kraal.

The treatment of the Kafir is a complicated question because it is wrapped up with politics, religion, education, civilisation, economics, ethics, social usages, as well as with apparently ineradicable and incompatible differences of temperament, tendency, ideal and outlook of several races. It is grave, because a failure on our part to solve the problem must end in a violent conflict and death-struggle. If the clash of racial interest should ever end in war, tens of thousands of lives will be lost, unimaginable sufferings and barbarities will be inflicted on thousands of innocent women and children; incalculable damage will be done to property; immense sums of money will be squandered in war; and, no matter which side wins, a whole sub-continent will be left in ruins. To put the matter on the lowest plane, we cannot afford the cost of a united native rising.

Again, it is grave because in no other country in the world, where the climate is suitable for the rearing of healthy European families, has a coloured aboriginal race been able to rise in the scale of civilisation, and permanently to survive and increase, in contact with a white race. The story is the same no matter what country we choose: wherever the climatic conditions are suitable to the European, the natives suffer. America, Australia, New Zealand, Tasmania, Canada—all tell the same dreary tale. As Mr. Benjamin Kidd says: "The fate of all races occupying territories of this kind has been identical. Whether wars of extermination have been waged against them, or whether they have been well treated and admitted to citizenship, they have always tended to disappear before the more vigorous incoming race." * No less an historian than Mr. Bryce has told us that: "For the last three thousand years this latter process (that of reducing the number of types through the killing off or assimilation of the weaker) has been the prevailing tendency over all or nearly all the earth. It is more energetic to-day than ever before, for barbarism was not more pitiless than is civilisation, even where civilisation may wish to spare." † The Native Problem in South Africa is therefore invested with a unique interest because, since all other aboriginal races in healthy climates have vanished, or are vanishing, before the

* "Social Evolution," p. 304. † "Romanes Lecture," p. 14.

presence of the white man, it presents civilisation with a last chance of atoning for the past, and of retrieving its character.

South Africa is the one solitary exception to the melancholy rule of the destructive effect of civilisation. It is surely nothing less than the irony of fate that it should be the one country in the whole world to be picked out for virulent abuse concerning its relation to its aborigines; and that Natal, in which the native population has increased to the incredible—and I believe unparalleled—extent of seventy-fold in seventy years * should be the one colony in South Africa to be held up to peculiar scorn. All this is the more remarkable since in South Africa the problem is complicated in the most unique fashion. In no other country have the conditions been so complex and adverse. The fact that after more than a century of intimate contact between the races in South Africa—I ignore the preceding centuries so as to concede as much as possible to objectors—the backward races are increasing in numbers more rapidly than are the whites by birth and immigration combined, is, on the one hand, an unanswerable, complete, and final vindication of the moral character of the colonist, and, on the other hand, the ground of gravest fears as to the future. The South African colonist may well ignore the ignorant and malicious libels recently levelled at him, for he is a sturdy person well able to take care of himself: and he may trust history, which judges racial problems not in a peddling but in a broad manner, to take care of his reputation.

* See the Report of the recent Native Commission, p. 5, where it is stated that in 1838 there were in Natal about 10,000 natives, while in 1906 there were 700,000—*exclusive of Zululand.*

Since the Boer War, difficulties have multiplied rapidly—partly owing to the excitement that war always awakens in primitive peoples, and partly owing to increased Home interference. No responsible colonist wishes to deny that every colonial problem—in common with every Home problem—has an Imperial bearing, for even a local parliamentary election in the Transvaal, or a revision of taxation, has such a bearing. However, that fact does not of necessity imply the need of Home interference. But the colonist says that the Native Problem is predominately a domestic affair that cannot be understood in England in an adequate manner. It is to be hoped that the Party in England that has tried to make so much profit out of South African affairs has learnt the unwisdom of making South Africa an asset of Party politics, and will now leave her to solve her own problems in her own way. The one thing that the colonist needs is that steadying and sobering sense of responsibility that ever arises when a man realises that for better or for worse he must solve his own vital problems.

Dawn is breaking in the Dark Continent, and the Kafirs are stirring in their sleep. Democratic Individualism is disturbing the Socialism that has reigned undisputed for ages. We need to be free from all embarrassing interference from Home—which takes our eyes away from the main problem, and fixes them on irritating side-issues—so that we may be able wisely to help the Kafir to make the best of his new day. South Africans are engaged in what is perhaps the most difficult sphere of human activity—the wise government of a backward race. Those who are holding the reins, as they seek to negotiate their team of horses round the curves of a dangerous pass, should not have their hands twitched by nervous passengers in the back seat of the coach, even though such timid people think the driver fails to see the danger. The safest plan is to hold tight and trust the driver. Considering that civilisation, with its somewhat disreputable reputation with regard to its relation to the backward races of mankind, is faced with its last opportunity of redeeming its character, we shall do well to stop hiding the real issues of the problem by dragging it into the arena of political strife, and to remember the sententious Kafir proverb which says, the dawn does not come twice to awaken a man.